"Kim offers a fitting text for our pluralistic times and presses essential questions for preachers and worship leaders. More than a foundation for preaching in diverse contexts and a set of strategies, this book is a call to participate in the sweeping and surprising work of the Holy Spirit."

—Donyelle McCray
Assistant Professor of Homiletics
Yale Divinity School

"Eunjoo Mary Kim believes that an imaginative, eschatological vision of wondrous diversity can transform the ways that we worship and preach. This vision is seen and felt in every sentence of this hopeful and practical book. The reader not only feels invited into Kim's kaleidoscopic vision but also is given perspectives and tools for practicing preaching and worship in ways that rehearse this vision each week, across all traditions and cultures."

—John S. McClure
Charles G. Finney Professor of Preaching and Worship
Vanderbilt Divinity School

"At last, someone has provided a detailed guide for how to make multicultural preaching and worship a reality. In her book, Eunjoo Kim challenges mainline Protestants to rethink their exclusive theologies and use non-Christian sacred texts and stories to broaden and illumine theological implications. In addition to providing sound theoretical foundations and samples of sermons and worship services, she also walks her readers, step-by-step, through the processes of multicultural biblical interpretation, liturgy formation, and sermon preparation. This is a must-have text for those who are committed to worship that truly reflects for reign of God."

—Debra J. Mumford
Frank H. Caldwell Professor of Homiletics
Louisville Presbyterian Theological Seminary

"Eunjoo Kim offers solid theological grounding and much practical wisdom for transforming worship in contemporary multicultural contexts. She skillfully weaves together theological and liturgical studies from a wide range of Christian traditions. Her book should be studied—and used—by all who seek to develop ways of worship suitable in a time of incredible cultural diversity."

—Ruth Meyers
    Dean of Academic Affairs and Hodges-Haynes Professor
        of Liturgics
    Church Divinity School of the Pacific

Christian Preaching and Worship in Multicultural Contexts

A Practical Theological Approach

Eunjoo Mary Kim

Foreword by
Mark R. Francis, CSV

A PUEBLO BOOK

Liturgical Press   Collegeville, Minnesota

www.litpress.org

A Pueblo Book published by Liturgical Press

Cover design by Ann Blattner. Photo © Thinkstock by Getty.

Library of Congress Cataloging-in-Publication Data

Names: Kim, Eunjoo Mary, author.
Title: Christian preaching and worship in multicultural contexts : a
   practical theological approach / Eunjoo Mary Kim ; foreword by Mark R.
   Francis, CSV.
Description: Collegeville, Minnesota : Liturgical Press, 2017. | Includes
   bibliographical references and index.
Identifiers: LCCN 2017009669 (print) | LCCN 2017030065 (ebook) | ISBN
   9780814663455 (ebook) | ISBN 9780814663202
Subjects: LCSH: Preaching. | Cultural pluralism—Religious
   aspects—Christianity. | Cultural fusion. | Public worship. | Christianity
   and culture.
Classification: LCC BV4211.3 (ebook) | LCC BV4211.3 .K54 2017 (print) | DDC
   251—dc23
LC record available at https://lccn.loc.gov/2017009669

Contents

Acknowledgments

Researching and writing a book in a professional field is often the journey of a lone star. It was, however, not the case with this book project. I had numerous companions who walked with me along the journey from start to finish. In 2009, the Wabash Center for Teaching and Learning in Theology and Religion granted me funding for research on multicultural worship, with which I could invite Drs. Paul Huh and Susan Smith to my worship class for some profound conversation with them. Since then, I have had countless discussions about Christian preaching and worship from the multicultural perspective with numerous scholars in various areas of theological study. In particular, my colleagues at Iliff were my most critical and constructive dialogue partners. Some of them had their own writing projects on race, ethnicity, and culture and challenged me to think in depth about cultural diversity and the future of the human community.

Most of my chapter drafts were discussed either at Iliff faculty summer retreats or at professional guilds such as the Academy of Homiletics, the North American Academy of Liturgics, *Societas Homiletica*, and the Society of Biblical Literature. Without their encouragement and support, as well as insightful feedback from the members, this book project might not have been accomplished as it is. Moreover, the Iliff students who took my course, Worship in Multicultural Contexts, read some portions of the rough draft of the manuscript as required texts and affirmed its value for teaching and learning preaching and worship in multicultural contexts.

My gratitude extends to the many churches and theological institutions that invited me to preach and lead worship services for their special events, through which I was able to test the theories that I have proposed in the book. Their invitations contributed to improving the quality of the book, making it more practical and effective for the actual ministry of preaching and worship.

The generous grant of a year-long sabbatical from the school enabled me to complete the writing project in a timely manner for the publisher. Kathy Frey and Beverly Leach, who diligently proofread the entire manuscript, made my writing much clearer for the readers. Through the interest and support of Peter Dwyer and Hans Christoffersen at Liturgical Press, this book became an ecumenical resource for Christian preaching and worship.

Blessings to all of them from my deepest heart!

Foreword

It would not be an exaggeration to say that the most serious task of the Christian churches in the twenty-first century is the challenge of nurturing disciples of Jesus in a world that has become culturally and religiously diverse. The churches that trace their origins from Christianity in Western Europe are confronted everywhere with men and women who seek to live out their faith in a manner that reflects their own cultural background and that respects the context of their daily life where they rub elbows with friends and relations of many faiths—or of none at all. Today, for the first time in centuries, Western Europe is experiencing unprecedented levels of immigration from around the world that parallels the historic movement of peoples to the Americas and Australia that continues from the nineteenth and twentieth centuries. This has led Christian leaders and theologians to explore the largely unprecedented question of bringing women and men of diverse cultural backgrounds together in the same assembly / congregation to worship "in spirit and in truth."

While there have been some antecedents of culturally diverse assemblies in Christian history—fourth-century Jerusalem as described by the pilgrim Egeria, for example—there have been very few *intentionally* multicultural historical examples of worship. In Roman Catholic and mainline Protestant history, culture, race, and language have more often than not divided Christians, especially when they gather to pray. On the one hand, this is understandable especially for those groups who sought to maintain their cultural identity in a very complex and sometimes hostile culture. This was the principal cause for the growth of "national parishes" of Irish, Germans, Italians, and others in nineteenth-century Roman Catholicism, of Lutheran congregations founded by synods that trace their origin to Germany and the

Scandinavian countries, and of Dutch Calvinists. On the other hand, at least in the United States, this has reflected social, ethnic, and racial divisions even among cultural groups of the same denomination. In a lecture given at Western Michigan University in 1963, Dr. Martin Luther King's words are tragically still true today. "We must face the fact that in America," he said, "the church is still the most segregated major institution in America. At 11:00 on Sunday morning when we stand and sing and Christ has no east or west, we stand at the most segregated hour in this nation. This is tragic."

Whether we care to admit it or not, today in our globalized world, we all live amid cultural diversity—even the most isolated regions in the United States are receiving people from Latin America, Asia, and other areas of the world. It is not unusual in the course of our day to run into a wide variety of people of different national and ethnic backgrounds. This raises the obvious question, "If we are living our daily public lives in a multicultural context, shouldn't our worship reflect that reality?"

I first met Eunjoo Mary Kim in an annual seminar group of the North American Academy of Liturgy dedicated to studying liturgy and culture. As a participant in that group she brings a unique and valuable perspective on worship that has enriched our discussions every year. Her position as professor of homiletics and liturgics at Iliff School of Theology in Denver and as a native of Korea affords her a privileged vantage point from which to look at the crucial enterprise of preparing preachers and liturgists in US congregations that are becoming increasingly multicultural. She is also a wide-ranging ecumenical scholar, conversant in the literature on liturgy and culture inspired by the range of Christian denominations.

The approach of this book to the topic of multicultural preaching and worship is appropriately interdisciplinary. In the following pages the reader will be exposed not only to theological foundations for understanding multicultural worship but also to specific hermeneutical (interpretive) considerations that are being developed by scholars working in light of new developments in biblical, intertextual, postcolonial, feminist, and ritual studies. These discussions inform the six examples given in the appendixes that offer the reader concrete ways of applying the theoretical treatment of multicultural worship contained in the chapters of the book.

This book is the fruit of study, experience, and dialogue. It takes the event of worship seriously as an especially important *locus theologicus* or theological context for appreciating the movement of the Spirit of God in the Christian churches in a more profound way. By writing this book Eunjoo Kim has made an invaluable contribution to the ongoing mandate we have received from God to celebrate the Christian message through culturally sensitive preaching and worship in our globalized world.

Rev. Dr. Mark R. Francis, CSV
President and Professor of Liturgy
Catholic Theological Union at Chicago

Introduction

Thinking about Christian preaching and worship in a multicultural context is not a new approach. The Christian church has always been situated in multicultural circumstances and worshiped God in diverse ways by incorporating cultural elements. As Richard Niebuhr summarizes in *Christ and Culture*, the church has always related to the surrounding culture in a variety of ways.[1] Obviously, Christian preaching and worship are the best illustrations of the relationship between culture and the Christian faith.

In the twenty-first century's globalized world, most people are living in multicultural environments, locally and globally, and it is inevitable that the church take seriously this changing cultural context for its ministry. A few years ago, a student in my worship class insisted that he was serving a monocultural congregation composed of only White European Americans in a rural area of Colorado, so he did not need to consider the multicultural issue. When we look deeper, however, even his White European American congregation is not culturally homogeneous. The Roman Catholic scholar, Mark R. Francis, CSV, convinces us that churches built by the original national groups of the early settlers in the United States have largely disappeared into mainstream US society, and nowadays they worship with people who are culturally different.[2] This situation represents not only the Roman Catholic Church but Christian churches in general

---

[1] Richard H. Niebuhr, *Christ and Culture* (New York: Harper and Row, 1956).

[2] Mark R. Francis, *Shape a Circle Ever Wider: Liturgical Inculturation in the United States* (Chicago: Liturgical Training Publications, 2000); *Liturgy in a Culturally Diverse Community: A Guide Towards Understanding* (Washington, DC: Federation of Diocesan Liturgical Commissions, 2012), 2.

in the United States. Even among Asian and other non-European American communities that have relatively short histories of immigration, an increasing number of people, particularly second and third generations, actively interact with different cultural groups and search for a worship community where they can experience meaningful and memorable worship across racial and ethnic boundaries.

One of my colleagues asked why I was interested in multicultural preaching and worship, since for her, as a Jew, the reason she attended her religious services was to pray, sing, and listen to scriptures in her mother tongue with people of her own race and ethnicity. As a first-generation Korean American, I understand what she means. Whenever I worshiped with people of my own race and ethnicity in my native language, following their unique liturgical tradition, I could immediately feel connected to the worship service and reaffirm my racial and cultural roots. Nonetheless, the more I attended my ethnic worship services, the more I felt that the monocultural worship was theologically exclusive and liturgically limited, due to its primary task of serving the interest of a particular racial and cultural group.

This experience raised for me a theological and liturgical question that Francis eloquently phrases, "Is culturally exclusive worship 'consistent with Christ's challenge for us to look beyond our own cultural limitations and prejudices to the universality of the Kingdom of God?'"[3] This question is a challenge to all ethnic minority churches, as well as majority European American congregations. I maintain that even when the congregants have the same racial and cultural backgrounds, their worship should not be limited to themselves, but their theological concerns and liturgical experiences should be extended beyond their limited worldview and culturally embedded spiritual practices.

Over the half century after Martin Luther King Jr. critically reminded us that Sunday worship time was the most segregated time of the week in the United States, the demographics of American congregations have slowly changed, and now they are no longer sharply divided by race and ethnicity. Their liturgies, however, still are. Most churches have not made intentional efforts to break

[3] Ibid., 3.

through the racial and cultural divides but have struggled to maintain the monocultural worship service. One reason for this reality is that it is difficult for pastors and congregations to think about their worship services outside of their traditional practice, for they were neither trained nor exposed to celebrating Christian worship from multicultural perspectives.

It is true that many theological schools in the United States have a number of students who have grown up in racially and culturally different liturgical environments, and many churches where they serve and will serve are located in a no longer racially and ethnically monolithic culture. Yet, most theological schools and seminaries still maintain the monocultural approach in their curricula. Their preaching and worship courses narrowly focus on the homiletical and liturgical practice in the tradition of the European American churches, on the assumption that their liturgical traditions are monolithic. Such a pedagogical direction is neither appropriate nor effective to celebrate Christian worship in our pluralistic, multicultural world. It is, therefore, urgent for the church to reform the ministry of preaching and worship to make it more relevant to our culturally diverse contexts.

How, then, can Christian preaching and worship in multicultural contexts be more faithful to the Christian gospel and more meaningful and memorable to the worshipers? This book takes into account this theological and liturgical concern and proposes a paradigm shift from monocultural to multicultural preaching and worship. The primary goal of this book is to help preachers and worship leaders, as well as homiletics and liturgics scholars, seek theological and biblical wisdom for and homiletical and liturgical insights into preaching and worship. Only in this way can their ministry participate in a life worthy of living together in our multicultural context.

For this purpose, the basic approach of the book is practical theological. It critically reflects on current theories and practices of preaching and worship from the multicultural perspective and aims to construct a new homiletical and liturgical paradigm that is effective to answer probing questions about and possibilities for the future of Christian preaching and worship. In the practical theological discipline, interdisciplinary dialogue is the key method. Dialogue with social sciences such as sociology, politics, cultural studies, anthropology, interreligious dialogue, and ritual theories, as well as with such areas of theological studies as doctrinal theology, biblical studies, and church history, broadens and deepens our understanding of the nature and function of preaching and worship in our multicultural world.

While a variety of approaches are available for interdisciplinary dialogue, Richard Osmer summarizes them into three models: the correlational, the transformational, and the transversal. According to his brief description, the correlational model regards theology and nontheological disciplines as equal dialogue partners,[4] and the transformational model considers them "standing in an asymmetrical bipolar unity."[5] The transversal model, originally proposed by J. Wentzel van Huyssteen as a postfoundationalist approach to interdisciplinary studies,[6] means conversation "ad hoc, moving back and forth between the disciplines to discover areas of convergence and divergence in ways that cannot be determined in advance but are specific to the disciplinary perspectives being engaged at any given time."[7] This last model leads the homiletical and liturgical study to overlap with a number of scientific studies. Moreover, its approach enriches conversation about a specific topic discussed in each chapter of the book, by providing resources for and insights into the renewal of Christian preaching and worship from the multicultural perspective.

The book is composed of four parts, with seven chapters. In "Part 1: Seeking Theological Foundations," chapter 1 explains multiculturalism as a socio-cultural and political movement to transform our multicultural society into a better world, in conversation with politics and sociology. Next, the chapter proposes a theology of diversity as the foundation of theological discourse on multiculturalism and

---

[4] Richard Osmer, "A New Clue for Religious Education?," in *Forging a Better Religious Education in the Third Millennium*, ed. by James Michael Lee (Birmingham: Religious Education Press, 2000), 187.

[5] Ibid., 188.

[6] J. Wentzel van Huyssteen, *Alone in the World: Human Uniqueness in Science and Theology* (Grand Rapids: Eerdmans, 2006), 9, 32–34.

[7] Osmer, "A New Clue," 195. The term "transverse" means to lie across, as a pile of beams might lie across one another at odd angles. The term suggests a fluid and dynamic understanding of the disciplines in which they intersect at some points and move apart at others.

human diversity, by exploring such traditional Christian doctrines as the image of God, the Trinity, and Creation from the multicultural perspective. Chapter 2 engages in conversation with cultural studies and anthropology to analyze and examine various liturgical cultures from three cultural views—the premodern, the modern, and the postmodern. It also presents the essence of Christian preaching and worship relevant to our multicultural world in a threefold way as the divine invitation to the community of friends, the human response to the invitation through praying and doing justice, and a fiesta, the eschatological celebration.

In "Part 2: Exploring Multicultural Hermeneutics," chapter 3 reexamines Christian scripture in our multicultural and pluralistic world and proposes multicultural hermeneutics as an alternative to the exclusive view of *sola scriptura*. Multicultural hermeneutics is not limited to Christian scripture and traditions but employs such critical methods as literary criticism, feminist and other social critical theories, postcolonial criticism, and intertextuality, in order to search for the wisdom of God, through dialogue with other religions and through intertextuality. Moreover, the chapter provides four hermeneutical principles for the practice of multicultural hermeneutics for preaching and worship in multicultural contexts. Chapter 4 exercises multicultural hermeneutics with the miracle story in Luke 7:11-17. As historiography or a historical narrative, the theological meaning of the text evolves through multicultural hermeneutics, particularly through the intertextual dialogue with the Buddhist story, "The Parable of the Mustard Seed."

In "Part 3: Searching for New Liturgical Models," chapter 5 first discusses why liturgical renewal is necessary and how it can be done effectively, in dialogue with ritual theories, and then reviews renewal movements of preaching and worship in the history of the Christian church from the multicultural perspective. Based on interdisciplinary study with ritual theories and church history, the chapter provides homiletical and liturgical insights into the renewal of preaching and worship in our multicultural context. Chapter 6 introduces five liturgical models—the melting pot, the salad bowl, the mosaic, the kaleidoscope, and the metamorphosis—and assesses each model with its strengths and weaknesses, in order to develop models of multicultural worship effective in particular liturgical and cultural contexts.

In "Part 4: Practice in Multicultural Contexts," chapter 7 proposes the reflective practical theological method as the process of the renewal of preaching and worship in an actual ministerial setting. In the reflective practical theological method, theory and practice dialectically relate to each other through the spiral movement of four stages—empathetic imagination, prayerful and contemplative imagination, creative imagination, and visionary imagination. Each stage is illustrated with a sample sermon and liturgy that I prepared and performed in a particular liturgical setting.

The last chapter is followed by appendixes in which my own sermons and worship orders are included. Throughout, introductory words are footnoted, briefly describing the liturgical context with its specific homiletical or liturgical information. These are just a few examples of multicultural preaching and worship. My intention with these examples is to provide preachers and worship leaders with some clues about how to practice the new paradigm of preaching and worship proposed in this book and to encourage them to practice it creatively in their particular liturgical contexts.

PART 1

Seeking Theological Foundations

CHAPTER 1

A Theology of Diversity

Multiculturalism and Its Challenges

The ministry of Christian preaching and worship cannot be considered without reflecting on its particular socio-cultural and historical context. It is true that contemporary Christian worshipers live in a most complex world, culturally, socially, and religiously. Within and beyond the church, they encounter many racially and ethnically different people who have various religious and cultural backgrounds. In particular, people in the West are aware that they live in a distinct historical epoch, no longer the age of Christendom, but moving toward post-Christendom, in which they are exposed to diversity in race, ethnicity, culture, and religion. Such diversity often affects power dynamics and causes tensions and conflicts between the culturally dominant group and other ethnic minority groups. This reality challenges all parties to reexamine their identities, worldviews, and faith traditions and practices and to be open to the possibility of transformation.

The term "multiculturalism" has been broadly used in relation to today's multicultural society. It often refers to a present social condition, "a state or condition of being multicultural,"[1] or "our historical fate to be living now."[2] Yet, multiculturalism is a loaded term. In fields within the social sciences such as politics, sociology, anthropology, and cultural studies, it is involved in "a variety of ideological

---

[1] www.dictionary.com/browse/multiculturalism. Accessed April 17, 2016.
[2] Eileen Ka-May Cheng uses this phrase to describe postmodernism in her book, *Historiography: An Introductory Guide* (New York: Continuum, 2012), 127.

constructs"[3]—political, social, and cultural. Many conservatives, as Henry Giroux points out, use the term in a negative sense "to signify a disruptive, unsettling, and dangerous force" against the dominant racial and ethnic group in a multicultural society.[4] In mainstream liberal discourse, however, multiculturalism is considered an affirmative and constructive "social model for the future,"[5] in which people are equally recognized and mutually respected regardless of their differences in race, ethnicity, culture, and religion. In this position, David Goldberg defines multiculturalism as the ideology of "political correctness,"[6] which is "critical of and resistant to the necessarily reductive imperatives of monocultural assimilation."[7] Jürgen Habermas also understands multiculturalism as "liberation movements" in political and cultural terms, that is, "the struggle of oppressed ethnic and cultural minorities for the recognition of their collective identities" and a way of "overcoming an illegitimate division of society."[8]

It is worth noting that Bhikhu Parekh distinguishes multiculturalism and interculturalism in conceptual and policy frameworks. According to him, both are social and political movements that pursue "developing commonalities rather than just the differences, and evolving a shared identity based on shared experiences" among diverse racial and ethnic groups in society. Yet, their approaches are different in the sense that multiculturalism is "a pro-minority provenance and orientation" while interculturalism is "biased towards the majority":[9]

[3] Henry E. Giroux, "Insurgent Multiculturalism and the Promise of Pedagogy," in *Multiculturalism: A Critical Reader*, ed. David Theo Goldberg (Cambridge: Blackwell, 1994), 336.

[4] Ibid.

[5] Giancarlo Collet, "From Theological Vandalism to Theological Romanticism? Questions about a Multicultural Identity of Christianity," in *Christianity and Cultures*, ed. Norbert Greinacher and Norbert Mette (Maryknoll, NY: Orbis Books, 1994), 28–29.

[6] David Goldberg, "Introduction: Multicultural Conditions," in Goldberg, *Multiculturalism: A Critical Reader*, 1.

[7] Ibid., 7.

[8] Jürgen Habermas, "Struggles for Recognition," in *Multiculturalism*, ed. Amy Gutmann (Princeton, NJ: Princeton University Press, 1994), 117.

[9] Bhikhu Parekh, "Afterword: Multiculturalism and Interculturalism—A Critical Dialogue," in *Multiculturalism and Interculturalism: Debating the Dividing*

Interculturalism . . . emphasizes robust intercommunal exchanges and has little sympathy for the minorities that want to lead relatively self-contained lives. . . . It is uncommon for them to feel nervous, diffident, overwhelmed by the all-pervasive majority culture. They then need the space and the resources to build up their self-confidence and strength, to explore and draw inspiration from their heritage, to debate among themselves and form a view of their own on public issues. Multiculturalism is acutely aware of this; interculturalism is not. Multiculturalism appreciates the symbolic significance and cultural value of sponsoring and publicly funding minority or single-identity artistic, religious, linguistic and other organisations and projects; interculturalism is in varying degrees antipathetic to them. . . . Multiculturalism is acutely aware of the ease and arrogance with which Western societies have historically judged and condemned non-Western cultures, and urges caution and humility. Interculturalism for the most part shared no such inhibition.[10]

In sum, multiculturalism is a socio-cultural and political movement that aims to change the multicultural society into a better world where people who differ in race, ethnicity, culture, and religion can live peacefully with equally respected recognition of their diverse cultural identities. In order to construct such a community, "a two-way process involving changes in both the majority and the minorities"[11] is imperative. It is an effort to "delicately [balance] the identity demands of the majority and the minority"[12] by generating "spaces within which different communities are able to grow at their own pace" and "interact [with and] enrich the existing culture." Ultimately, multiculturalism aims to create "a new consensual culture in which all recognize reflections of their own identity."[13]

The conceptualization of multiculturalism discussed in the social sciences is an invaluable source to deal with Christian preaching and

Lines, ed. Nasar Meer, Tariq Modood, and Ricard Zapata-Barrero (Edinburgh: Edinburgh University Press, 2016), 277.

[10] Ibid., 277–78.

[11] Ibid., 269.

[12] Ibid., 274.

[13] Homi Bhabha and Bhikhu Parekh, "Identities on Parade: A Conversation," *Marxism Today* (June 1989): 4, quoted from Giroux, "Insurgent Multiculturalism," 337.

worship in multicultural contexts. If multiculturalism is to become a subject matter of Christian preaching and worship, fundamental issues of multiculturalism need to be probed theologically in relation to such questions as: What does it mean to be a human as we relate to God and others? How can it be possible to recognize and respect racially and culturally different people? And, what kind of world do we envisage in our multicultural contexts? Considering that theology is basically tasked to explore possible interpretations of human experiences and articulate new possibilities for experience, these questions demand creative theological thinking rather than conventional theological assumptions. Profound theological answers to these questions will not only deepen the understanding of multiculturalism but also enrich the theology and practice of preaching and worship in multicultural contexts.

In relation to these questions, the rest of the chapter focuses on developing a theology of diversity. This has been one of the major topics in my recent research. For example, in the essay, "A Theology of Preaching in Post-Christendom: Seeking a New Paradigm," I presented a theology of diversity as a work-in-progress to respond to the problem of divine revelation in the pluralistic context of post-Christendom.[14] The following three sections advance the conceptual framework and content of the theology of diversity in depth and propose it as the theological foundation for preaching and worship in multicultural contexts. The theology of diversity fundamentally deals with the intrinsic value of human beings on the basis of their primary identity created in and according to the image of God and understands human diversity to be based on the trinitarian concept of God. Accordingly, such traditional Christian doctrines as the image of God, the Trinity, and Creation are revisited and critically evaluated from a multicultural perspective to envisage a future of human community. Consequently, the theology of diversity challenges preachers and worship leaders to examine their basic assumptions about human identity and diversity and encourages them to practice the ministry of preaching and worship in a theologically profound way.

---

[14] Eunjoo M. Kim, "A Theology of Preaching in Post-Christendom: Seeking a New Paradigm," in *Viva Vox Evangelii–Reforming Preaching*, ed. Jan Hermelink and Alexander Deeg (Leipzig: Evangelische Verlangsanstalt, 2013), 263–80.

The Image of God and Human Identity

What does it mean to be a human as we relate to God and others? The central Christian response to this question belongs at the heart of any discussion about the biblical statement of the *imago Dei*. Genesis 1:26-28 speaks of God creating humankind as male and female in and according to the image of God and giving them dominion over other creatures. Throughout the history of Christian theology, the biblical notion of the image of God has prompted numerous controversial and richly diverse debates. Still, those debates have not yet really resolved what image bearing means, and it remains an open-ended theological topic. This situation requires of us profound theological reflection on what the image of God means and awaits a fresh new interpretation crucial to our multicultural contexts for preaching and worship.

In *Alone in the World? Human Uniqueness in Science and Theology*, J. Wentzel van Huyssteen summarizes the rich history of interpretation of the image of God in three phases: "substantive interpretations" that understand the image of God as such individual "property or capacity" as "reason, rationality, and intellect";[15] "functional interpretations" that stress "the role of human action" as "God's representatives" in relation to the task of "dominion over the earth";[16] and "relational interpretations" that identify the image of God as the "amazing ability or gift to be in a relationship with God."[17] While these three views have contributed to understanding the meaning of the image of God in certain ways, states Huyssteen, all of them have weaknesses: The substantive view leads to "a mind/body dualism,"[18] the functional view is controversial "in light of the current ecological debate,"[19] and the relational view is not grounded in "the original *imago Dei* texts."[20]

---

[15] J. Wentzel van Huyssteen, *Alone in the World: Human Uniqueness in Science and Theology* (Grand Rapids: Eerdmans, 2006), 126.

[16] Ibid., 134–35.

[17] Ibid., 136.

[18] Ibid., 133.

[19] Ibid., 135.

[20] Ibid., 137.

In addition to these three hermeneutical views, Huyssteen elaborates on two contemporary views on the *imago Dei*: the *imago Dei* as embodied self and the *imago Dei* as future-oriented. According to Robert Jenson, explains Huyssteen, human beings are unique because they have communications with God through rituals: "[A]s embodied prayer, ritual is the complement to that address of God that posits our ontologically specific humanity. And as such, we humans are the praying animals."[21] In other words,

> To be human . . . is to have a body, and as this embodied person to be open and available to God and to one another. . . . The image of God thus consists in the action of prayer, but it is faith that performs this action through love for the other. Ultimately it is in *love*, then, that we find the true *imago Dei*.[22]

The image of God as the embodied self does not mean the present condition of the human being, but it is "'self-transcendent,' a 'future-open' entity that now is itself only as it projects what it is not yet."[23] This eschatological perspective is reinforced by Wolfhart Pannenberg. For him, the image of God is "both an original gift and a future destiny for humankind."[24] In line with this, Jürgen Moltmann argues that the true image of God "is to be found not at the beginning of God's history with human kind, but in true eschatological fashion at its end."[25]

The embodied eschatological view has become the key theological approach among contemporary evolutionary theologians. For example, in *Life, Love, and Hope: God and Human Experience*, Jan-Olav Henriksen attempts to create the relevant meaning of the image of God for contemporary believers who are living in the modern scientific world, based on theological insights gained from the embodied eschatological view. For him, the image of God, primarily granted to humans in creation, is not rationality but love for the other, and

---

[21] Robert Jenson, "The Praying Animal," *Zygon: Journal of Science and Religion* 18, no. 3 (September 1983), quoted from Huyssteen, *Alone in the World*, 146.

[22] Huyssteen, *Alone in the World*, 147.

[23] Ibid.

[24] Ibid., 141.

[25] Ibid., 152.

it is in the evolutionary process of completion through interaction with others. In other words, human beings are created in the image of God, as the embodied being, to be available to love one another, and called to complete the love-relationship with others, which is the divine intention for the creation of the world.[26]

In fact, love is God's mode of being (1 John 4:16) that implies the human being's mode of being created in and according to the image of God. John Zizioulas expands on this notion as follows:

> Love is not an emanation or "property" of the substance of God . . . but is *constitutive* of His [*sic*] substance, i.e. it is that which makes God what He is, the one God. . . . Love as God's mode of existence "hypostasizes" God, *constitutes* His being. Therefore, as a result of love, the ontology of God is not subject to the necessity of the substance. Love is identified with ontological freedom.[27]

The expression of God as love signifies that God is personal. The personal God has created human beings in and according to the divine image to love and to be loved and invites them to the love-relationship with God and others, regardless of their biological, social, and religious differences. As Henriksen claims, the whole world created by God "is conceived of in faith as the place where love should be promoted, witnessed, expressed, fulfilled, expected, and anticipated."[28]

The fulfilled state of the image of God or the love-relationship with God and others is the *telos* of humanity. In Genesis 1, when God was creating the universe, the goodness of the world was subsequently affirmed by the words, "God saw that it was good." This statement is, as Henriksen asserts, not a once-upon-a-time historical fact of the world but "a testimony to the basic conditions that are required if the world is to be as God intended it to be."[29] Celia Deane-Drummond extends the eschatological dimension of the goodness of the world to nonhuman creatures. In *The Wisdom of the Liminal: Evolution and Other*

---

[26] Jan-Olav Henriksen, *Life, Love, and Hope: God and Human Experience* (Grand Rapids: Eerdmans, 2014).

[27] John Zizioulas, *Being as Communion: Studies in Personhood and the Church* (Crestwood, NY: St. Vladimir's Seminary, 1985), 46.

[28] Henriksen, *Life, Love, and Hope*, 118.

[29] Ibid., 112.

Animals in Human Becoming, she explains that the fullness of creation means to bring forth harmony and balance among all the creatures that God has created in and for the world. She also insists that the image of God should be understood in light of the "intersectionality of human evolution and other animal lives"[30] rather than simply emphasizing human dominion over other creatures.

In this eschatological evolutionary view, the image of God is a promise or a destiny that has not yet been reached but is in the process of fulfillment. Contrary to the traditional Christian theology, in which the image of God is understood as a human nature that was given by God at the time of creation and either was lost as a result of the Fall, according to Protestant theology, or still remains in us as our essential nature even after the Fall, according to Roman Catholic theology,[31] the eschatological evolutionary view liberates the image of God to be open-ended toward fulfillment in the future.

If the image of God means the embodied love-relationship with God and others, it is crucial to deepen our understanding of love. Love is generally perceived as having three distinct forms—*agape, philia,* and *eros. Agape* is God's unconditional sacrificial love, which is the ultimate level and beyond human capacity to reach, while *philia* is conditional friendship among people, and *eros* is an expression of feelings based on sexual attraction. Insightfully, however, Deane-Drummond contends that all three forms of love should not be separated but be interconnected to represent the holistic concept of love:

> *Agape* is a more generalized version of love that makes more sense if it deliberately allows for the possibility of other forms of love to be qualified within it. Hence, *philia* may have destructive tendencies, but when guided by *agape* it can lead to an overall love that is open rather than closed. . . . The *eros* hovering in the background of love as *agape,* then, can be thought of as directed toward valuation of an ultimate end as the object of desire so as to promote overall

---

[30] Celia Deane-Drummond, *The Wisdom of the Liminal: Evolution and Other Animals in Human Becoming* (Grand Rapids: Eerdmans, 2014), 21.

[31] Leroy Howe, *The Image of God: A Theology for Pastoral Care and Counseling* (Nashville: Abingdon Press, 1995), 56.

flourishing, even in the face of immediate difficulties, setbacks and hostilities.[32]

In the holistic view of love, *philia* "guided by *agape*" stands out as the form of love that humans need to practice in the relationship with God and others. It denotes "human friendship with God"[33] that results in promoting "loving others as God loves, so inviting greater openness and hospitality to others," by including every stranger "in a circle of friendship."[34] This notion of *philia* is distinct from that of Aristotle's, which is prevalent in the popular understanding of friendship. For Aristotle, "*philia* consists . . . more of loving than of being loved, and the best expression of friendship occurs when a friend is loved according to that friend's worth."[35] *Philia* guided by *agape*, however, occurs in an unequal relationship between God and "the people God saves," by divine initiation (John 15:15). As Thomas Aquinas elaborates, "Grace raises us to a new connaturality with God. . . . God creates friends for himself [*sic*]. And we can love God for what God is, according to his 'worth,' because God has made us able to do so."[36] Initiated by the grace of God, *philia* as the love of friendship

> presupposes the ability not only to love oneself, but also to perceive another as an individual subject; hence the person who loves her friend wills the friend's good and not her own, though not necessarily more than her own good. The closest friendships will therefore be with those who are considered other selves who share the same basic capacities and interests in flourishing. In this sense, another's good becomes part of our own good. In biological terms, this ability to recognize depth of connection is sometimes called a form of "deep engagement."[37]

Philia as a form of deep engagement with others plays a major role in the formation of human identity. Who we are and what we

---

[32] Deane-Drummond, *The Wisdom of the Liminal*, 294–95.

[33] Ibid., 297.

[34] Ibid., 298.

[35] Pamela M. Hall, *Narrative and the Natural Law: An Interpretation of Thomistic Ethics* (Notre Dame, IN: University of Notre Dame Press, 1994), 76.

[36] Ibid., 77.

[37] Deane-Drummond, *The Wisdom of the Liminal*, 298.

become as human beings are defined in continuity with other human beings who are different from ourselves and can be fulfilled by living a life of love with and for others as God loves them. Human identity, therefore, is a communal product, and the fruit of friendship is "a new harmony"[38] or a peace with others through the transforming power of love.

The communal sense of human identity grounded in the love of friendship leads preachers and worship leaders to think theologically about the matter of diversity in our multicultural society. Diversity is, in fact, a challenge for everyone, for it is not easy to make friends (or to love others and to be loved by them), particularly with those who are most unlike ourselves in the backgrounds of race, ethnicity, culture, social status, and religion. If preaching simply stresses the significance of love for others without considering such a reality, that kind of sermon is too idealistic; if worship celebrates diversity without taking seriously problems caused by such diversity, that kind of worship is inauthentic. How, then, can the reality of diversity in human communities be articulated in preaching and expressed in worship in theologically appropriate ways? How can preaching and worship recognize and respect racially and culturally different people? In relation to these questions, the trinitarian framework of who God is and what God is doing illuminates theological directions and insights.

The Trinity and Human Diversity

Christian faith is based on the confession that the very essence of God belongs to the Trinity of God. If preachers and worship leaders faithfully follow the lectionary texts for their Sunday worship services, Trinity Sunday will always highlight and celebrate the mystery of the Trinity. The doctrine of the Trinity has traditionally focused on exploring the mystery of the Trinity in relation to the uniqueness of each Person and the internal relationship of the three Persons of the Trinity. Indeed, the concept and relationship of the three Persons in the Trinity is a mystery that surpasses human understanding.

---

[38] Hall, *Narrative and the Natural Law*, 78.

The internal relationship of Father, Son, and Holy Spirit has been described by the Greek term *perichoresis*, derived from the Greek *peri* ("around") and *chorein* ("contain"). It was first used to express the relationship between the divine and human natures of Christ and later became the technical term to describe the reciprocal relationship of the three Persons of the Trinity. [39] In the *perichoresis*, explains Leonardo Boff, each distinctive Person of the Trinity penetrates each of the others without losing the distinctive character as Creator, Liberator, and Sustainer "to be *for* the others, *through* the others, *with* the others and *in* the others." [40] To put it another way, the trinitarian Persons "do not exist in themselves for themselves: the 'in themselves' *is* 'for the others.'" [41] They interpenetrate one another as "not independent, nor even interdependent identities who influence one another, but rather, . . . [as] *personally interior* to one another." [42] The *perichoretic* relationship of the Trinity, which means "the unity and plurality of the being of God," [43] is the divine mode of living, through which the divine unity is actualized by realizing the differences of the others and sharing love in the lives of the others.

The manifestation of the *perichoresis* of the Trinity, which is the ultimate state of unity-in-difference, is ineffable. In limited human language, such terms as "glory" and "beauty" may be used to express, partially, the sublime of the mystery and the depth of the divine unity-in-difference. As Boff reminds us, in Christian worship, doxology is an important liturgical component to express "adoration, thanksgiving and respect in the face of the mystery of the Trinity." [44] The entire worship service is actually supposed to be doxological, through which worshipers may experience the glory and beauty of the *perichoresis* of the Trinity and praise the wonderful work of the Trinity for the world.

[39] https://en.wikipedia.org/wiki/Perichoresis. Accessed June 28, 2016.

[40] Leonardo Boff, *Trinity and Society*, trans. Paul Burns (Maryknoll, NY: Orbis Press, 1988), 127.

[41] Ibid., 128.

[42] Andrew Shepherd, *The Gift of the Other: Levinas, Derrida, and a Theology of Hospitality* (Eugene, OR: Pickwick Publications, 2014), 110.

[43] Ibid.

[44] Boff, *Trinity and Society*, 158.

If humans were created as communal beings in and according to the image of God, the *perichoretic* relationship of the Trinity is "the prototype of the human community."[45] Henriksen uses the term "a double-*perichoresis*"[46] to describe the communal relationship of humanity grounded in the *perichoretic* relationship of God. According to him, the double-*perichoretic* relationship implies that just as the difference of the three Persons of the Trinity does not mean separation or opposition among them but enables them to enrich the divine essence of love, so human difference is created by God to be not obstacles but enrichment for human lives. In this manner, the unity-in-difference of the Trinity models the mode of living for the human community in God: "Father, may they be one in us, as you are in me" (John 17:21-23). Such unity is possible through the practice of *philia*, the love of friendship, as the three Persons of the Trinity unite through interpenetration, by loving the others.

The genuine love of friendship is the opposite of tolerance. As Jacob Neusner points out, the former actively engages thoroughly with the otherness of the other and changes both of them to become more mature humans in and according to the image of God, while the latter "works only in a climate of indifference."[47] Practicing the love of friendship thus makes it possible to recognize and respect otherness. Elizabeth Johnson reminds us that Jesus exemplified how to practice the love of friendship:

> Jesus-Sophia is the incarnation of divine friendship, hosting meals of inclusive table community and being hospitable to people of all kinds, even responding to prodding to widen his circle of care, as in the case of the Canaanite woman whose daughter was ill (Mt 15:21-28). He calls the women and men of his circle not children, not servants, and even disciples, but friends (Jn 15:15).[48]

---

[45] Ibid., 7.

[46] Henriksen, *Life, Love, and Hope*, 11, 230.

[47] Jacob Neusner, "Shalom: Complementarity," in *Ministry and Theology in Global Perspective: Contemporary Challenges for the Church*, ed. Don A. Pittman, Ruben L. Habito, Terry Muck (Grand Rapids: Eerdmans, 1996), 471.

[48] Elizabeth A. Johnson, *She Who Is: The Mystery of God in Feminist Theological Discourse* (New York: Crossroad, 1993), 217.

By making friends with others and loving them as God loved them, Jesus manifested God's goodness and love and became the true image of God (2 Cor 4:4-6; Col 1:15-20; Heb 1:3, etc.).

It would be hard to overemphasize that, in the life and work of Jesus, the Spirit of God was present in, with, and for him (Matt 1:18; Mark 1:10; Rom 1:4; Heb 5:5; 13:33; Phil 2:6-11, etc.). Even in Jesus' circle of friends, the Holy Spirit was deeply involved in their lives during his ministry and even after his death and resurrection. The Spirit also became the source of life and energy of the fledging Christian church (Acts 2) and has continued to work in the world by inspiring and encouraging people to practice the love of friendship with and for others as Jesus did. In the same manner, the Holy Spirit encourages us not to limit the love of friendship to the inner circle of friends of our own race and ethnicity in our multicultural society but to extend it to others, even to strangers and foreigners.

The mode of living following the lead of the Holy Spirit, who is the agent of "the double-*perichoretic* movement,"[49] represents the way of Christian life and suggests that Christian ethics should not be the ethics of a particular racial or ethnic group but one that "transcend(s) borders between groups."[50] Through the acts of love and responsibility in a widened circle of friendship, including those who are different from us in racial, cultural, social, economic, and religious backgrounds, we can become "true image bearing."[51]

For preachers and worship leaders who recognize the double-*perichoretic* movement of the Spirit, the task of Christian preaching and worship is to witness to the love of God in every face of God's creatures and to encourage the worshipers to cross their racial and cultural boundaries and break through the borderlines of their community of love. In order to accomplish this task, preachers and worship leaders need to open their eyes to see the image of God in every human face and recognize the presence and work of the triune God in the human community.

[49] Henriksen, *Life, Love, and Hope*, 345.
[50] Ibid., 255.
[51] Deane-Drummond, *The Wisdom of the Liminal*, 306.

Creatio Continua

If preachers and worship leaders see human identity and diversity as based on the communal sense of the image of God and the unity-in-difference of the Trinity, their homiletical and liturgical concern will be how to theologically articulate human responsibilities for the fulfillment of the image of God and how to project a vision for a new world. Regarding the vision for a new world, Boff describes the ultimate state of the human community or "a utopia"[52] as follows:

> A society that is without conflicts and that consists of an interplay of relationships in which the common good is placed above individual good because the members of such a society feel bound up with each other and completed in each other, through each other and by each other. This utopia, even though never achieved in the conditions of history as we know it, is eminently meaningful in both social and anthropological terms, since it continually unleashes energies directed at bringing about social changes in the direction of more balanced and participatory forms of living together.[53]

While Boff understands the utopian society as an ideal human community in which all the people live together peacefully with recognition and respect,[54] Deane-Drummond expands its dimension by including nonhuman creatures. She expresses the condition of peaceful coexistence with the Hebrew term "shalom," which means "right relationships with God and with every other creature."[55] Shalom "represents not just an absence of hostility, but enjoyment in relationships,"[56] which is the eschatological vision for all the creatures of God (cf. Isa 65:25; 11:6; Eph 2:10, etc.).

If the ministry of preaching and worship is responsible for achieving this visionary world, it is because of God's gracious invitation to the work of creation that still continues (*creatio continua*). As Henriksen explains,

[52] Boff, *Trinity and Society*, 130.
[53] Ibid.
[54] Ibid., 119, 130.
[55] Deane-Drummond, *The Wisdom of the Liminal*, 316.
[56] Ibid., 317.

God as the Creator is the originator of every moment, not only of the beginning of time, but of every moment since then. As such, God's *creatio prima* and *creatio continua* cannot be fully separated. Furthermore, God's creative work also implies change and process. Creation not only makes change possible in the first place, but it also makes it possible for God to create in, with, under, and through change.[57]

Niels Henrik Gregersen sums up this evolutionary view of Creation as this: "At each moment, God creates both *ex nihilo* (out of nothing) and *ex ovo* (out of the potentialities of the past) and for the purpose of letting something new come into being (*ad novum*)."[58] To God's *creatio continua*, preachers and worship leaders are invited to work together with their imagination of and passion for a new world.

In order for preaching and worship to be part of God's *creatio continua*, preachers and worship leaders need to discern the image of God in our multicultural society. In this regard, Henriksen states that "we are in a position to see Christ in the face of every other human—as the one who calls us to mercy, compassion, and love."[59] This declaration may sound alien to many Protestant believers. Since the sixteenth-century reformers emphasized the loss of the image of God at the time of the Fall, Protestant preaching has proclaimed that the image of God cannot be found in human beings, not "in the face of every other human," but only in the restored image of God, in those who confess Jesus Christ as their personal savior. It is, however, important for preachers and worship leaders to remember that the image of God as love is not an object that was once lost and then found but rather a mode of being and living in the communal life of human beings. All human beings are created in the image of God to love and to be loved as God intends, so the image of God is not only the primary state of being in creation but also in the process of becoming human—*creatio continua*.

[57] Henriksen, *Life, Love, and Hope*, 142.

[58] Niels Henrik Gregersen, "Special Divine Action and the Quilt of Laws," in *Scientific Perspectives on Divine Action: Twenty Years of Challenges and Progress*, ed. Robert J. Russell, et al. (Notre Dame, IN: University of Notre Dame Press, 2008), 192, quoted from Henriksen, *Life, Love, and Hope*, 144.

[59] Henriksen, *Life, Love, and Hope*, 267.

Conclusion

The theology of diversity, based on fresh new understanding of the image of God, the Trinity, and Creation from the eschatological evolutionary view, is the theological foundation for reflection on human identity and diversity in our multicultural society. It is a "public theology" in the sense that it contributes to "public discussion by witnessing to a truth which is relevant to what is going on in the world and to the pressing issues facing peoples and societies today."[60]

The theology of diversity as a public theology awakens Christian preachers to pay special attention to multiculturalism and provides them with a new interpretive lens through which they may critically examine their theological assumptions of the pressing issues emerging from the multicultural context within and beyond the church. In addition, it offers direction to the ministry of preaching and worship by challenging them to imagine a new world.

In this sense, the theology of diversity is theological imagination of the hope for a new world that is in *creatio continua*. This hope is not a daydream but inspiration grounded in the faith that the triune God of love is still at work to fulfill the image of God in humanity. Preachers and worship leaders are invited to manifest God's continuing work of love in our multicultural world. Their preaching and worship as *creation continua* have the power to inspire the worshipers to participate in God's *creatio continua* through practicing the love of friendship with and for others. By the grace of God, therefore, the whole Christian community, as well as preachers and worship leaders, is invited to the divine mission of *creatio continua* toward the actualization of hope for the entire world.

The sermon "Can We Love Our Enemies?," which is included in appendix 1, illustrates how Christian preaching can participate in God's *creatio continua*. I prepared this sermon to preach at the commemoration service of the death of Martin Luther King Jr. at Virginia Theological Seminary. The sermon tackles complexities of the racial conflicts and prejudices we have experienced locally and globally and evokes the listeners' imagination to envision the future of the

---

[60] Duncan B. Forrester, *Truthful Action: Exploration of Practical Theology* (Edinburgh: T&T Clark, 2001), 127.

human community from the perspective of the theology of diversity. Through the sermon, they are encouraged to love even their enemies, as Jesus did.

CHAPTER 2

Preaching, Worship, and Culture

The previous chapter explored the theology of diversity and presented it as a pertinent theological foundation for preaching and worship in multicultural contexts. It presupposes multicultural environments as an inescapable reality of our historical time and affirms the significance of multiculturalism in seeking theological directions for the well-being of God's creatures in the world. This chapter makes an effort to deepen the theological understanding of Christian preaching and worship from a cultural perspective, based on the theology of diversity.

Preaching and worship are liturgical acts formed in particular cultural milieus. Just as the anthropological understanding of culture suggests that "theology be viewed as a part of culture, as a form of cultural activity . . . historically and socially conditioned," so Christian preaching and worship are human cultural activities in the sense that they are "something that human beings produce"[1] in a particular socio-cultural and historical context. They not only represent the individual congregational culture and identity but also make an effort to change them, implicitly or explicitly.

In order to understand Christian preaching and worship from a cultural perspective, the first section of this chapter aims to explain the formation of liturgical cultures, based on the framework of Kathryn Tanner's three views on culture—the premodern, the modern, and the postmodern—expounded in her book, *Theories of Culture: A*

---

[1] Kathryn Tanner, *Theories of Culture: A New Agenda for Theology* (Minneapolis: Fortress Press, 1997), 63.

New Agenda for Theology.[2] The second section proposes the essence of Christian preaching and worship in multicultural contexts with three theological implications for multicultural worship—the divine invitation, praying and doing justice, and the eschatological celebration. These theological understandings of multicultural worship are fundamental to the practice of preaching and worship in multicultural contexts.

Three Views of the Liturgical Culture

Preaching and worship are inextricably associated with culture. Through culture, we not only express our faith in liturgy but also interpret liturgical acts. The term "culture" does not have one fixed meaning. Rather, as Giancarlo Collet informs us, more than three hundred definitions of culture are available.[3] Among them, Tanner's understanding of culture stands out as helpful to critically reflect on liturgical cultures. She classifies the various concepts of culture into three categories based on three different views—the premodern, the modern, and the postmodern—and explains them in chronological order.[4]

While her diversified views are suitable to deal with the complexity of Christian liturgical cultures, it should be admitted that her approach has some limitations when used for the analysis of liturgical culture. One is that her three views of culture are exclusively based on the historical context of Western Europe and North America. Other parts of the globe have not gone through the same intellectual stages in their cultural histories and may have used different norms in studying culture. Another limitation of Tanner's approach is that her chronological understanding of the three views is not quite accurate to explain cultural complexities in the Christian church and the larger world. In our daily lives, we often witness that the three views

---

[2] Ibid., 3–60.

[3] Giancarlo Collet, "From Theological Vandalism to Theological Romanticism? Questions about a Multicultural Identity of Christianity," in *Christianity and Cultures*, ed. Norbert Greinacher and Norbert Mette (Maryknoll, NY: Orbis Books, 1994), 32.

[4] Tanner, *Theories of Culture*, 3–60.

of culture do not exist diachronically but coexist in our contemporary context, not only synchronically, but also progressively, multiplying into various modified views of culture by interacting and interconnecting with one another. Nonetheless, the three views of culture provide a framework to analyze the diversity of Christian liturgical cultures and evaluate their influences on preaching and worship.

The Premodern View

In this view, the term "culture" is often used as a synonym for cultivation or civilization. Just as people "cultivate crops or animals in order to better them," so humans can cultivate their capacities or faculties through intellectual and aesthetic training.[5] In this sense, culture refers to "a process of individual education and refinement, and by extension, to the products of such processes (works of art and literature)."[6] Culture as cultivation or civilization means "the high culture achievements promoted and sustained by discrete social institutions" without associating it with "organic holism."[7] This conception of culture creates a hierarchy by dividing people into elite high culture and popular low culture groups, each of which has a unified singular form of culture.

The premodern conception of culture has influenced the formation of Christian liturgical culture through the Middle Ages, which is in stark contrast to those of the primitive and early churches. Biblical texts and early church history evidence that, in the fledging stage of the church, its worship was culturally diverse and preaching was "spontaneous," "allowing lay people to preach."[8] In this early stage, Christian preaching and worship promoted an egalitarian and participatory community in which gender, race, economic status, and social class were not discriminatory factors (cf. Gal 3:28). Throughout the medieval period, however, Christian worship was divided into high class liturgy and low class devotional practices. Liturgical

---

[5] Ibid., 4.

[6] Ibid., 5.

[7] Ibid., 16.

[8] Alden Bass, "Preaching in an Early Christian Church," in *A Handbook for Catholic Preaching*, ed. Edward Foley (Collegeville, MN: Liturgical Press, 2016), 54.

components, including sacraments, preaching, songs, prayers, etc., were formalized based on medieval doctrines; the primary agent of worship was not the assembled community but professionally trained "cultured" clergy. Peasants and illiterate commoners had to remain passive onlookers in the liturgy and be content with their popular devotional practices.

During the medieval period, preaching gradually became a professional ministry requiring formal education that was available for only male clergy. Lay preaching was rarely authorized, permitted only in special situations. Clergy were trained to master "a systematic reflection on the text according to some scholastic method";[9] sermons were normally written and preserved in Latin even though they were delivered to the laity in the vernacular.[10] Priests and bishops often read homilaries, which are collections of authoritative patristic sermons, in worship rather than preaching their own sermons.[11] Such a practice of preaching contributed to the formation of an elite high culture in the Christian liturgy.

The elite culture of liturgy has been transmitted to and retained in many Protestant denominational churches, particularly those connected to high church traditions. Their theological schools and seminaries train clergy according to the unified knowledge and format of their liturgy. Clergy, as cultural elites, are supposed to "perform" the liturgy that they have learned, regardless of the particular congregational culture. In such a liturgical culture, worshipers are treated as a passive audience rather than as active participants.

The Modern View

In the beginning of the twentieth century, the premodern conception of culture as individual maturity gained by intellectual and aesthetic training was challenged by such emerging social sciences as anthropology, ethnology, and sociology. They commonly understand culture at a communal level rather than as an individual achievement.

---

[9] Edward Foley, "The Homily," in Foley, *A Handbook for Catholic Preaching*, 157.
[10] Carolyn Muessig, "Medieval Preaching," in Foley, *A Handbook for Catholic Preaching*, 65.
[11] Foley, "The Homily," 157.

The modern view, which is an outcome of such social-scientific studies, conceptualizes culture as "traditional behavior which has been developed by the human race and is successfully learned by each generation."[12] In other words, culture is the attribute of a particular social group, that is, "social consensus . . . what every member of the group more or less shares" in the mode of life, including "social habits and institutions, rituals, artifacts, categorical schemes, beliefs and values."[13] In this view, each social group has its own distinctive corporate culture that has been historically transmitted to the community. Human culture is thus neither singular nor unified, but it is as diverse as human communities are.

The modern conception of culture has contributed a great deal to contemporary liturgical studies. For example, Vatican II documents on liturgy admit the "plurality of cultures" and acknowledge the "relativity of cultural expression" in worship.[14] Even in the Protestant tradition, many resources to learn about the racial and ethnic diversity of Christian worship have been published. C. Michael Hawn's book, *One Bread, One Body: Exploring Cultural Diversity in Worship,*[15] and Charles E. Farhadian's edited volume, *Christian Worship Worldwide: Expanding Horizons, Deepening Practices,*[16] are just a couple of them. In addition, African American, Asian American, and Latino American scholars have contributed to introducing distinctive cultural characteristics of their ethnic worship lives.[17]

[12] Margaret Mead, *Cooperation and Competition among Primitive Peoples* (New York: McGraw-Hill, 1937), 17, quoted from Tanner, *Theories of Culture,* 28.

[13] Tanner, *Theories of Culture,* 27.

[14] Mark Francis, *Liturgy in a Multicultural Community* (Collegeville, MN: Liturgical Press, 1991), 13.

[15] C. Michael Hawn, *One Bread, One Body: Exploring Cultural Diversity in Worship* (Bethesda, MD: Alban Institute, 2003).

[16] Charles E. Farhadian, ed., *Christian Worship Worldwide: Exploring Horizons, Deepening Practices* (Grand Rapids: Eerdmans, 2007).

[17] Cf. Melva W. Costen, *African American Christian Worship,* 2nd ed. (Nashville: Abingdon Press, 2007); Russell Yee, *Worship on the Way: Exploring Asian North American Christian Experience* (Valley Forge, PA: Judson Press, 2012); Justo L. González, ed., *¡Alabadle! Hispanic Christian Worship* (Nashville: Abingdon Press, 1996).

In relation to preaching, it is worth noting that in *Preaching as Local Theology and Folk Art*,[18] Leonora T. Tisdale emphasizes the significance of the particular congregational culture. Based on the modern view of culture, she reminds us that each congregation has its own unique "subculture" expressed by an idiom or a web of signs and symbols. Like an anthropologist, insists Tisdale, the preacher's task is to identify and interpret the congregation's "subcultural identity" with its distinctive "worldview, values, and ethos"[19] in order to make preaching engage and appeal to the particular congregation. The modern view of culture has also encouraged ethnic minority scholars in the United States to research distinctive characteristics of their own racial and ethnic preaching. As a result, resources for teaching and learning about African American preaching, Asian American preaching, and Hispanic preaching have been available since the late twentieth century.[20]

It is epochal that the modern view of culture has shifted the understanding of Christian preaching and worship from the unified expression of the elite clergy culture to distinctive cultural expressions of racially and ethnically different faith communities. The modern view, however, has its own limitations in comprehending the liturgical culture. First of all, by observing distinctive cultural phenomena of a geographically restricted space and synchronically limited time frame, the modern view defines "a particular slice of the historical sweep of things as cultural consensus."[21] It assumes that individual members of a society are born into a culture as its "passive porters"[22] and are responsible to preserve and transmit it to the next generations. This static understanding of culture leads local churches to

---

[18] Leonora T. Tisdale, *Preaching as Local Theology and Folk Art* (Minneapolis: Fortress Press, 1997).

[19] Ibid., 77.

[20] Cf. Henry Mitchell, *Black Preaching: The Recovery of a Powerful Art* (Nashville: Abingdon Press, 1990); Eunjoo Mary Kim, *Preaching the Presence of God: A Homiletic from an Asian American Perspective* (Valley Forge, PA: Judson Press, 1999); Kenneth Davis and Jorge Presmanes, eds., *Preaching and Culture in Latino Congregations* (Chicago: Liturgical Training Publications, 2000).

[21] Tanner, *Theories of Culture*, 35.

[22] Ibid., 29.

regard their identities and cultural expressions in preaching and worship as fixed and closed and discourages them from including other cultures in their preaching and worship in order to preserve their cultural homogeneity. Consequently, the worship life of a particular congregation tends to be exclusive rather than inclusive, static rather than dynamic, and regressive rather than progressive.

The second limitation of the modern view of culture is that its approach is still monocultural in the sense that it searches for the unified culture of a community. [23] The monocultural approach makes preachers and worship leaders assume that an individual church has a unique subculture representing its communal ethos and worldview. No community, however, even if it is racially homogeneous, has one unified subculture. Instead, every community has a multilayered culture or subcultures representing different subgroups in age, gender, class, sexuality, ethnicity, etc. If the community has a unified culture, that would be the culture of the dominant group, which suppresses and marginalizes the other subculture groups within the community. And if preachers and worship leaders regard the liturgical culture as that of the dominant group in the congregation, they participate, consciously or unconsciously, in maintaining the status quo of the cultural hegemony within the church.

The third limitation of the modern view is with the agents of socio-anthropological studies. In the past century, these were people of Western colonialist nations. As outsiders, they defined the culture of the colonized by observing its surface level and overlooked the complexity of the cultural dynamics within a community. Their space-oriented, atemporal approach increased the prejudice that non-Western cultures did not have a past, therefore rendering them inferior to historically civilized Western culture. [24] This biased attitude contributed to promoting imperialism and colonialism in the West and reinforced Eurocentrism in Christian liturgical culture. For example, Western missionaries and denomination leaders imposed their liturgical theology and practice on non-Western churches as the norm and forced them to change their cultural identities and expressions by adopting Western liturgy. Ethnic minority churches in North America

[23] Ibid., 46.
[24] Ibid., 41.

and churches in once- and still-colonized countries in other parts of the globe remain under the influence of the Euro-centered liturgy, and many theological schools and seminaries still teach preaching and worship courses based on the Western tradition, identifying it as the universal knowledge and practice of Christian preaching and worship.

The Postmodern View

In today's twenty-first-century colonial and postcolonial era, people struggle with the dichotomous dilemma of living in a globalized multicultural world with no sharp geographical boundaries between cultures, and their own communal desire to "protect a homogenous, stable, and unified whole from outside dissension and disruption."[25] In this particular historical time, racial and ethnic cultures are so fluid that our own racial and ethnic culture, which is supposed to be distinctive to our particular racial and ethnic community, is widely open to change through active interaction and exchanges with other cultures. Such internal and external factors as advanced information technology, the development of transportation, global job markets, and the increase of refugees, migrant workers, and immigrants have spurred "a cultural hybridity."[26] In other words, people face in daily life cultural negotiation through which their cultural identities are formed as hybrid, rather than being rooted in one particular racial and ethnic culture. Indeed, it is hard to find in our multicultural world a racially and ethnically pure culture that has not been mixed with other cultural factors.

This situation contributes to the primary distinction between the modern and the postmodern views on culture. Like the modern view, the postmodern view understands that culture may be formed "by stable configurations of cultural elements" to "be shared by all persons affiliated with a particular culture and thereby serve to solidify their social relations."[27] Unlike the modern view, though, the postmodern view does not assume that one community has one unified

[25] Ibid., 53.
[26] Homi K. Bhabha, *The Location of Culture* (New York: Routledge, 2004), 5.
[27] Tanner, *Theories of Culture*, 56.

culture. Instead, it focuses on the "interactive process and negotiation, indeterminacy, fragmentation, conflict, and porosity" of culture and takes into account diversity, complexity, and contradictions, not only among cultures, but also within cultures.[28] As a result, while the modern view regards cultural consensus as "a common focus of *agreement*" on a set of beliefs, values, and sentiments,[29] the postmodern view disagrees on that. If there is a possibility to consider cultural consensus in the postmodern view, it is "extremely minimalistic," because "it forms the basis for conflict as much as it forms the basis for shared beliefs and sentiments."[30] If not, the postmodern view of cultural consensus may be "a common focus for *engagement*"[31] in shared concerns of people who live in the process of becoming a "hybrid, relational affair, something that lives between as much as within cultures" in the multicultural society.[32]

The postmodern view of culture convinces preachers and worship leaders that the congregational culture should not be considered a unified culture and that the liturgical culture should no longer be conditioned by only one subculture of the congregation. Just as their congregational culture is multilayered and has the potential to be enriched through intersecting and interchanging with diverse subcultures of the congregation, so their liturgical culture has possibilities to evolve through cultural hybridity and thereby express the shared concerns of the worshipers in more appropriate ways. The cultural identity expressed in preaching and worship is supposed to represent the Christian identity of the worshipers. If the former is fixed in liturgical expression, the latter is hardly open to transformation. The postmodern view of culture, therefore, encourages preachers and worship leaders to reconsider their role in relation to the transformation of the liturgical culture and Christian identity of the worshipers. It challenges them to be vulnerable by opening themselves to learning about different cultures within and beyond their congregational liturgical traditions and to prepare the worship service with creativity across

---

[28] Ibid., 38
[29] Ibid.
[30] Ibid., 57.
[31] Ibid.
[32] Ibid., 57–58.

cultural boundaries. This challenge is also serious for theological schools and seminaries, for they need to train future preachers and worship leaders to be culturally competent and pastorally sensitive to changing cultural contexts for preaching and worship.

The Essence of Christian Preaching and Worship

Understanding the liturgical culture from the postmodern view directs us to rethink the nature and function of Christian preaching and worship in our multicultural context. While resources are scarce for conducting a theological and liturgical conversation from the postmodern view of culture, at least two books are valuable for considering how to transform Christian preaching and worship. One is Mark Francis's *Liturgy in a Multicultural Community*, written from a Roman Catholic point of view, and the other is Brian Blount and Tisdale's coedited volume, *Making Room at the Table: Invitation to Multicultural Worship,*[33] contributed by Protestant theologians. The former provides the historical knowledge of and liturgical insights into multicultural Christian worship, and the latter develops biblical and theological foundations of "multicultural worship." Based on these resources, the essence of Christian preaching and worship can be articulated in a threefold way: the divine invitation to the community of friends, the human response to the invitation through praying and doing justice, and the eschatological celebration here and now.

The Divine Invitation

In his monograph, Francis critically evaluates the modern view of culture that was the conceptual guideline for Vatican II documents on worship. While the modern conception of culture helps the church acknowledge the plurality and relativity of liturgy, argues Francis, it degenerates liturgy into a simple act of translation of the Christian message into the symbolic language of the congregation—verbal and nonverbal—by ignoring "the present movement of God's spirit."[34]

---

[33] Brian K. Blount and Leonora T. Tisdale, eds., *Making Room at the Table: An Invitation to Multicultural Worship* (Louisville: Westminster John Knox Press, 2001).

[34] Francis, *Liturgy in a Multicultural Community*, 17.

For him, culture is "a lens through which we look at the world and interpret reality" and express our faith.[35] Thus, culturally sensitive worship should be "much more than translation" and involve "more than bilingualism"[36] to be "a conscious attempt at helping all members of the assembly feel 'at home' at worship."[37]

The challenge of Francis's statement of culturally conscious worship is compelling, for making worship in which people who are genuinely different in race and culture feel at home is realistically a daunting task for the preacher and worship leaders. Donald H. Juel uses the image of a stranger in describing how challenging it is for culturally different people to live together and feel at home:

> Strangers pose a challenge not only in terms of physical violence. Encountering a stranger is genuinely unsettling. . . . It is remarkably difficult, because significant opinions about life's major questions are presupposed by the culture and taken to be common sense. As "common sense," they are never subjected to scrutiny. Those opinions, in turn, provide the very conditions for perceptions and judgments. Those raised in another culture—"strangers"—can raise questions that constitute a deep challenge to notions that we take to be foundational to everything we think and do.[38]

In spite of such difficulties, Juel reminds us that there is the potential for "real friendship" among the strangers through "a growing recognition of and respect for remarkably different ways of viewing and experiencing the world."[39] Although all of us are strangers—a genuine threat to and source of fear of one another in certain ways—we may became friends because the initiator of friendship is God. God, as the host, is willing to extend hospitality to all of us strangers to form a "community of strangers" in which differences are recognized as "a great gift."[40] Christian worship, according to Juel, is

[35] Ibid., 50.

[36] Ibid., 49.

[37] Ibid., 49–50.

[38] Donald H. Juel, "Multicultural Worship: A Pauline Perspective," in Blount and Tisdale, *Making Room at the Table*, 51.

[39] Ibid., 53.

[40] Ibid.

supposed to be multicultural, "a primary locus for this welcoming of strangers," because it is "a central place at which God is at work breaking down 'the dividing wall, . . . the hostility' (Eph. 2:14)."[41] What makes multicultural worship possible is, asserts Juel, the "God who claims us and promises that 'neither death, nor life, nor angels, nor rulers, nor things present, nor things to come, nor powers, nor height, nor depth, nor anything else in all creation, will be able to separate us from the love of God in Christ Jesus our Lord' (Rom. 8:38-39)."[42]

Sang Hyun Lee expresses God's invitation to the community of strangers as the experience of "liminality."[43] By observing worship services in Korean immigrant churches, he understands worship as "a ritual process that can be truly communal and transforming only when the participants are led to experience a structural ambiguity or openness by being liberated for a moment from social roles, status, and hierarchy."[44] This ritual process, according to Lee, is called an "in-between" or "liminal" state in Victor Turner's term, in which "one has left behind the 'culturally defined encumbrances of role, status, reputation, class, caste, sex or other structural niche'" and is "freed up temporarily from all that binds [one] in society."[45] For Lee, the "egalitarian relationship among persons" in the liminal state is powerful enough to lead the worshipers to feel free to "reflect on their lives or society, envision new ideas and ways of doing things and dream new dreams."[46] He identifies this "creative state"[47] as the experience of "leaving home, a pilgrimage,"[48] in which transformative change can happen in the community, as well as in the individual person, and defines multicultural worship as the ritual experience of this liminal state.

[41] Ibid., 55.

[42] Ibid.

[43] Sang Hyun Lee, "Worship on the Edge: Liminality and the Korean American Context," in Blount and Tisdale, *Making Room at the Table*, 96–107.

[44] Ibid., 97.

[45] Ibid., 98.

[46] Ibid.

[47] Ibid.

[48] Ibid., 104.

Multicultural worship as hospitality to the stranger or as the experience of a pilgrimage may be a wild experience, since it requires the worshipers to give up their ownership or leave home. Nonetheless, feeling at home in multicultural worship may be possible if the community of strangers or pilgrims turns into a community of friends where the strangers or pilgrims experience "real friendship" with one another. More precisely, extended hospitality, not as mannerism, but as the practice of genuine love of friendship, makes it possible for strangers and pilgrims to feel at home. Here, feeling at home should be distinguished from being in a comfort zone, a secure position, or a dominant status. Instead, it means a joyful experience through which our spiritual life is enhanced and enriched, even in the midst of conflicts and hardships.

Feeling at home in multicultural worship is not gained by chance but by intentional efforts of the preacher and worship leaders. In other words, the love of friendship is a prerequisite to authentic multicultural worship. By making friends with those strangers who have racially and culturally different backgrounds, the preacher and worship leaders may learn about the distinctive characteristics of their spiritual lives and incorporate the songs, prayers, and stories of the strangers into the worship service in effective ways that appeal to racially and culturally diverse worshipers. By making an effort to recognize and respect difference in multicultural worship, we encounter the living God in creative and harmonious ways beyond our conventional expectations. This kind of practice makes preaching and worship a liminal experience (the divine invitation to the community of strangers) and participates in the fulfillment of the image of God—the community of friends—that is in *creation continua*.

Praying and Doing Justice

Praying and doing justice are integral in worship, for the glory of God is manifested in the prayerful and just life of the worshipers (cf. Amos 5:21-24; Matt 6:1-18, etc.). Francis stresses this notion particularly in multicultural liturgical contexts. According to him, liturgy should encourage worshipers to question justice, to live justly in solidarity with others who are treated unjustly, and to share the faith that "God can and does liberate us" from the burdens of unjust acts.[49] Thus, Christian worship in multicultural contexts should be not merely culturally balanced liturgical expressions but a sharing of passion for justice and faith in the presence and work of the divine Spirit among us.

As vanThanh Nguyen defines it, justice means "to be in right relationship with God, with oneself, with one's neighbor, and with creation as a whole."[50] In this sense, justice and peace are a pair. They go together hand-in-hand:

> The word "peace" (Gr., *eirene*, Heb., *shalom*)—which means "wholeness," "perfect welfare," or "complete harmony"—appears very frequently in the gospels. When Jesus used the word peace, he implied more than just the absence of war. It is rather a state of wholeness or reconciliation with God and people. . . . What is peace for Jesus? It is, primarily, restoring people to a "right relationship" with God and with people. It is making people and society completely whole, a state "wherein greed will end, exploitation will cease, and an entirely new social order will take over" (Fuellenbach 1997, 168).[51]

Christian preaching and worship, understood as praying and doing justice, exchange ethical concerns through prophetic preaching and the liturgy of reconciliation. As Jorge Presmanes adequately defines it, prophetic preaching is a "dialogue between God and people . . . based on divine anger against the injustice that perpetuates human and environmental suffering of the oppressed."[52] It is deeply rooted in biblical narratives, both in the Hebrew Bible and the New Testament, in which God initiates it by calling preachers to share the divine pathos for the oppressed and preach against injustice in their particular historical time and place. Prophetic preaching requires prayerful and critical discernment of how God senses our reality and what God is doing in order to make human life more human.

---

[49] Robert W. Hovda, "The Amen Corner," *Worship* 63 (1989): 462, quoted from Francis, *Liturgy in a Multicultural Community*, 55.

[50] vanThanh Nguyen, "Preaching in the New Testament," in Foley, *A Handbook for Catholic Preaching*, 44.

[51] Ibid.

[52] Jorge Presmanes, "Prophetic Preaching," in Foley, *A Handbook for Catholic Preaching*, 210.

"Out of sympathy with God's pathos,"[53] states Presmanes, prophetic preachers proclaim "the emancipating truth of God's Word" and call for "concrete action on behalf of justice in the world."[54] The message of prophetic preaching, addressing sin and forgiveness, aims to liberate not only the oppressed or marginalized but also the oppressive or dominant group in society, by inviting them to live in and according to the image of God. In this sense, all preaching is to be prophetic, particularly in our multicultural context.[55]

According to Ruth Duck, "liturgies of reconciliation" are "the church's ancient ministry of addressing sin and forgiveness, woundedness and healing through worship and ritual."[56] In the multicultural context, one of the greatest sins is racial and cultural discrimination and its destructive consequences. In many cases, forgiveness is possible by grace only, and reconciliation through grace has the power to restore true friendship with God and one another. Duck explains what reconciliation means in our multicultural context, as follows:

> The life, death, and resurrection of Jesus Christ bring reconciliation, so that people from diverse nations and cultures become one body. For Paul, that meant breaking down the dividing walls between Jews and Gentiles; in the North American context, it means bringing together people of many races and cultures. In many countries, Christians seek common ground with their neighbors in the wake of prejudice, disaster, civil war, and violence.[57]

In the liturgy of reconciliation, the worshipers are invited not only to the inward confession of sin by naming specific sins but also to the outward act of doing justice at both individual and corporate levels. At this point, every worship service should fundamentally be the liturgy of reconciliation. Such liturgical components as the

---

[53] Ibid., 218.

[54] Ibid., 219.

[55] It is notable that Tércio B. Junker stresses that liturgy itself should be prophetic, by functioning as an "agent of transformation" in "social, political, and economic life" of the individuals and communities in his book, *Prophetic Liturgy: Toward a Transforming Christian Praxis* (Eugene, OR: Pickwick Publications, 2014), xv.

[56] Ruth Duck, *Worship for the Whole People of God: Vital Worship for the 21st Century* (Louisville: Westminster John Knox Press, 2013), 243.

[57] Ibid.

confession and pardon, the passing of the peace, the Eucharist, litanies of lament, the prayers of the people, pastoral prayer, charge and benediction, as well as preaching, are supposed to be effectively crafted to call the worshipers to reconciliation.[58] Following is an example of the prayer of confession that I crafted for the closing worship service of the Presbyterian Women Racial Ethnic Dialogue:

> (In Unison): O God, you have created the peoples of the earth to be one universal family. We bear the imprint of your face; the colors of our skin are your design. But, we have been torn and pulled apart by hate because of our race and ethnicity. We, as the Church, have often forgotten that in Christ's reconciling love, you already broke down every form of discrimination based on racial or ethnic differences. We judge and are judged against your will and dishonor your living face on earth. Forgive our sins and help us live according to your gracious calling to the ministry of reconciliation.[59]

In relation to the liturgy of reconciliation, it is also important to take into account reconciliation with nature. The respectful relationship with nature is an urgent issue for us as we face climate changes and other critical ecological crises. Native American prayers to the four directions of the Earth are some of the liturgical expressions of respecting and caring for nature.[60] Such prayers are not merely a token expression of cultural diversity but genuine conduits for us to express our sincere desire for reconciliation with nature.

The Eschatological Celebration

In his essay "The Apocalypse of Worship," Blount claims that "in the Gospel of Mark, Jesus is a preacher of multicultural worship."[61] He explains that multicultural worship is actually an urgent demand

[58] Ibid., 256.

[59] The Presbyterian Women Racial and Ethnic Dialogue was offered by the Presbyterian Church (USA) as an annual conference for three years (2010–2012), in order to educate female lay leaders of local churches on racial and ethnic issues. The worshipers were a racially and ethnically diverse group.

[60] Cf., "Prayers to the Four Directions," by Chief Seattle, in *Four Directions— Native American Prayers, Poems and Sayings* on www.starstuffs.com. Viewed on August 16, 2016.

[61] Blount, "The Apocalypse of Worship," in Blount and Tisdale, *Making Room at the Table*, 16.

for the promise of God's reign, because it is an apocalyptic reality in which God's promise of justice is "immediately" fulfilled as a historical reality.[62] He illustrates Jesus' table fellowship as a model of multicultural worship, in which socially and culturally diverse people are invited to the apocalyptic reality of the kingdom of God. In addition, he interprets Jesus' act of cleansing the temple (Mark 11:15-18) as the apocalyptic eschatological event that premises multicultural worship (v. 17: "And as he taught them, he said, 'Is it not written: "My house will be called a house of prayer for all nations"?'"). For Blount, therefore, multicultural worship is "the apocalypse of worship, the realization of its end-time, multicultural reality."[63]

While monocultural worship maintains the status quo by preserving the identity of the community of faith as racially and socially exclusive, multicultural worship from the apocalyptic eschatological perspective demands a radical transformation of our current worship life by including all the people of God, even the "foreigners" (Isa 56:6), in its celebration.[64] This kind of worship is possible when the community of worship is open to reformulating its identity as the inclusive eschatological community of strangers, who eventually become friends through worship. To put it another way, multicultural worship is a human response to the critically realistic call to the kingdom of God; it is an eschatological event, a foretaste of the realization of the end of history.

In *Theology of Play*, Jürgen Moltmann gives insight into how multicultural worship might be imagined from the eschatological point of view:

> Christian eschatology has never thought of the end of history as a kind of retirement or payday or accomplished purpose but has regarded it totally without purpose as a hymn of praise for unending joy, as an ever-varying round dance of the redeemed in the Trinitarian fullness of God, and as the complete harmony of soul and body.[65]

---

[62] Ibid., 19–22.

[63] Ibid., 27.

[64] Ibid., 22.

[65] Jürgen Moltmann, *Theology of Play*, trans. Reinhard Ulrich (New York: Harper & Row, Publishers, 1972), 34.

Just as Moltmann defines Christian eschatology as a joyful celebration, so Christian worship as an eschatological event is to be a celebration with praising songs and dance. In Justo L. González's term, it is a "fiesta." It is "a celebration of the mighty deeds of God. It is a get-together of the family of God."[66] According to him, "the goal of Christian worship is that day when 'a great multitude that no one can count, from every nation, from all tribes and peoples and languages,' will worship together, 'standing before the throne and before the Lamb' (Rev. 7:9)."[67]

This kind of worship, states González, is manifested in Latino worship, in which the celebrant is not a professionally trained clergyperson, but "all participants are 'celebrants,' in that they are gathered to celebrate the fiesta of God and God's people."[68] It is a model of multicultural worship in unity-in-difference:

> In a fiesta, as in a steak dinner, we are not required to understand everything that goes on. We are not even expected to agree with everything that everyone says. We are simply invited to join the party, to allow ourselves to be carried and defined by it, to make our own contribution, whatever that might be, and above all to celebrate whatever the fiesta is about. . . . We have learned how to worship together in congregations in which people come from radically different strata of society, where some speak mostly English and very little Spanish, while others know mostly Spanish and very little English, and where there are several different variants of Spanish spoken. We have learned to worship and celebrate together even across significant theological lines. We have learned how to do this by combining a spirit of fiesta with a profound sense of mystery. The fiesta makes us all participants, and thus leads to the mystery of transgenerational, transclass, and transcultural communication. The mystery reminds us of the otherness of God, and thus makes it possible for all to celebrate the glory of one another's otherness.[69]

---

[66] Justo L. González, "Hispanic Worship: An Introduction," in González, ¡Alabadle!, 20.

[67] Ibid., 24.

[68] Ibid., 21.

[69] Ibid., 25–26.

The experience of Christian worship as a fiesta must not be restricted to Latino congregations. Instead, it should be extended to every Christian church, for worship as an eschatological fiesta can be imagined as the expression of the amazement, joy, adoration, and praise of God's glory through various liturgical components by all the worshipers, who are from different racial and religious backgrounds in the presence of divine beauty. It is "a symbolic play"[70] expressed in the diverse human capacities of imagination and creativity. It is also a play of "the game of eschatological surprises" or "the game of grace in which the loser wins and the lost are saved, the poor are filled and the rich are left empty-handed."[71] Therefore, multicultural worship as an eschatological celebration is both a sign that the world is more than what is present at hand and a fountain of hope for worshipers to envision the future of the human community in the multicultural world.

The liturgy of the Iliff community worship, included in appendix 2, is a good example of fiesta worship. The entire Iliff community—the students, the professors, the board of trustees, the staff, and friends of Iliff—was invited to the service, and many of them participated in prayers, songs, dance, and preaching. In the service, multiple languages—English, Spanish, Korean, German, and Chinese—were used in harmony. The worship service generated the mood of a fiesta, a joyful celebration, through the active participation of the worshipers. It was a foretaste of the eschatological banquet.

Conclusion

The understanding of the liturgical culture from the postmodern view leads us to consider the transformation of our liturgical culture. It is fluid and open to transformation and invites the preacher and worship leaders to think collectively about how it can be changed in order for Christian preaching and worship to participate in transforming our globalized, multicultural society into a world in which racially and culturally different people live together in justice and peace.

[70] Henriksen, *Life, Love, and Hope: God and Human Experience* (Grand Rapids: Eerdmans, 2014), 348.
[71] Moltmann, *Theology of Play*, 24.

38

In reality, however, most Christian churches still hold premodern or modern views of culture, in which their liturgical cultures are monocultural or ethnocentric, exclusive to other racial and ethnic cultures. In this situation, for preachers and worship leaders who want to transform their liturgical cultures, the first step is to critically evaluate the power dynamics among the congregational subcultures and discuss with the congregation the Christian identity in a changing cultural context. The next step for the transformation of the liturgical culture is to engage in conversation with the worshipers on the renewal of their liturgical culture and their worship life, reflecting on the racial and ethnic diversity within and beyond the church. Based on such conversations, the preacher and worship leaders may help them imagine more theologically appropriate and culturally relevant Christian preaching and worship in multicultural contexts.

PART 2

Exploring Multicultural Hermeneutics

CHAPTER 3

The Bible and Multicultural Hermeneutics

Sola Scriptura and a Multicultural Context

George E. (Tink) Tinker, an American Indian theologian and ordained Lutheran minister, wrote an essay in the Lutheran journal *Dialogue* about Reformation theology and its understanding of the Bible from the postcolonial perspective.[1] One of the issues Tinker tackles in the essay is the impact of the doctrine of *sola scriptura*, which is the hallmark of Lutheran and other Protestant churches rooted in the Reformation. According to Tinker, Martin Luther's emphasis on *sola scriptura* made perfect sense in his own historical time for the reformation of the church. However, states Tinker, throughout the later history of the Protestant church, *sola scriptura* has been used as a device for validating the Western invasion and colonization of the two Americas and other parts of the globe.[2]

As Tinker rightly points out, the Bible was the divine weapon for Luther and other reformers to fight the corrupted power of the papacy and liberate Christian believers from the oppression of the late medieval church. Luther's reading of the Bible focused on the theme of justification by faith alone against papal pardon and the efficacy of indulgences. For him, the central message of the Christian gospel

---

[1] George Tinker, "Decolonizing the Language of Lutheran Theology: Confessions, Mission, Indians, and the Globalization of Hybridity," *Dialogue: A Journal of Theology* 50, no. 2 (Summer 2011): 193–205.

[2] Ibid., 202.

was the doctrine of forgiveness by grace, by which believers could be liberated from the fear of punishment for sins. Luther's theology of justification by faith, however, is based on some selective biblical passages in the New Testament, particularly the Epistle to the Romans and other Christocentric Pauline texts. Luther identified them as the kernel of the Christian scriptures and thus as the substance of *sola scriptura*, while regarding the Hebrew Bible and other biblical texts as merely husks of scripture and "shadows" of the gospel of Jesus Christ.

The doctrine of *sola scriptura* has led many Protestant churches to understand that biblical preaching is to proclaim that God's saving grace was fully revealed through the life, death, and resurrection of Jesus Christ. Unfortunately, their preaching has often misguided listeners to understand the meaning of salvation as an exclusive property gained by professing their belief in Jesus Christ. Consequently, their preaching has contributed to Christian exclusivism against other religions and spurred the mission of the church in the direction of Christian triumphalism.

Our world is rapidly changing toward a globalized, postcolonial, and multicultural community. North America is one of the best examples of this reality, in which once- and still- colonized people live together with the descendants of their colonizers—European Americans—as citizens and neighbors. In this globalized multicultural society, we frequently experience racial tensions and hate crimes related to differences in appearance, skin color, language, and religion, at individual and communal levels. Moreover, our society is radically imbalanced socially and economically between descendants of the colonizer and diasporas of the colonized, and the gap between the privileged and the marginalized is getting wider and wider.

While the major theological concern of sixteenth-century reformers was the salvation of individual souls from their personal sins, our globalized multicultural society requires preachers and worship leaders to consider how their preaching and worship can contribute to fostering values of communal commitment to public well-being. In relation to this concern, the Reformation doctrine of *sola scriptura* needs to be critically reexamined in order for the ministry of preaching and worship to be more relevant to our multicultural context. One of the crucial tasks for contemporary preachers and worship leaders is to think about how they can liberate the Bible from the exclusivist view of *sola scriptura* and make it play a major role in reforming the church again in our particular historical time.

As a way to reappropriate Christian scripture to our contemporary context, this chapter proposes multicultural hermeneutics as an alternative to the Christocentric approach to *sola scriptura*. In multicultural hermeneutics, culture is understood not as fixed or static but as dynamic and flexible, as perceived in the postmodern view. As was explained in chapter 2, the modern view understands culture as a precondition of social behavior, including rituals and beliefs that are already formed, finished, and attributed to a particular social group and "a historically transmitted pattern of meanings embodied in symbols."[3] In this static view of culture, religion is often identified as "a cultural system,"[4] that is, "a system of inherited conceptions expressed in symbolic forms."[5] In our pluralistic and multicultural environment, however, religion and culture are not always identical; rather, they are very complex. The complexity of the relationship between religion and culture can be explained by the postmodern view of culture. It helps us realize that culture is not a unified entity but a constantly changing dynamic pattern of society, mutually influencing other cultures that coexist in society. And, just as culture is fluid, so is religion. The more multicultural a society is, the more its religions are pluralistic and do not necessarily identify with a single particular culture. That is to say, one of the major characteristics of multicultural society is that multiple religions coexist, influencing one another, loosely connected to their original cultures.

Multicultural hermeneutics understands this complexity of the relationship between culture and religion in our multicultural society and recognizes that their relationship is traversal rather than in a one-to-one identification. In the traversal relationship, diverse religions and cultures pass across, over, or through to meet points of contact through dialogue. Based on this vital relationship, multicultural hermeneutics considers different religious texts and cultural traditions to be dialogue partners seeking the relevant meaning of humanity in our multicultural world. This kind of dialogue is

---

[3] Clifford Geertz, *The Interpretation of Cultures* (New York: Basic Books, 1973), 89.
[4] Ibid., 87–125.
[5] Ibid., 89.

possible only when the nature and function of the Bible is understood not exclusively but inclusively, in a fresh new way. The rest of the chapter presents a renewed understanding of the Bible as a source of wisdom and proposes methods and principles of multicultural hermeneutics.

The Bible as a Source of Wisdom

In sixteenth-century Christendom, reformers emphasized *sola scriptura* as the source of liberation from ecclesiocentrism. Multicultural hermeneutics, however, redirects Christian scripture into pluralistic contexts and liberates it from Christocentrism to be a dialogue partner with different religious texts and traditions. This seemingly radical approach does not diminish the Christian faith grounded in the interpretation of the life, death, and resurrection of Jesus Christ, because, as Thomas Groome asserts, "affirming Jesus as the apex of God's self-disclosure and saving action in human history does not preclude openness to and appreciation for God's revelation in traditions and cultures that are 'other,'" and its "surplus of meaning" will never be exhausted.[6]

Among many views of the Bible within the church—the Bible as the inerrant Word of God, the Bible as a historical record, the Bible as the canon of the Christian community, the Bible as a classic, the Bible as a historical prototype, etc.—the view of the Bible as a source of wisdom opens an avenue for the Bible to engage in dialogue with other sacred texts and cultural traditions.[7] In fact, the view of the Bible as a source of wisdom has been least attractive to preachers. As Alyce McKenzie indicates in her book *Hear and Be Wise*, "Christian preachers neither view the substance of their preaching as wisdom nor think

---

[6] Thomas Groome, "Inculturation: How to Proceed in a Pastoral Context," in *Christianity and Cultures*, ed. Norbert Greinacher and Norbert Mette (Maryknoll, NY: Orbis Books, 1994), 124.

[7] R. S. Sugirtharajah supports this view by claiming that the wisdom tradition is "universal," in his essay, "Inter-faith Hermeneutics: An Example and Some Implications," in *Voices from the Margin: Interpreting the Bible from the Third World*, ed. R. S. Surgirtharajah, 2nd ed. (Maryknoll, NY: Orbis Books, 1997), 316.

of their vocations as learning and teaching wisdom."[8] Perhaps this is because wisdom is generally regarded as mere knowledge of nature or an understanding of conventional moral principles or veiled secrets hidden in puns and riddles or special skills and artisanship.[9] In addition, Christians often misunderstand the term wisdom as a synonym for passionless "speculative intelligence," as opposed to the passionate faith of following Jesus Christ as his disciples.[10]

When I insist that the Bible should be understood as a source of wisdom, I mean a totally different concept of wisdom. I am suggesting a comprehensive and holistic perception of a way of approaching life. In other words, wisdom is concerned with a way of living or a way of assessing life in relation to who we are and what we ought to do as members of the human family. In this sense, wisdom is, in essence, the substance of the Christian scriptures. Reading the Bible as a source of wisdom means that we read biblical texts "to become able to read life more clearly, more truthfully, with a sense of solidarity, humility, and awe."[11] Approaching the Bible this way, we learn to discern the ways of God toward the actualization of personal and communal well-being in our pluralistic, multicultural world.

Biblical scholarship generally limits the study of wisdom to Wisdom literature in the Hebrew Bible (i.e., Proverbs, Job, and Ecclesiastes)[12] and Jesus' parables in the gospels. Yet, the wisdom of God,

[8] Alyce M. McKenzie, *Hear and Be Wise: Becoming a Preacher and Teacher of Wisdom* (Nashville: Abingdon Press, 2004), xv.

[9] Ben Witherington III, *Jesus the Sage: The Pilgrimage of Wisdom* (Minneapolis: Fortress Press, 1994), 4.

[10] Colin Crowder, "Wisdom and Passion: Wittgenstein, Kierkegaard, and Religious Belief," in *Where Shall Wisdom Be Found?*, ed. Stephen C. Barton (Edinburg: T&T Clark, 1999), 371–72.

[11] Charles F. Melchert, *Wise Teaching: Biblical Wisdom and Educational Ministry* (Harrisburg, PA: Trinity Press International, 1998), 58–59.

[12] As Silvia Schroer rightly points out in her essay, wisdom literature in the Bible is more open to other cultures: "The Wisdom schools and wisdom literature in Israel had long had a certain international character; the authors were aware of their links with other cultures and had less anxiety about coming into contact with them than, say, the Deuteronomistic tradition" (Silvia Schroer, "Transformations of Faith: Documents of Intercultural Learning in the Bible," in Greinacher and Mette, *Christianity and Cultures*, 8).

which is the ultimate wisdom of humanity, is in fact the main theme of the scriptures. Throughout the Bible, wisdom has been revealed in a variety of modes such as conventional wisdom in Proverbs and James, subversive wisdom in Jesus' Beatitudes and the Sermon on the Mount, wisdom as an alternative vision for human life in Jesus' parables, and revelatory wisdom of the Christ in John and the Pauline letters.[13] Moreover, as McKenzie affirms, the gospels describe Jesus as a "subversive sage."[14] He voluntarily suffered and died to do justice to his teaching and way of life, in which he identified himself with the outcasts of his day and publicly challenged people in power and authority. Wisdom revealed in Jesus' teaching and his life, death, and resurrection is "not good advice, but good news, a vision of reality present but also yet to come."[15]

Most biblical texts, even historical records of Israel or compilations of Jewish laws and principles, are also sources of wisdom at a deeper level. For example, the book of Judges has been considered a historical record of "heroes and moral exemplars."[16] The book is, however, hard to read as a source for learning morality because it is replete with a series of violent, blood-soaked episodes involving morally ambiguous characters.[17] Rather, as Roy Heller argues, the storyline of the book as a tragedy reminds us that we also live in a violent and unjust world, just as when the book was composed,[18] and that the reference of the stories challenges readers to reflect on what wisdom of humanity does the book imply from God's point of view in relation to our identity and actions toward others. Reading the book of Judges in this way provides us with wisdom in seeking a responsible way of living more fully in our racially, culturally, and religiously diverse community.

Wisdom revealed in biblical texts is an expression of the presence and guidance of God, subject to divine mystery and sovereignty

[13] Cf., Witherington.

[14] Ibid., 36.

[15] McKenzie, *Hear and Be Wise*, 149.

[16] Roy L. Heller, *Conversations with Scripture: The Book of Judges* (New York: Morehouse Publishing, 2011), 5.

[17] Ibid., 5–6.

[18] Ibid., 10.

revealed in a particular historical time and place. It is partial, fragmentary, and incomplete. Its truth is thus not absolute but conditional and contingent. While these characteristics are the limits of wisdom revealed in the Bible, they are also the reasons why the Bible should be open to dialogue with different human experiences and religious traditions. Through the dialogue with them, it is possible for biblical wisdom to be appropriated more holistically and profoundly.

Like the Bible, religious texts contain the wisdom of living life as the core of their teaching. Buddhism calls it Buddhahood, and its scriptures are used as a vehicle to access that wisdom. In Taoism, the term "Tao" means "way," "path," or "principle" of humanity, and its vast writings are concerned with instructions of Tao. Confucian classics serve as a medium for learning the way of humanity, called sagehood. Hindu people consider their religion the inseparable companion and guide of their daily lives. In Islam, the Qur'an has served as an agent for the community to deal with personal and communal problems of life.[19] American Indian religions also aim to give ethical guidelines to a way of life toward "the personal, communal, and eventually cosmic balance."[20] In association with these religious teachings, George Buchanan reminds us that "the early Christian movement was first called, 'the way' . . . in which it was necessary for Christians 'to walk' (Acts 9:2; 19:9, 23; 22:4; 24:14; 24:22; cf. also 2:28; 14:16; 16:17; 18:25-26)."[21]

As David Tracy confirms, most religious traditions instruct some way of life and have "a built-in dynamism toward the other through religious principles of justice, compassion, love."[22] It is, however, significant to recognize that the history of religions shows that all religious traditions have their own dark side too, for they are subject

[19] Wilfred Cantwell Smith, "The Study of Religion and the Study of the Bible," in *Rethinking Scripture: Essays from a Comparative Perspective*, ed. Miriam Levering (Albany: State University of New York Press, 1989), 21.

[20] Tinker, "Decolonizing the Language," 195.

[21] George Buchanan, *Introduction to Intertextuality* (Lewiston, NY: Mellen Biblical Press, 1994), 16.

[22] David Tracy, "Western Hermeneutics and Interreligious Dialogue," in *Interreligious Hermeneutics*, ed. Catherine Cornille and Christopher Conway (Eugene, OR: Cascade Books, 2010), 14, 16.

to power dynamics in their particular socio-historical and cultural situations. As a result, just as biblical wisdom is partial, contingent, and incomplete, so is the wisdom revealed in other religious texts. In order for wisdom not to be perpetuated in its own tradition and to evolve to promote the common good or public well-being of communities, it must open itself to critical conversation with other religious and cultural traditions. At this point, the view of the Bible as a source of wisdom encourages all religious people, including Christians, to engage in dialogue with others and critically evaluate the understanding and interpretation of their particular religious texts and traditions.

Multicultural hermeneutics is concerned with searching for the wholeness of wisdom beyond the limits of particular religious texts and cultural experiences and proclaiming the divine wisdom for the transformation of the world. In other words, the task of multicultural hermeneutics is the service of proclamation,[23] by encouraging Christian and other religious preachers to have dialogue with different sets of experiences, beliefs, and values. Contrary to *sola scriptura* that demands Christian preachers discover the absolute truth claim within the Christological events, critical and meaningful dialogue with different religious texts and traditions may liberate them from their limited religious and cultural frameworks. Preaching and worship based on such a dialogue may contribute to transforming our multicultural world into a better world in which racially, culturally, and religiously different people live together with recognition of and respect for their differences. Basic attitudes that multicultural hermeneutics requires of preachers and worship leaders are openness, humility, and vulnerability in order to make room for strangers—other sacred texts, traditions, and experiences—in their own space. In doing so, they can deepen and widen the Christian gospel by addressing questions people face today in our pluralistic, multicultural society and by seeking answers to those questions by trying to live a life together worthy of a human being.

---

[23] Richard Hays reminds us that the original *Sitz im Leben* of Christian biblical interpretation is not a scholarly discourse but preaching in his book, *Echoes of Scripture in the Letters of Paul* (New Haven: Yale University Press, 1989), 184.

Methods of Multicultural Hermeneutics

How, then, are we to engage other religious texts and cultural traditions in dialogue? One answer is to see multicultural hermeneutics as interdisciplinary and employ such critical methods as literary criticism, feminist and other social critical theories, postcolonial criticism, and intertextuality. In the practice of multicultural hermeneutics, these methods intersect.

Like other critical methods, literary criticism is multifaceted, interconnected with narrative, rhetorical, and other biblical criticisms. Literary criticism presupposes that the meaning of biblical narratives is indeterminate, remaining latent. The "indeterminatedness"[24] or unfinished quality of the stories demands from the reader an act of interpretation. Narrative and rhetorical criticisms that focus on narrative artistry, genre, the social function of a narrative, plot, setting, characters, the communication process, etc., help readers analyze and appreciate the stories in depth.

With whatever various literary genres have been used to enlighten humanity, stories are a universal tool for teaching wisdom in most traditions of human communities. Multicultural hermeneutics takes biblical narratives and other stories in different religious traditions as important sources to discern the wisdom of life and encourages preachers and worship leaders to be familiar with those stories. When they read the stories, they need first to follow the stories' particular plots in their specific historical and cultural settings and then connect characters analogically with contemporary worshipers. In the process of interaction between the world of the story and the world of the worshipers, imagination plays a key role in discerning God's wisdom for today.

Among social and cultural criticisms, feminist critical theories are particularly helpful for multicultural hermeneutics. Considering that most religions in the world have oppressed women in some way, no religious traditions are immune from the criticism of sexism. As a result, one of the primary concerns of multicultural hermeneutics is fostering women's liberation by using a feminist interpretation.

---

[24] Ronald F. Thiemann, *Constructing a Public Theology: The Church in a Pluralistic Culture* (Louisville: Westminster John Knox Press, 1991), 50.

Feminist interpretation as "a set of approaches to texts that resists patriarchy—the ideology that legitimates social structures that privilege men and disempower women"[25]—deconstructs traditionally fixed meanings of texts and reconstructs the meaning by reading all religious texts critically and by retrieving the silenced voices of women in the texts. In order to retrieve the voices of women that are suppressed in most religious traditions, it is necessary to critically reconstruct the feminine image of divinity in Christianity, for example, the feminine image of Jesus as the prophetic sage of Sophia,[26] as well as in other religions. Such an effort means that multicultural hermeneutics reads scriptures not only to interpret the world differently but also to change it into a new human community.

Postcolonial criticism is a relatively recent critical theory. R. S. Sugirtharajah defines postcolonialism "not [as] a homogenous project, but [as] a hermeneutical salmagundi, consisting of extremely varied methods, materials, historical entanglement, geographical locations, political affiliations, cultural identities, and economic predicaments."[27] Like postmodernism, postcolonialism rejects "excessive reverence for reason, a spurious belief in objective truth, savage control over the environment, and less-critical respect for such institutions as the nation-state."[28] Unlike postmodernism, which is "Eurocentric in its conceptual and aesthetic thrust," postcolonial critics question Eurocentric beliefs and values dominating the process of meaning-making of Christian texts and deconstruct prescribed ways of reading them. They understand that it is a mistake to identify the colonialists' interests and values as universal interests and values and instead attempt to help the colonized acquire "a new identity" through the renewed interpretation of the biblical texts.[29]

[25] Kevin Vanhoozer, *Is There a Meaning in This Text? The Bible, the Reader and the Morality of Literary Knowledge* (Leicester: Apollos, 1998), 167.

[26] Elisabeth Schüssler Fiorenza, *Jesus: Miriam's Child, Sophia's Prophet* (New York: Continuum, 1994), 157.

[27] R. S. Sugirtharajah, *Asian Biblical Hermeneutics and Postcolonialism: Contesting the Interpretations* (Maryknoll, NY: Orbis Books, 1998), 15.

[28] Ibid.

[29] Ibid., 16.

In postcolonial hermeneutics, the Bible is "a literary product of the ancient world"[30] that is supposed to be read "along with other communally inspired sacred narratives" as an "intertextual continuum."[31] As a result, postcolonial readers reject the postliberal approach of "intratextuality"[32] and replace it with "intertextuality"[33] between the Christian text and other sacred texts and traditions. While the intratextuality of postliberal theology is used to preserve the Christian identity based on "conformity to 'a normative cultural-linguistic framework,'"[34] intertextuality is based on the proposition that human beings are not the products of particular written texts but "hermeneutical creatures who are involved in a creative way with the process of giving meaning"[35] and that the Christian identity is open-ended to new meanings of the text generated in the interactive hermeneutical process with other sacred texts. Multicultural hermeneutics encourages preachers and worship leaders to read the Bible from the postcolonial perspective and use the intertextual approach in their practice of preaching and worship. Those who use the intertextual approach beyond the boundary of Christian scripture trust that the God who spoke through the Christian scriptures has spoken through

[30] Ibid., 19.

[31] Ibid., 23.

[32] George A. Lindbeck, *The Nature of Doctrine: Religion and Theology in a Postliberal Age* (Philadelphia: Westminster Press, 1984), 114.

[33] The term "intertexuality" is generally used to refer to the way of interpreting a biblical text in relation to other biblical texts and the term "extratextuality" as a way of relating the biblical text to other religious and cultural texts or experiences among European American biblical scholars (cf. Steve Moyise, "Intertextuality and the Study of the Old Testament in the New Testament," in *The Old Testament in the New Testament*, ed. Steve Moyise [(Sheffield: Sheffield Academic Press, 2000)], 14; Lindbeck, *The Nature of Doctrine*, 114). However, non-European American biblical scholars, especially postcolonial scholars use the term "intertextuality" broadly by including extrabiblical resources and ways of interpreting a religious text in dialogue with other religious texts (cf. Sugirtharajah, *Asian Biblical Hermeneutics*, 116). In multicultural hermeneutics, the term "intertextuality" means the latter.

[34] Marianne Moyaert, "Absorption or Hospitality: Two Approaches to the Tension between Identity and Alterity," in Cornille and Conway, *Interreligious Hermeneutics*, 72.

[35] Ibid., 73.

other sacred texts so that they can be helpful to draw out "the divine meaning latent in Scripture."[36]

Biblical scholarship has proved that the Christian scriptures are the product of intertextuality. According to Daniel Boyarin, Dennis MacDonald, and other scholars, large numbers of biblical texts are interconnected with more than one text, either in Jewish religious and cultural traditions or in those of neighboring people who lived in different religious and cultural environments.[37] More precisely, the Bible is "a preeminent example" that "the text is always made up of a mosaic of conscious and unconscious citation of earlier discourse."[38] This notion confirms the validity of using intertextuality in preaching and worship. Like biblical texts, sermons can be in dialogue with other texts, not only within, but also beyond the Christian scriptures, so that the plain sense of the biblical text may grow and change through the dialogue and eventually provide worshipers a fresh new meaning of the wisdom of life.

With regard to how intertextual dialogues can happen in a constructive and fruitful way in the liturgy, the intertextual tactics and strategies that the biblical authors employed are useful. For example, allusion, echo, quotation, juxtaposition, typology, irony, Midrash, allegory, and metaphor[39] can be used in constructing intertextual relationships between biblical texts and other sacred texts in sermons and other liturgical components. In addition, it is worthwhile to pay attention to Jean Delorme's suggestion that texts should be consid-

[36] Vanhoozer, *Is There a Meaning?*, 115.

[37] It is notable that, while most biblical scholars who are interested in intertextuality have researched intertextual relationships within the Bible, Dennis MacDonald explores the influence of extrabiblical texts on the New Testament in his two books, *The Homeric Epics and the Gospel of Mark* (New Haven: Yale University Press, 2000) and *Does the New Testament Imitate Homer? Four Cases from the Acts of the Apostles* (New Haven: Yale University Press, 2003).

[38] Daniel Boyarin, *Intertextuality and the Reading of Midrash* (Bloomington: Indiana University Press, 1990), 12. Julia Kristeva also mentions that "every text builds itself as a mosaic of quotations, every text is absorption and transformation of another text" in *Semiotike* (Paris: Éditions du Seuil, 1969), 146, quoted from Boyarin, *Intertextuality*, 22.

[39] Cf. Vanhoozer; Hays; Boyarin.

ered "partners capable of entering into dialogue," rather than merely "documents, sources of information":[40]

> The text enters the world of texts with a certain autonomy permitting it to dialogue with others without allowing itself to be absorbed by them or absorbing them itself. New meanings can come forth from their encounter permitting a further fresh reading and new interpretations of them. . . . To consider the Bible as an intertext . . . would mean to establish between them a network of similitudes, tensions and transformations more beneficial to the reader than any synthesis.[41]

Intertextual dialogue in the process of sermon formation aims not merely to analyze or compare biblical texts with partner texts but to generate new meaning. This semiotic process of intertextual dialogue is possible when the dialogue is mutually critical and dialectical. As Groome succinctly explains, the term dialectical means "a threefold dynamic of affirming and cherishing, of refusing or questioning, and of moving on to new and transformed possibilities."[42] That is, the symbolic world of a biblical text that has been cherished by Christian believers collides with that of other religious texts and is vulnerable to criticism and interpretation by the other, and vice versa. Eventually, the conventional meaning of each text may be transformed to a new meaning relevant to contemporary listeners through interaction with the preacher's vision for the world. This dialectical process of affirming, challenging, and transforming the text enriches the substance of the sermon by creating the surplus meaning or the meaning "latent in scripture."

The creation of new meaning also requires worshipers' active participation in the intertextual dialogue. As Daniel Chandler rightly states, "Information or meaning is not 'contained' in the world or in books, computers or audio-visual media. Meaning is not 'transmitted' to us—we actively create it according to a complex interplay of codes

---

[40] Jean Delorme, "Intertextualities about Mark," in *Intertextuality in Biblical Writing*, ed. Sipke Draisma (Kampen: Uitgeversmaatschappij J.H. Kok, 1989), 37.
[41] Ibid., 35.
[42] Groome, "Inculturation," 121.

or conventions of which we are normally unaware."[43] In this vein, Ellen van Wolde elaborates on the role of the reader in the process of meaning-making like this:

> Even though a text creates its own world or context, this world can only emerge when the reader actualizes it, i.e., relates it to his [or her] own referential (living- and reading-) world. The text only contains potential referential worlds that become actualized when they are read. A possible world, therefore, is not a present but an absent world and it only becomes present when it is actualized by the reader. Intertextual relationships are thus a part of the reader's general semiotic actualization process. . . . The reader achieves intertextual semiosis through logical and analogical reasoning in interaction with the text. . . . These relationships do not concern the similarity between text and referent but the ability of the reader to conceive of the worlds of the text as possible or to reconstruct them, or in other words, to give them contents by relating them to his [or her] own living- and reading-experience. In this way, the reader turns the possible worlds of the text into realities.[44]

Wolde's description of the active role of the reader in the process of meaning-making echoes the role of the worshipers in the liturgical context. How they engage in texts or stories used in a sermon or in other liturgical components directly relates to the process of meaning-making. For example, the worshipers naturally engage in the intertextual process when they listen to scripture readings or a sermon. Even if the sermon is related to one particular biblical text, their minds often interconnect the text to other texts or stories that are familiar to them. In other words, they enter into a dialogue, consciously or unconsciously, with the possibilities the sermon offers them and have hermeneutical freedom to use the possibilities of the sermon by relating it to what they have experienced in their own lives. The meaning of a sermon is thus not restrained by the preacher but is finalized through the reasoning and imagination of the individual listener, who is "the product of various cultural codes."[45] As a

[43] Daniel Chandler, *Semiotics: The Basics* (London: Routledge, 2002), 14.

[44] Ellen van Wolde, "Trendy Intertextuality," in Draisma, *Intertextuality in Biblical Writing*, 48.

[45] Vanhoozer, *Is There a Meaning?*, 154.

result, the meaning of a sermon is polyvalent. Even the meanings of extrabiblical resources that are used in a sermon as partner texts are polyvalent. They offer certain possibilities that the listener can assign meaning in relation to his or her own *"stream of interpretants, i.e., the residue of previous processes in which he [or she] has assigned meaning,"* [46] and the infinite stream of interpretants makes the total number of possible meanings of the texts inexhaustable.

Consequently, preachers may need to deconstruct their own existing understanding of the text and be open to a strange new meaning created by the listeners. Just as "neither Priests, who supposedly speak for God, nor Philosophers, who supposedly speak for reason, should be trusted," [47] so preachers, who supposedly speak the truthful meaning of the text, should give up their privileged perspectives and deconstruct it. Deconstruction is different from destruction in the following sense:

> Deconstruction is a strategy for resisting closure. Undoing is a half-serious, half-playful attempt to take things apart in order to show that there are different ways of putting them together. . . . It is not simply a matter of demolishing something through external force, but of disassembling it. Deconstruction is a painstaking taking-apart, a peeling away of the various layers—historical, rhetorical, ideological—of distinctions, concepts, texts, and whole philosophies, whose aim is to expose the arbitrary linguistic nature of their original construction. Deconstruction is an intense analytical method, occasionally perversely so, that results in the collapse from within of all that it touches. It is an "analysis" in the etymological sense of the term (Greek: *analusis*): an "un-loosing" or "un-tying." Deconstruction is thus best understood as a kind of undoing, with all the attendant connotations that the term implies: untying, undermining, and ruining. [48]

While affirming "a plurality and undecidability of meaning" [49] of the sermon, it is important to emphasize that the preacher who uses the intertextual approach is unlike the radical "deconstructor" who

[46] Wolde, "Trendy Intertextuality," 47.
[47] Quoted from Jacques Derrida in Vanhoozer, *Is There a Meaning?*, 22.
[48] Ibid., 40, 52.
[49] Ibid., 111.

"celebrates the arbitrariness of meaning and truth by dancing on the tomb of God,"[50] for at least two reasons. One is that, in multicultural hermeneutics, the literal sense (or *"the sense of a literary act"*[51]) of a text functions as "a space of variations that has its own constrains."[52] The other is that how to interpret a text for a sermon is inextricably connected to the theological and ethical concerns that were explored in relation to the theology of diversity in chapter 1 of this volume. Therefore, the literal sense of the text and the theological and ethical concerns of the theology of diversity are criteria for discerning the relevance of meaning. In addition, preachers who use the intertextual approach need to pray for the guidance of the Holy Spirit to aid in the listener's process of meaning-making.

Hermeneutical Principles

While the critical methods of literary criticism, feminist interpretation, postcolonial criticism, and intertextuality are hermeneutical tools to practice multicultural hermeneutics for preaching and worship in a multicultural context, the following four hermeneutical principles are significant for preachers and worship leaders to keep in mind when practicing multicultural hermeneutics.

The first hermeneutical principle is that dialogue partners in multicultural hermeneutics must not be limited to written texts. This is because multicultural hermeneutics is concerned with discerning the wisdom of God through the interpretation of human life described not only in sacred texts but also in symbols, stories, and rituals. While Christianity is a text-based religion in the tradition of *sola scriptura*, many other religions in the world do not depend on written materials.

For example, Tinker explains that American Indians gain the personal and communal direction of life from "the spiritual experience or the experience of a spirit in the vigil."[53] Sugirtharajah also informs

---

[50] Ibid., 50.

[51] Ibid., 312.

[52] Ricoeur, "World of the Text, World of the Reader," in *A Ricoeur Reader: Reflections and Imagination*, ed. Mario J. Valdes (London: Harvester Wheatsheaf, 1991), 496, quoted from Vanhoozer, *Is There a Meaning?*, 108.

[53] Tinker, "Decolonizing the Language," 202.

us that Hinduism and other indigenous religions in India and other parts of Asia are not text-oriented; rather, the key carrier of their religious teachings is oral tradition.[54] Their information reminds us that God's mysterious and unfathomable nature cannot be confined to written texts or books since God is free from human limitations in articulating or explaining divine wisdom. In order to discern God's ways for humanity, multicultural hermeneutics invites preachers and worship leaders to dialogue not only with the scriptures of other religions but also with their orally transmitted stories, rituals, and lived experiences of the Holy.

The sermon "Weeds and the Wheat," included in appendix 3, searches for the wisdom of God through a dialogue between various experiences of the Christian faith in the history of Korean Christianity and the biblical text, Matthew 13:24-30. The text is first interpreted through the lens of the historical and cultural stories of Korean Christians. Then, three Iliff faculty members from racially and culturally different backgrounds are invited into the conversation to enrich the meaning of the text by sharing their theological views. Eventually, the newly created meaning of the text becomes theological and spiritual guidance or the wisdom of God for the people of God who gathered at the worship service.

One of the issues related to the first principle would be the ethical question of "religious ownership and property."[55] Preachers and worship leaders may wonder whether it is legitimate to borrow other religious and cultural stories, rituals, and disciplines into their ministry of preaching and worship. In this regard, David Eckel explains that "religious borrowing"[56] is a natural phenomenon, through which religious and cultural identities and ideas continuously grow for mutual enrichment, rather than being confined within a particular religious and cultural tradition.[57]

---

[54] Sugirtharajah, *Asian Biblical Hermeneutics*, 13.

[55] Cornille, "Introduction: On Hermeneutics in Dialogue," in Cornille and Conway, *Interreligious Hermeneutics*, xviii.

[56] David Eckel, "Show Me Your Resurrection: Preaching on the Boundary of Buddhism and Christianity," in Cornille and Conway, *Interreligious Hermeneutics*, 155.

[57] Ibid., 159–62.

The second principle of multicultural hermeneutics is that it is to be used as context-oriented[58] within and beyond the church. When preachers and worship leaders use multicultural hermeneutics for once-colonized Christian communities, it is crucial for them to critically examine available commentaries and other preaching and worship resources from the postcolonial perspective, and then question from whose perspective the particular biblical text has been interpreted. Moreover, their task is to discover the congregation's native cultural and religious elements that were eradicated during the colonial period and bring them into conversation with a biblical text as a dialogue partner. If a church is a multicultural and multiracial community, subcultures of the congregation and their power dynamics should be analyzed in the process of biblical interpretation in order to make room for hearing culturally marginalized voices within the community of faith. When multicultural hermeneutics happens beyond the church—for example, if the church is socially and racially homogenous but seeks to broaden and deepen the Christian gospel in a larger cultural and religious context—the preacher and worship leaders need to evaluate the existing interpretation of biblical texts applied to sermons, hymns, and prayers and make an effort to reinterpret them from the perspectives of people of other races and religions.

The third principle of multicultural hermeneutics relates to understanding differences among religious and cultural traditions. Differences are often regarded as contradictory opposites that generate nonnegotiable conflicts. In the worst case, they result in hate crimes

[58] At this point, multicultural hermeneutics is broader than interreligious hermeneutics. Interreligious hermeneutics seeks a dialogue beyond Christian communities, which is one of the approaches of multicultural hermeneutics. It is also notable that Monica Jyotsna Melanchthon uses the term "multifaith" hermeneutics as a synonym for multicultural hermeneutics in her essay, "Akkamahadevi and the Samaritan Woman: Paradigms of Resistance and Spirituality," in *Border Crossings: Cross-Cultural Hermeneutics*, ed. D. N. Premnath (Maryknoll, NY: Orbis Books, 2007), 36. My definition of multicultural hermeneutics, however, is not only in dialogue between different religious or faith traditions but also in dialogue with different life experiences of Christian believers who are racially and culturally different. Therefore, multicultural hermeneutics is for both within and beyond the Christian communities.

and other violent actions against each other. Differences, however, do not actually mean binary opposites but rather polarities that complement and reinforce each other. Like in the Taoist view, they are "neither opposite nor the same, but correlative toward the wholeness."[59] This understanding of difference corresponds to the conception of unity-in-difference of the Trinity, expounded in chapter 1 of this volume. Differences represent pluralistic, multiple, and endless flexibilities of human realities that are created by the triune God and are intended to contribute to harmony and balance toward the wholeness of humanity. This positive view of differences leads preachers and worship leaders to be confident when facing differences in the practice of preaching and worship between Christianity and other religions. Likewise, this view encourages confidence among the congregants as they face their racial and cultural differences and deal with such differences constructively and without fear.

The last but most fundamental principle of multicultural hermeneutics is that the Bible should be treated as a book not closed but dynamically open to dialogue with other sacred texts. For many preachers and worship leaders, especially those who were trained within the Reformation tradition of *sola scriptura*, the use of other religious texts in Christian preaching and worship may be a genuine risk-taking venture, because it challenges the traditional understanding of the Bible as the canon of the Christian community. Generally, canon refers to "a list of recommended or authoritative books"[60] or "the sets of books that contain a wealth of moral knowledge about the nature and meaning of the human condition"[61] for a particular community. This definition of canon often misleads the Christian community to regard the Bible as a prescribed, fixed book that creates "an interpreter-free zone" with the Reformation dictum, "Scripture interprets Scripture."[62] Multicultural hermeneutics, however, breaks "the centripetal constraint of canon"[63] and makes it centrifugal by engaging in dialogue with other religious texts, practices, and experiences.

---

[59] Tracy, "Western Hermeneutics," 39.
[60] Vanhoozer, *Is There a Meaning?*, 134.
[61] Ibid., 165.
[62] Ibid., 135.
[63] Ibid.

Through dialogue, the authority of the Bible as the canon of the Christian community lies in its ability to evoke new possibilities of human existence in our multicultural context.

Conclusion

Multicultural hermeneutics is indispensable in our contemporary globalized multicultural world. It is an effort to liberate God from the confinement of *sola scriptura* to the freedom of divine revelation and to free Christian believers from their religious superiority and Christian triumphalism to a just and peaceful coexistence with people of other religions and cultures. In order to appropriate the biblical text as a source of revealing God's will for humanity or wisdom of life at a deeper level, preachers and worship leaders are encouraged to have a passion for and an interest in learning about what God has been doing in other racial and cultural groups within and beyond the Christian church.

Perhaps the most challenging issue of multicultural hermeneutics is with theological education. Many theological schools and seminaries do not pay enough attention to teaching other religious texts and cultural traditions. Instead, they train students in a monocultural and "monoreligious way." [64] Even though some schools include interreligious or interfaith dialogue courses, their teaching is limited to academic and ecumenical debate rather than relating the dialogue to a real-life situation. If preachers and worship leaders had gained at least a basic knowledge of and experience with different religions and cultures at school, they could have been more accessible to multicultural hermeneutics. At this point, multicultural hermeneutics challenges theological schools and seminaries to reevaluate their educational goals and consider curriculum reform. They should be reminded that the ultimate purpose of theological education is to transform lives and to empower the work of religious communities—not only the Christian church, but also other religious communities—by following the lead of the Holy Spirit, who is "not an essence or an abstract theo-

[64] Hendrik Vroom, "Hermeneutics and Dialogue Applied to the Establishment of a Western Department of Islamic Theology," in Cornille and Conway, *Interreligious Hermeneutics*, 207.

logical concept but the daily experienced mode of God's powerful presence in human communities."[65] Multicultural hermeneutics also encourages preachers and worship leaders to continue to study and research different religions and cultures as a lifelong process of learning, since no one can be an expert at different religious traditions and practices through a short-term study.

[65] Hays, *Echoes of Scripture*, 150.

CHAPTER 4

A Practice of Multicultural Hermeneutics
Luke 7:11-17

This chapter aims to demonstrate how to practice multicultural hermeneutics for preaching and worship in a particular ministerial setting. For this purpose, the miracle story in Luke 7:11-17 is chosen as the text to create a new meaning through multicultural hermeneutics. Christianity is not the only religion involving miracle stories; nor is its religious community the only body to infer meaning in life from the transmission and interpretation of those stories. Buddhism, Hinduism, Islam, and other religious traditions also involve many and various kinds of miracle stories such as healings, feedings, rescues, blessings, punishments, the raising of the dead, and an ascension into heaven.[1] These stories have functioned to break through the mundane world in which people understand the truth partially and to offer them glimpses of the wholeness of the truth.

In addition to stories in sacred texts, contemporary life experiences are also important resources for Christian preachers to address the questions people face today in relation to miracles. We live in a multicultural and pluralistic society. In our globalized world, cultural and religious diversity is an everyday life experience in our local communities, which are microcosms of the global village. How do my next door neighbors, who came from different parts of the globe, view miracles through the lens of their life experiences? How might my colleagues

---

[1] Kenneth L. Woodward, *The Book of Miracles* (New York: Simon & Schuster, 2000), 35–36.

and friends who grew up with different religious teachings understand the miracle stories in the Bible? These questions will be a conversation starter in the process of multicultural hermeneutics to seek answers in an effort to live a life together that is worthy of a human being.

The chapter includes four sections: The first summarizes how Christian churches have dealt with the miracle stories in the Bible in their preaching and worship. The second section proposes that the literary genre of these miracle stories is not parable but historiography, and that they should be read as historical narratives. The third section interprets Luke 7:11-17, which is the miracle story of Jesus raising a widow's dead son in Nain. The text is assigned in the Revised Common Lectionary on Sunday of the Season after Pentecost, Proper 5, Year C, paralleled with the miracle story of Elijah in 1 Kings 17:8-24. While most biblical commentaries use the intertextual approach, juxtaposing the miracle story in Luke 7:11-17 with Elijah's miracle story in 1 Kings 17:8-24 or the miracle story of healing a centurion's servant in the previous paragraph of Luke 7:1-10, this section goes beyond Christian scripture. It extends the intertextual dialogue to the Buddhist story of the Parable of the Mustard Seed and creates relevant meaning for contemporary listeners. The last section provides homiletical and liturgical strategies for the effective use of multicultural hermeneutics in preaching and worship.

The process of multicultural hermeneutics for the interpretation of Luke 7:11-17 uses the intertextual approach as its major tool, along with literary criticism, feminist theories, and postcolonialism. This practice is only the tip of the iceberg. It intends to encourage preachers and worship leaders to practice multicultural hermeneutics, through which they may appreciate the profound wisdom of God and share it with their worshipers.

Miracle Stories in the Christian Church

According to research by Kenneth Woodward, religion editor of *Newsweek* magazine, eight out of ten Americans identify themselves as Christians and believe that "even today, God continues to work miracles."[2] No wonder that, even at my suburban, liberal Presbyterian

---

[2] Ibid., 21. According to the Pew Forum's US Religious Landscape Survey conducted from May 8 to Aug. 13, 2007, 78.4 percent of Americans identify

church, more than 80 percent of the prayer requests at every Sunday worship service involve the expectation of God's miraculous work for physical, mental, psychological, spiritual, and social healing. Even though we live in a scientifically and technologically advanced country, many of us eagerly wait for something miraculous to happen in order to make our personal and communal lives better.

In relation to this reality, it is remarkable that, compared with other major religions in the world, Christianity is the one that most emphasizes miracles. For example, in the Gospel of Mark, 47 percent of the verses—which means 200 out of 450 verses—involve miracles, and the four gospels together include six exorcisms, seventeen healings (including three raisings from the dead), and eight so-called nature miracles.[3] The book of Acts and the Hebrew Bible also contain miracle stories. The miracle stories in the Bible, in fact, have been a source of controversy in the history of the Christian church. Although Augustine was witness to a miraculous cure,[4] the medieval church gradually dismissed the practice of liturgies and rituals of miraculous healing as its faith in healing miracles waned. When Gregory the Great called sickness "a discipline sent from God, something to be accepted rather than healed,"[5] such liturgical components as prayers with laying on of hands and anointing of the sick with oil was dropped from the Christian liturgy. Instead, anointing of the sick became a rite for the dying, not for the living.[6]

In the Protestant church, the influence of the sixteenth-century Protestant reformers' attitude to miracle stories in the Bible is substantial. As Ruth Duck concisely summarizes, the reformers were not consistent in dealing with miracle stories in preaching and worship. Martin Luther at first dismissed the healing service in Christian liturgy but later wrote a service of healing after observing a miraculous

---

themselves as Christians (http://religions.pewforum.org/reports, viewed on October 22, 2014).

[3] Woodward, *The Book of Miracles*, 104, 118.

[4] Avery Brooks, *Healing in the Landscape of Prayer* (Harrisburg, PA: Morehouse, 1996), 22–23, quoted from Ruth Duck, *Worship for the Whole People of God: Vital Worship for the 21st Century* (Louisville: Westminster John Knox Press, 2013), 233.

[5] Ibid.

[6] Ibid.

physical healing. John Calvin rejected rituals of healing, ridiculing the oil of anointing as "a putrid and ineffectual grease,"[7] although he pronounced somewhere that God continues to heal. In England, Thomas Cranmer first included a service for the visitation of the sick in *The Book of Common Prayer*, but it was deleted in a later edition.[8]

Since the Reformation, the Protestant tradition has tended to deny that any miracles have occurred since those recorded in the book of Acts.[9] The miracle stories in the Bible were even "demythologized" by Rudolf Bultmann, Martin Dibelius, and other modern biblical scholars due to an inability to prove them as historical facts.[10] As a result, theologically liberal preachers have been encouraged to preach the miracle stories as "tales" or "pious fictions,"[11] while conservative and charismatic preachers still try to prove the facticity of the miracle stories in the Bible based on their literalistic interpretation. They also stress in their sermons that such miraculous events can be replicated in the lives of contemporary believers.

In his essay "Preaching the Miracles of Jesus,"[12] Stephen Wright names the former rational approach "cessationist" and the latter charismatic approach "restorationist."[13] In addition, Wright reminds us of two other approaches to preaching the miracles of Jesus: one according to modern Roman Catholic theology and the other as narrative theology. Modern Roman Catholic theology, explains Wright, comprehends that the miracles of Jesus "point forward . . . to the continued signs of God's kingdom coming."[14] In this view, the preacher's

---

[7] John Calvin, *Institutes of the Christian Religion*, ed. John T. McNeill, trans. Ford Lewis Battles (Philadelphia: Westminster Press, 1960), 1467–69, quoted from Duck, *Worship for the Whole People*, 233.

[8] Ibid.

[9] Woodward, *The Book of Miracles*, 21.

[10] Rudolf Bultmann, *The History of the Synoptic Tradition* (New York: Harper & Row Publishers, 1963), 209–44; Martin Dibelius, *From Tradition to Gospel* (London: Ivor Nicholson and Watson, 1934), 70–103.

[11] Ibid., 70; Woodward, *The Book of Miracles*, 21.

[12] Stephen Wright, "Preaching the Miracles of Jesus," in *Preaching the New Testament*, ed. Ivan Paul and David Wenham (Downers Grove, IN: IVP Academic, 2013), 59–72.

[13] Ibid., 65.

[14] Ibid., 66.

role is to help listeners discern the signs of God's continued work of grace and bear witness to them. This sacramental recognition provides theological guidance for the interpretation of miracle stories.

Narrative theology focuses on the literary character of the story. Like other stories, the miracle stories in the Bible have a "narrative quality"[15] that enables the reader to connect the ancient text and the contemporary context. With this notion, Wright suggests that the miracle stories in the Bible should be read as "parables." For him, just like preaching parables in the Bible, preaching the miracle stories as parables helps the preacher prepare a sermon to offer "neither simple 'proof' of Christian claims, nor the possibility of rationalization," but to "catch their provocative, unsettling tone, rather than taming them or making them 'obvious.'"[16]

The Miracle Story as Historiography

As Wright explains, parables have the power to evoke the reader's imagination to create a new meaning, and, like parables, the miracle stories in the Bible have such parabolic power. It seems that categorizing the miracle stories as parables solves the hermeneutical dilemma with miracle stories. This solution, however, is problematic in terms of the historicity of the miracle stories. It is true that once historical events are handed down to the community of faith in oral or written form, they go through a process of change by various storytellers for different audiences. Eventually, the narrative quality overrides the factuality of the events and makes them open to multiple new meanings. Treating the miracle stories as parables, however, completely avoids their historicity and risks overlooking the significance of their function as signs of God's continuing works of grace in human history. As Gerd Theissen convinces us, history tells that Jesus was indeed a charismatic miracle worker and that his miracle stories were "testimonies to a unique event in the past."[17] In other words, the miracle stories in the Bible were not created purely by the authors' imaginations, like parables, but were grounded in historical

[15] Ibid., 67.

[16] Ibid., 70.

[17] Gerd Theissen, *The Miracle Stories of the Early Christian Tradition*, trans. Francis McDonagh (Philadelphia: Fortress Press, 1974), 276–78.

events. At this point, it seems more legitimate to consider the miracle stories as historiography than parables.

According to the *Encyclopedia Britannica*, historiography is the narrative presentation of history through the critical examination of selected sources.[18] Peter Burke advocates the value of historiography in the study of history by indicating that many historical sources are, in fact, "stories told by particular people," rather than an "objective reflection of the past," and that historians' work "does not reproduce 'what actually happened' so much as represent it from a particular point of view." [19] Thus, historiography is, on the one hand, rooted in the historical event and is concerned with the historicity of the story, that is, its historical meaning in its original historical and cultural context. On the other hand, historiography is a narrative that has parabolic power in meaning-making. It is descriptive rather than analytical, is concerned with people rather than abstract ideas or circumstances, and deals with particular and specific examples rather than statistically verified empirical regularities.[20] As a historical narrative, historiography "mediates between the events reported in it on the one side and pregenric [*sic*] plot structures conventionally used in our culture to endow unfamiliar events and situations with meanings, on the other." [21]

With regard to this, it is worth noting that Wendy Cotter classifies the miracle stories in the Bible as anecdotes,[22] "a short obscure historical or biographical account," [23] like testimonies. An anecdote has some narrative elements and "serves a community *Sitz im Leben*," by functioning as "an exempla story that provides some virtues to

[18] http://www.britannica.com/EBchecked/topic/267436/historiography. Accessed October 22, 2014.

[19] Peter Burke, "History of Events and the Revival of Narrative," in *New Perspectives on Historical Writing*, ed. Peter Burke, 2nd ed. (University Park: Pennsylvania State University Press, 2001), 284.

[20] http://en.wikipedia.org/wiki/Historiography#Narrative. Accessed October 22, 2014.

[21] Hayden White, *Tropics of Discourse: Essays in Cultural Criticism* (Baltimore: Johns Hopkins University Press, 1982), 88.

[22] Wendy J. Cotter, *The Christ of the Miracle Stories: Portrait through Encounter* (Grand Rapids: Baker Academic, 2010), 4–15.

[23] http://dictionary.reference.com/browse/anecdote?s=t. Accessed October 22, 2014.

be admired and imitated by the community."[24] In other words, a miracle story, as an anecdote, is a paraphrase of a historical event or "representation of the past . . . filtered through the cultural, socio-ideological matrix"[25] of the present readers in order to achieve a certain intention of the author.

In addition, "microhistory" or "micronarrative," in Burke's terminology, is another concept suitable for understanding miracle stories in the Bible as historiography. Burke explains that microhistory is "an approach that focused on a small community or locality, often using the story of a single ordinary individual or event to illuminate something larger about the culture." For him, micronarrative is "a kind of microhistory" that tells "a story about ordinary people in their local setting," in opposition to "what is often called 'Grand Narrative,' the story of the rise of nations, the growth of liberty, the modernization of the economy and so on."[26]

The historiographical approach to the miracle stories in the Bible suggests that their interpretive process should not ignore the particular historical context, either by prioritizing the narrative quality or hastily relating them to contemporary readers' situations. Instead, it should first take the story as "the other" that happened in a particular socio-cultural and historical context and then try to find the connector between the world of the story and the world of the reader by exploring the literary and rhetorical function of the story. In this process, it is helpful to discern the connector through such questions as: In what historical and cultural situation did Jesus work that miracle? How is the plot designed to make the miracle happen? How can the biblical scene be imagined analogically in our contemporary context? From whose perspective among the worshipers should the story be read? How and for what? These hermeneutical and theological questions lead the preacher to a dynamic interaction between text and context. From the to-and-fro movement between them, which

[24] Cotter, *The Christ of the Miracle Stories*, 9.

[25] Daniel Boyarin, *Intertextuality and the Reading of Midrash* (Bloomington: Indiana University Press, 1990), 12. It is worth noting that Boyarin claims that the Bible itself must be read as "ideologized historiography" (90).

[26] Burke, "History of Events," 292.

is not value-neutral but is closely related to the preacher's purpose of preaching, a new meaning emerges.

The Intertextual Approach to Luke 7:11-17

When we approach the miracle story in Luke 7:1-17 as an anecdotal historical narrative, it functions as a lens through which we can discern what God is doing in human history in order to make human life more human. The intertextual approach exclusively bound to intertextuality within the Christian scriptures is not sufficient to be used as an interpretive tool to discern God's humanizing activity in the world, for it is not limited to the Christian community and its stories. So, it is incumbent on the preacher to choose a partner text beyond the Christian scriptures. For many Christian preachers, however, that may be a challenge because major world religions involve so many miracle stories that finding one with the same literary elements—such as genre, characters, plot, setting, motivations, theme, etc.—may not be readily available.

Facing this problem, the functional approach sounds feasible. In his book *The Miracle Stories of the Early Christian Tradition*, Theissen explains the functional approach to the miracle stories with three symbolic actions: the social, the religio-historical, and the existential.[27] According to him, the social function of the miracle stories is to vitalize people who live under oppression and hopelessness in a particular socio-cultural and historical context. For example, in primitive Christianity and ancient society, people lived in the "extreme situations of suffering, hopelessness and injustice,"[28] and miracle stories functioned as "collective symbolic actions by which distress was remedied and in which the members found strength to combat it in their ordinary lives."[29] The religio-historical function of miracle stories is based on the assumption that they are "part of general expansion of ancient belief in miracles"[30] through which religious communities interpreted the world in a new way. The cosmic world

---

[27] Theissen, *The Miracle Stories*, 231–301.
[28] Ibid., 29.
[29] Ibid., 251.
[30] Ibid., 31.

was not turned upside down, but in the interpreted world through miracle stories, the way of life distinguishes itself from all existing ways of life "by its claim to absoluteness."[31] Miracle stories also have an existential function as symbolic action in relation to perennial human predicaments. Human beings experience "'timeless' existential situations of distress such as illness and despair," and they cannot endure "the reality which confronts them unless they try to transcend it by means of symbolic actions in order to transform it into a human world of meaning."[32] For them, miracle stories function as "a revelation of the sacred in tangible form,"[33] through which "the real negativity of existence is transcended."[34]

The three functions of the miracle stories as symbolic actions imply that a criterion for selecting a partner text for intertextuality should be "homologies of function"[35] between the two texts. Just as the goal of interreligious dialogue is to seek homologies of function that reflect "a common purpose" of humanity,[36] according to Jay Garfield, so is that of intertextual dialogue. This functional approach avoids narrowly comparing the literary elements of different religious texts or stories at the surface level. It also avoids the potential pitfall of ignoring the distinctive essences and profundity of other religious stories in the intertextual dialogue.

Feminist and postcolonial perspectives also provide criteria for selecting a partner text for intertextual dialogue. The perspective of the lives of women and other marginalized or colonized people in multicultural society needs to play an important role in selecting a partner text. It is crucial for the preacher to deconstruct the conventional meaning of the story interpreted and appreciated by socially privileged people and reconstruct new life-giving meaning from the point of view of the socially unprivileged or underprivileged. Such

---

[31] Ibid., 286.

[32] Ibid., 33.

[33] Ibid., 302.

[34] Ibid., 289.

[35] Jay L. Garfield, *Empty Words: Buddhist Philosophy and Cross-Cultural Interpretation* (Oxford: Oxford University Press, 2002), 259.

[36] Ibid.

reading makes it possible for the preacher to see more clearly where God is, what God is doing, and how God is working in human history.

Following the functional approach, the Buddhist story "Kisa Gotami and the Mustard Seed," which is one of the most famous stories in the Pali Canon,[37] is chosen as a partner text to Luke 7:11-17. The story is also known as "The Buddhist Parable of the Mustard Seed" and has a variety of versions. While the two stories tell different miracles—the miracle of resuscitation in Luke's story and the miracle of psychological and mental healing in the Buddhist story—they have commonalities in symbolic actions or homologies of function. Moreover, both stories include marginalized people as main characters, although commentators have not paid primary attention to this fact.

Once the partner text is selected, the preacher needs to be aware that, as postcolonial criticism legitimately points out, intertextual or interreligious hermeneutics conducted by Western theologians and philosophers has, consciously or unconsciously, been based on a colonial mentality that treats other cultural and religious traditions and scriptures as inferior to that of Christianity through the comparison of doctrinal substance among different religions.[38] Even in studying the miracle stories in the Bible, some Western biblical scholars have used the extrabiblical approach as a hermeneutical tool. But their goal was to prove the uniqueness of the biblical stories[39] or demonstrate the distinctiveness of Jesus' miracles as superior to others.[40] In this

[37] http://www.accesstoinsight.org/tipitaka/kn/thig/thig.10.01.than.html; http://www.clear-vision.org/Schools/Students/Ages-4-7/story-of-Kisa.aspx. Accessed October 22, 2014.

[38] Cf., R. S. Sugirtharajah, *Asian Biblical Hermeneutics and Postcolonialism: Contesting the Interpretations* (Maryknoll, NY: Orbis Books, 1998).

[39] For example, Dibelius, Herman Hendrickx, Benjamin E. Williams, and other biblical scholars have compared similarities and dissimilarities between miracle stories in the Bible and those in Rabbinic and Hellenistic literature based on literary and redaction criticisms and presented the uniqueness of the miracle stories in the Bible. Cf. Dibelius; Herman Hendrickx, *The Miracle Stories of the Synoptic Gospels* (London: Geoffrey Chapman, 1987); Benjamin E. Williams, *Miracle Stories in the Biblical Book Acts of the Apostles* (Lewiston: Edwin Mellen Press, 2001).

[40] Murray J. Harris, "'The Dead are Restored to Life': Miracles of Revivification in the Gospels," in *Gospel Perspectives: The Miracles of Jesus*, vol. 6, ed. David Wenham and Craig Blomberg (Sheffield: JSOT Press, 1986), 302–3.

situation, the Christian preacher needs to keep in mind that the intertextual dialogue between Luke 7:11-17 and the Buddhist Parable of the Mustard Seed must be conducted through a mutually critical conversation in humility to discern what God is doing for the well-being of humanity, not only within, but also beyond the boundary of Christian communities, rather than to prove the superiority of the miracle of Jesus.

Both the Lukan and the Buddhist stories include some characters in common, such as a widow, her only son who is dead, the community of people, and the miracle worker. Their storylines are similar in following the "basic narrative syntagm . . . a linear temporal model composed of three phases—*equilibrium-disruption-equilibrium*," [41] or from the beginning through crisis and climax toward denouement. In Luke, the story begins with Jesus entering into Nain, a village of Galilee (*equilibrium*). At the gate of the town, Jesus encounters the widow, who has lost her only son, and the people of her community who accompany her on the way of the funeral process (*disruption*: the crisis). Moved by compassion for her, Jesus resuscitates her dead son from death (*disruption*: the climax), and the story ends with words of praise by the people of the community for Jesus' miraculous work (*equilibrium*: the denouement).

In the Buddhist story, a young woman, Kisa Gautami, has a son (*equilibrium*). Then, suddenly her son dies. Unable to accept her son's death, she goes from house to house throughout the village, holding her son's dead body in her arms and begging for medicine to bring him back to life. Feeling sympathy for her lunatic behavior, a person from the community tells her to visit the Buddha. Upon meeting the Buddha, she asks him for medicine to resuscitate her dead son (*disruption*: the crisis). Moved by compassion, the Buddha tells her to bring him some mustard seeds from any family in which there has never been a death, to be used as ingredients for this medicine. She eagerly visits each house in the village to acquire the mustard seeds but fails to find a single house without death. Instead, she hears numerous stories about death from the villagers and eventually realizes the truth that suffering is part of life and that nothing is permanent (*disruption*:

---

[41] Daniel Chandler, *Semiotics: The Basics* (London: Routledge, 2004), 90.

the climax). Finally, she takes her son's corpse away, returns to the Buddha, and becomes his follower (*equilibrium*: the denouement).

The two stories are similar, not only in their literary form, but also in their function. Even though they were told in different cultural and religious contexts, in different parts of the globe, at different times, homologies of their functions can be sought in relation to the symbolic actions of the stories: Both women lived in patriarchal societies in which their identity and value were determined only by virtue of their ability to procreate sons. The two stories present the predicament of women who have lost their only sons in their male-centered patriarchal societies, and both demonstrate how they were able to transcend their social and existential predicaments through different miracles performed by their religious leaders. Consequently, both stories provide their readers or listeners with wisdom to live a transformed life amid the negativity of their realities.

Despite such similarities, the two stories also have differences. While the climax of the Lukan story is the demonstration of Jesus' miraculous divine power, the climax of the Buddhist story is the widow's enlightenment, which is counted as a miracle. Considering this difference, it is no wonder that most authoritative biblical commentaries focus on Jesus as the protagonist in the story and regard the widow, her dead son, the community, and Jesus's disciples as supporting cast to highlight Jesus' miraculous power as a sign of the eschatological reality. They are passive onlookers in Jesus' work of the miracle but only at the end became witnesses to the miracle (vv. 16-17: "A great prophet has risen among us," "This word about him spread throughout Judea and all the surrounding country").

Unlike the Lukan story, the widow and the community of people in the Buddhist story actively participate in making the miracle happen in her life, although it is eventually a completely different miracle from what they expect. It is a stark contrast to the Lukan story in that the miracle happens through the widow's tireless efforts to search for the source of the miracle and the villagers' active role in the process by guiding her to the Buddha and sharing with her their stories of losing their own loved ones. Although it is hard to find written commentaries on the story, this is one of the most popular stories for Buddhists to illustrate the teaching of impermanence and the path to liberation from attachments.

These differences illumine the different worldviews of the two religious schools of thought. In Luke, human suffering and death are understood eschatologically in relation to power hegemony between the divine and the evil, and the miracle of Jesus in the story functions as a sign or foretaste of the nearness of God's reign, the cosmic victory of divine power. Based on this worldview, Luke describes the miracle as a solely divine intervention, leaving humanity—the widow, her community, and the disciples of Jesus—to remain passive onlookers, and gives his implied readers, supposedly people suffering economically, politically, culturally, and socially in a colony of the Roman Empire, hope and courage to live by looking beyond their present reality, based on the promise of God. This theological interpretation raises a homiletical question for the preacher: While the miracle in the Lukan story is a good reminder of the promise of God for contemporary listeners, how can the present time frame, in which the consummation of God's victory over death is still not fulfilled, be understood? In other words, what is the good news to those who anticipate the fulfillment of the eschatological reality in relation to the miracle that happened in the story?

In Buddhism, human suffering and death are perceived as being part of "the web of entanglement" woven in "the endless becoming and passing away according to *karma* (action)." The way to be freed from this fate into *nirvana* (the ideal condition of release from all forms of suffering) is "nonattachment to things," which is possible only through enlightenment.[42] Since life is impermanent, death is inevitable. In the Buddhist worldview, however, death is not the end but is followed by rebirth according to "the resultant karma (cause and effect)" or the results of one's past actions.[43] In this view, raising the dead is not a spectacular miracle, because all the deceased will be born again in a different body and live a new life. As a result, in the Buddhist Parable of the Mustard Seed, the miracle is perceived as

[42] Fritz Buri, "A Comparison of Buddhism and Christianity According to a History of Problems," in *Buddhist-Christian Dialogue: Mutual Renewal and Transformation*, ed. Paul Ingram and Frederick Streng (Honolulu: University of Hawaii Press, 1986), 16. The parenthesis is mine.

[43] Thich Nguyen Tang, "Buddhist View on Death and Rebirth," http://www.urbandharma.org/udharma5/viewdeath.html. Accessed April 10, 2016.

an event of human transformation, transcending—rather than over-coming—the reality of suffering and death through enlightenment. The widow's life is transformed, not through the resuscitation of her dead son by the miraculous power of the Buddha, but through the awakening to the truthful wisdom of life by the help of the Buddha and the people of her community.

Homiletical and Liturgical Strategies

The intertextual dialogue on Luke 7:11-17 challenges Christian preachers and worship leaders to think about how the two stories can be used effectively to help worshipers apperceive the wisdom of God for the life of humanity in multicultural contexts. Upon this challenge, three cultural approaches—the intercultural, the crosscultural, and the transcultural—give homiletical insights. They are context-oriented, depending on the particular context of the congregational culture, and are not necessarily mutually exclusive. More precisely, the same text can be used in three different approaches based on the preacher's pastoral sensitivity to her own congregational culture and her particular homiletical and liturgical intentions. The terms "intercultural" and "crosscultural" are often used as synonyms, and the term "transcultural" tends to be identified with the word "acul-tural" in academia and the church.[44] In multicultural hermeneutics, however, they are distinguished differently, as follows.

The intercultural approach is to invite other religious and cultural traditions into the Christian framework. This approach presupposes similarities or common grounds among different religious groups, as well as among racially and culturally different Christian groups in understanding humanity and its relation to divinity. Based on this approach, intercultural dialogue aims to deepen the understanding of a theological theme involved in a Christian text by engaging in a dialogue with other religious and cultural resources. They can be used as illustrations and examples in exploring and elaborating on a theological and biblical theme, so that worshipers may feel an

---

[44] Cf. Lutheran World Federation, "The Nairobi Statement in Worship and Culture (1996)," in *Worship and Culture: Foreign Country or Homeland?*, ed. Gláucia Vasconcelos Wilkey (Grand Rapids: Eerdmans, 2014), 137–42.

interconnectedness by recognizing that they share an ultimate religious and existential concern in common. The pitfall of this approach, however, is the danger of superficiality. That is, simple observation without critical reflection may lead the worshipers to ignore the distinctive essences and profundity of other religions and cultures.

The intercultural approach, however, can still be used carefully and subversively to help culturally exclusive congregations that are not open or friendly to other religious groups gradually become more receptive to them. Based on this approach when preaching Luke 7:11-17, the Buddhist Parable of the Mustard Seed can be used as an illustration of women's common predicaments in patriarchal society. The parable can reveal how their suffering lives share a common experience that will lead them all to witness the divine presence, regardless of their distinct worldviews. Considering that the worshipers are not fully open to other religious texts or stories, the preacher and worship leaders do not need to highlight the Buddhist story in the liturgy by including it in Scripture reading, but they can simply incorporate it into the sermon as an illustration. Such a strategy may avoid unnecessary conflicts with some worshipers who are confined to the exclusive view of *sola scriptura*.

While intercultural dialogue presupposes common ground among different religions and cultures, the crosscultural approach focuses on the differences between them. It invites worshipers to a different religious and cultural framework and encourages each to understand the other. For example, a Christian preacher immerses herself into understanding the Buddhist meaning of suffering by reading Buddhist texts and other resources following the Buddhist logic or its hermeneutical principles and appreciates the differences between the Buddhist perspective and the Christian perspective on suffering. The goal for the preacher is not to present a common ground for these different religious perspectives but to help the congregation perceive how various religions follow different paths in the search for wisdom. As a byproduct, the worshipers may critically evaluate their own religious and cultural tradition in comparison with others' and deepen the meaning of suffering. Yet, in many cases, the crosscultural approach may trouble the worshipers in applying the learning from other religious traditions to their Christian belief, without ignoring the value of the differences and without losing their built-in Christian identity.

The crosscultural approach is effective when the congregation is open to other religions and is curious about their truth-claims. If the preacher wants to use the crosscultural approach in preaching Luke 7:11-17, one way would be for the preacher to paraphrase the Lukan story and address the problematic fact that such a miracle in the story hardly happens in our lives. To resolve this dilemma, the preacher might suggest a different concept of miracle based on her knowledge of the Buddhist understanding of suffering and death and employ the Buddhist Parable of the Mustard Seed as a teaching tool. At the end, the preacher can lead the listeners to experience such a miracle in their personal and communal lives. Or they can be encouraged to find God's continuing work of miracles in their daily lives and participate in it. In the liturgical context, the Buddhist Parable of the Mustard Seed can be performed as an ensemble reading or a pantomime before or after the sermon.

In the transcultural approach, "trans-" means going "through" and "beyond" a local culture, rather than simply beyond all cultures, which implies acultural. On this conceptual basis, the transcultural approach means a critical conversation among racially and culturally different groups. It juxtaposes their different perspectives and critically examines each in order to create new spiritual and religious bearings for today. Therefore, the aim of the transcultural approach is to bring about a new understanding of the biblical text beyond its conventional meaning through dialogue from diverse religious perspectives. For example, the distinctively Christian note proclaiming the eschatological message of Jesus on the reign of God can reconfigure its theological meaning through a dialogue with other religious teachings about a vision for a new community and place it in a broader context in concert with others as a harmonious voice singing its unique tone.

While the transcultural approach makes it possible to reconfigure or reappropriate the understanding of the Christian gospel by expanding it through "the fusion of horizons," this approach first requires of preachers and worship leaders profound theological and religious knowledge about other religious sources and cultural traditions, as well as that of Christianity. If the congregation is open to learning about different religious stories and traditions, the transcultural approach may be helpful to preach Luke 7:11-17 in dialogue with the Buddhist Parable of the Mustard Seed. The mutually critical conversation between the two stories challenges the Christian preacher to read the Lukan story from multiple angles. For example, when the preacher reads it from the angle of the miracle, its theological meaning as a sign of God's imminent reign needs to be reinterpreted for contemporary listeners to gain relevant meaning in their particular time and space. In the process of meaning-making, Buddhist philosophy, embedded in the Buddhist Parable of the Mustard Seed, that nothing is permanent and that working a miracle is interconnected and interdependent, offers an insight into deepening the eschatological framework of Christian theology.

Such mutually critical dialogue also encourages the preacher to imagine Luke's story from different characters' perspectives, rather than exclusively focusing on the miracle worker, Jesus, who represents the divine power over death. When the story is read from the widow's or the community members' point of view in relation to the Buddhist Parable of the Mustard Seed, it not only reveals various theological meanings of the miracle but also illumines how it can be enacted in our contemporary lives. Through the sheer compassion of the divine and the people and shared wisdom among the members of the community, the miracles that were witnessed in the ancient stories can be experienced in a fresh new communitarian way in our reality.

For Buddhist preachers, it may be interesting to realize that while the Buddhist story tells that the widow makes every effort to solve her problem and finds the Buddha, the Christian story tells that Jesus (or the divine presence and power) graciously approaches the widow and initiates the solution to her problem. Moreover, the community's exclamation at the end of Luke's story, "God has come to help his people" (v. 17), may lead them, who are supposed to be atheist, to be confused, thereby allowing it to function like a "koan," or words of meditation on the metaphysical question about the relationship between the divine and the human in the process of enlightenment.

Preaching the miracle story in Luke 7:11-17 through multicultural hermeneutics encourages worship leaders to reconsider Christian liturgy in relation to the faith that God is still working miracles in many mysterious ways to transform our lives, and also to pay special attention to the significance of the liturgy of healing. It is worth noting that Duck laments, in her book *Worship for the Whole People of God*:

Vital Worship for the 21ˢᵗ Century, that "what has often been missing in our churches is intentional communal worship with the opportunity for prayer, laying on of hands, and anointing"[45] and emphasizes the importance of the healing ministry as follows:

> Healing is the transformation that may occur when humans encounter God at the point of their need . . . a transformation of perspective within which human life and relationships take on a new meaning unbounded by death. . . . Healing is the church's intentional ministry, through worship and pastoral care, of seeking God's presence with people experiencing grief, pain, suffering, and sickness. In some cases, the presence of God may bring physical cure, through prayer or medical processes. But, healing is not the same as cure. It may bring peace about memories of life's hurts or serenity in facing death. Healing may also occur through a community's change of attitude and behavior toward people with physical or emotional disabilities so all may freely worship and contribute their gifts to the human family. A congregation also does healing ministry when it challenges social injustice that harms people and communities. God is at work in many ways in life.[46]

Along with such various liturgical components of the healing liturgy as prayer with the laying on hands, anointing, preaching, and intercessory prayers, Duck stresses the significance of personal testimonies and thanksgiving. For her, the healing service should basically be "a witness to the way God continues to bring wholeness and hope even today."[47]

Regarding the role of the witness, Woodward informs us that, in major world religions, to witness to the continuing power of a God in the world is a common function of sainthood.[48] The definition of saint is multilateral and has been used in many different religious communities to refer to various people, such as members of religious communities, martyrs who died for their religious faith, hermits,

---

[45] Duck, *Worship for the Whole People*, 234.
[46] Ibid., 235.
[47] Ibid.
[48] Woodward, *The Book of Miracles*, 32.

monks, bishops, missionaries, and even pious kings and queens.[49] One of the commonalities of the saints, states Woodward, is that "they all work miracles,"[50] and their miracles have been recognized and interpreted in a variety of ways by their religious communities. In this sense, Christian preaching and worship that participate in and witness to God's continuous work of miracles are the work of the saints, who belong to "a great cloud of witnesses" (Heb 12:1) testifying to the continuing presence and work of God in human history.

Conclusion

Preaching the miracle story through multicultural hermeneutics intends neither to prove it as a historical fact that can be replicated in our contemporary context, nor to discover a timeless, perennial existential meaning of the story by demythologizing it. Instead, it is to help listeners discern what God is doing in human history and nurture their faith and hope that God is with us to heal us and make our lives whole in our difficult life situations. In the discerning process of God's humanizing activities, miracle stories in the Bible and other sacred texts function like a lens, through which we can zoom in and out to where God is and what God is doing for humanity in our multicultural world.

Following the lead of the Spirit to find where God is and what God is doing through the lens of the miracle stories, it is necessary for Christian worship to be a service of healing. Preachers and worship leaders are called to revalue the theological and pastoral significance of the traditional practice of the Christian healing service and develop it to be culturally more relevant to contemporary worshipers. Therefore, the miracles stories are ongoing challenges to preachers and worship leaders to ponder what the miracles mean and how they can be manifested in preaching and worship.

[49] Ibid., 137–38.
[50] Ibid., 32.

PART 3

Searching for New Liturgical Models

CHAPTER 5

The Renewal of Christian Preaching
and Worship

The search for a new paradigm of Christian preaching and worship relevant to our multicultural context requires the theological and biblical investigations that were explored in previous chapters. This and the next chapters tackle pragmatic issues in relation to the paradigm shift in Christian preaching and worship. It is not an easy task to change the liturgical model, for hundreds of Christian denominations have their own liturgical traditions, and many local congregations have their unique liturgical patterns embedded in their particular cultures. Tension between tradition and innovation becomes tangible whenever the worship committee or the pastoral leadership tries something new in order to invigorate congregational worship. In fact, some churches have the painful experience of having tensions escalate into "worship wars" and seeing how costly the renewal of worship can be.[1] Why, then, is liturgical renewal necessary? How can the tension surrounding the renewal of worship be transformed into energy that brings about a positive outcome? What kind of homiletical and liturgical insights would be helpful for the renewal of preaching and worship?

This chapter aims to respond to these questions through interdisciplinary studies with ritual theories and church history. The first section situates Christian worship within the broad context of ritual

[1] Cf. Thomas G. Long, *Beyond the Worship Wars: Building Vital and Faithful Worship* (Bethesda, MD: Alban Institute, 2001).

in general and presents a conversation with ritual theories in order to explore the possibility of changing liturgical patterns. The second section reviews a history of the renewal movements of Christian worship from the multicultural perspective, to learn how preaching and worship have been transformed in particular historical and cultural contexts. Together, these two sections provide homiletical and liturgical insights into the renewal of Christian worship in our multicultural context.

Ritual Theories and Liturgical Changes

Christian worship has often been regarded as a branch of historical studies, particularly the doctrinal history of the Christian church. It is significant, however, to approach worship as ritual, since it is a ritual performance that represents the identity and belief of the worshipers, as well as their doctrinal assumptions about God. Christian believers have ritualized passages of life and other great events as a way to relate to the community of which they are part, based on their lived theology and faith in God.

While the term "ritual" is too multifaceted and complex to be defined,[2] Robert Bellah helps us understand it in a threefold way— ritual as practice, play, and celebration—based on its primordial significance in the history of human evolution. According to him, ritual is "a form of practice" that includes not only sacred but also profane activities recurring regularly in the context of daily life, such as meals, sports, festivals, Sabbath observations, etc.[3] Ritual is also a play in the sense that it is an activity that has a beginning and an ending and requires "human cooperation" with "shared intentionality."[4] By playing "certain games, making sacrifices, singing and dancing,"[5] people create "a relaxed field"[6] where the ordinary pressures of life

[2] Catherine Bell, *Ritual Theory, Ritual Practice* (New York: Oxford University Press, 1992), 13–17.

[3] Robert Bellah, *Religion in Human Evolution: From the Paleolithic to the Axial Age* (Cambridge: Belknap Press of Harvard University Press, 2011), 9–10.

[4] Ibid., 74, 92.

[5] Ibid., 110.

[6] Ibid., 77.

and social tensions are suspended, and they "celebrate the solidarity of the group."[7]

Christian worship is a religious ritual, both sacred and human. It is sacred because it is the divine accommodation of the Transcendent to humanity. It is also profoundly human because it is based on a humanly created liturgical pattern. As Randall Collins sums up, it is "the doorway-to-the-transcendental approach of cultural anthropology."[8] Christian worship, therefore, is an empirical reality of communal interaction that happens through the formality of a ritual. Through ritual interactions, people enter into the community of faith and deepen their relationship with God and others. The formal pattern of the ritual plays a major role in forming the identity of the community and enhances its solidarity.

The primary concern of humanity in relation to ritual practice is with meaning-making. Roy Rappaport rightly states that human beings are "a species that lives and can only live, in terms of meanings,"[9] and meaning-making has to do with "religion's most general and universal elements, 'The Sacred,' 'The Numinous,' 'The Occult,' and 'The Divine' and with their fusion into 'The Holy' in ritual."[10] Meaning-making is not simply an intellectual or rational process of knowing, explains Michael Aune, but it is an interpretive process that occurs through "the real communication" in which "intellectual precision and passionate force" are joined.[11] Meaning-making at such a deep level occurs through participation or communal actions in the performance of a ritual.

Rappaport emphasizes the significant role of participants in ritual performance by distinguishing it from other performances. For him, those who are present at a ritual performance constitute a congregation that is invited to participate in the ritual by taking action, while

[7] Ibid., 94.

[8] Randall Collins, *Interaction Ritual Chains* (Princeton, NJ: Princeton University Press, 2004), 7.

[9] Roy A. Rappaport, *Ritual and Religion in the Making of Humanity* (New York: Cambridge University Press, 1999), 1.

[10] Ibid.

[11] Michael B. Aune, *To Move the Heart: Rhetoric and Ritual in the Theology of Philip Melanchthon* (San Francisco: Christian University Press, 1994), 69.

those who are present at other performances such as theatrical or athletic events are audiences that are allowed to only watch and listen to the performers.[12] Through participation, following the particular order of the ritual, explains Bellah, the congregation experiences "collective effervescence"[13] as the condition for meaning-making and perceives a "deeper reality"[14] or a " vision" that is "the [product] of hope and imagination" that transcends the present reality.[15] When a ritual is performed as an embodied event of the community through active participation, it has the power to transform the daily lives of the participants at an individual and communal level, by providing them with a new meaning of reality, and propels them to take action.

Worship as a ritual performance supposes that the participants interact with one another with "the physical presence of living bodies" in the same place at the same time. They perform "a series of prescribed motions" by repeating the fixed order of the ritual.[16] Such pattern-embodied participation encourages conservatism in the worshipers' reluctance to change their way of worship. Consequently, a fixed liturgy rarely changes, and any action to renew it should expect resistance, to a certain degree.

It is, however, worthwhile to pay attention to Collins's interaction ritual theory. According to his analysis, "the formality and the stereotyped activity" of a ritual are not natural but functional.[17] They are "not the crucial ingredients; they only contribute to the core process of intersubjectivity and shared emotion, which is to say the experience of collective consciousness and collective effervescence, insofar as they contribute to a mutual focus of attention."[18] In other words, "the formality" of a ritual performance is supposed to generate emotional energies and symbolic meanings. If it fails to fulfill this goal, change is inevitable. Collins eloquently articulates this functional view as follows:

[12] Rappaport, *Ritual and Religion*, 42–43.

[13] Bellah, *Religion in Human Evolution*, 17.

[14] Ibid.

[15] Ibid., 15–16.

[16] Mark Searle, "Ritual," in *The Study of Liturgy*, ed. Cheslyn Jones, et al. (New York: Oxford University Press, 1992), 56.

[17] Collins, *Interaction Ritual Chains*, 49.

[18] Ibid.

Religion is not simply a body of beliefs, but beliefs sustained by ritual practices. When the practices stop, the beliefs lose their emotional import, becoming mere memories, forms without substance, eventually dead and meaningless. By the same token, new symbols can be created; whenever the group assembles and focuses its attention around an object that comes to embody their emotion, a new sacred object is born.[19]

Catherine Bell also convinces us that, in spite of the general assumption that ritual is unchangeable with its intrinsic features of "formality, fixity, and repetition,"[20] it continues to change in order to better represent the contemporary participants' worldviews, religious beliefs, and cultural ethos:

Ritual is not primarily a matter of unchanging tradition. On the contrary . . . ritual [is] a particularly effective means of mediating tradition and change, that is, as a medium for appropriating some changes while maintaining a sense of cultural continuity. . . . Ritual can change as the conditions of the community change. . . . No ritual stands by itself. It is always embedded in a thick context of traditions, changes, tensions, and unquestioned assumptions and practices. . . . A community's attitudes and styles of ritualizing are inseparable from their worldview, and it is not hard today to find a great variety of communities, worldviews, and styles of ritualizing living in close proximity to each other.[21]

Rappaport is especially concerned with the possibility for the renewal of religious rituals. As a special mode of ritual communication, states Rappaport, a religious ritual transmits two different messages—"self-referential and canonical messages."[22] While the former is variant, conveying "information concerning the current states of the participants, often transmitted indexically rather than symbolically," the latter is invariant, conveying the concerns with "enduring aspects of nature, society or cosmos."[23] The seemingly changeless

[19] Ibid., 37.
[20] Bell, *Ritual Theory*, 91.
[21] Bell, *Ritual: Perspectives and Dimensions* (New York: Oxford University Press, 1997), 251–52.
[22] Rappaport, *Ritual and Religion*, 53.
[23] Ibid., 58.

message of the canonical information is transmitted symbolically, incorporating the self-referential information in a ritual form. In the process of transmission, explains Rappaport, if the participants feel that the ritual order makes the ritual "mere ritual" by not adequately conveying both messages, it is "likely soon to pass away," and a sudden and abrupt change possibly happens.[24] Therefore, the structure of the ritual cannot be guaranteed to remain unchanged. Rather, it is evolutionary, existing in "an unpredictably changing universe."[25] Once ritual change happens and engages the participants with "intellectual precision and passionate force," it generates energy that fuels personal and communal transformation and plays a significant role in changing the identity and role of the community.

Just as ritual changes, so Christian worship as a religious ritual is subject to change. It survives and also thrives, not through rigid formality, but by opening itself to interact with changing realities. When Christian worship loses the capacity for meaning-making and is unable to provide an intrinsic worship experience, it is challenged to transform its form and substance. Church history has been witness to numerous occasions of the renewal of worship that attempted to make Christian preaching and worship an event of meaning-making, intrinsic to worshipers in their particular historical time and place.

Renewal Movements in Church History

It would not be an overstatement that the history of the Christian church is at some point the history of the renewal of worship. Just like other religious communities, the Christian church tends to resist change in worship. Yet, changing social and cultural circumstances have caused liturgical traditions to be deliberately refashioned or invented. Church history shows that numerous movements to renew worship experiences took place, and new liturgical paradigms were created to be theologically and culturally more relevant to changing liturgical contexts. Following is a brief summary of the renewal movements of Christian preaching and worship from the multicultural perspective, over time.

[24] Ibid., 419.
[25] Ibid., 421.

The Early Period

In *The Search for the Origins of Christian Worship: Sources and Methods for the Study of Early Liturgy*,[26] Paul Bradshaw considers the Jewish synagogue liturgy to be the root of Christian worship, and he investigates the influence of the liturgical practice of Judaism on the fledgling practice of Christian worship. According to Bradshaw, the synagogue liturgy during the first century was diverse due to the variety of liturgical occasions and the geographical dispersion of the Jews. Some standardized forms included only general rules about the liturgical elements like benedictions, recitations, and general contents of the elements, rather than "their exact words."[27] Even these general liturgical rules and orders differed from place to place. One example of the diversity of synagogue worship is that the Babylonian Talmud prescribed that the entire Pentateuch should be read throughout a year's time, while the Palestinian practice was a three-year lectionary cycle, both for the Torah and for the Prophets.[28]

Bradshaw also informs us that liturgical manuscripts of the early church were not fixed materials but "living literature," a literary genre that includes the written material "which circulates within a community and forms a part of its heritage and tradition but which is constantly subject to revision and rewriting to reflect changing historical and cultural circumstances."[29] This implies that in the primitive and early Christian communities, their worship did not have an absolutely fixed liturgical form but was flexible to the changing cultural context. It was not static but dynamic, providing worshipers with intrinsic experiences in their particular cultural contexts on their particular theological stances.

Bell convinces us that the synagogue liturgical pattern—reading "portions of scripture," listening to "expository preaching," invoking "intercessory prayer," and closing with the "'amen' that Jews used to punctuate their petitions"—was also used in the primitive Christian church and gradually changed to make Christian worship

---

[26] Paul F. Bradshaw, *The Search for the Origins of Christian Worship: Sources and Methods for the Study of Early Liturgy* (New York: Oxford University Press, 1992).

[27] Ibid., 6.

[28] Ibid., 22.

[29] Ibid, 74.

more efficacious to express the theology of the Christian faith in particular historical and cultural environments.[30] It is, as John F. Baldovin guesses, "probable that in a large city like Rome, several Christian language groups with varying practices existed at least up until the end of the second century" and ritualized Christian experiences in diverse cultural ways.[31] They were, states Baldovin, open to reinterpret theological meanings of the liturgical elements based on their unique experiences in Jesus Christ and flexible to practice worship in various ways to actualize their "intelligible experience."[32] As a result, Christian worship varied considerably from place to place during the early period. Geographical difference and cultural fluidity led Christian churches to continuously renew their worship as a response to the changing cultural context for worship.

Baptism and the Eucharist are among the examples of liturgical diversity. Baptism, "originally derived from Jewish lustration rites of repentance for one's sins,"[33] and Jesus' last supper with his disciples as the practice of the Jewish "Passover seder"[34] were reinterpreted in diverse ways in order to provide relevant theological meaning to different racial communities. Likewise, rites were administered with different elements and in different ways through the ongoing process of cultural adaptation.[35] It is notable that Paul the Apostle relativized the practice of Jewish Christianity by admitting the importance of racial and cultural diversity among Christian believers. As Bell points out,

> Paul decided that Gentiles (persons who were neither Romans nor Jews) who wanted to become Christians did not need to convert first to Judaism and obey all its laws; they simply needed to profess belief in Jesus. . . . This step effectively made the message of belief in Christ independent of the cultural practices of a particular group,

[30] Bell, *Ritual*, 212.

[31] John F. Baldovin, "Christian Worship to the Eve of the Reformation," in *The Making of Jewish and Christian Worship*, ed. Paul F. Bradshaw and Lawrence A. Hoffman (Notre Dame, IN: University of Notre Dame Press, 1991), 156.

[32] Ibid.

[33] Bell, *Ritual*, 213.

[34] Ibid., 212.

[35] Baldovin, "Christian Worship," 46–47, 56–57.

although Christianity continued to appropriate both Jewish and non-Jewish practices as its own.[36]

Preaching was also culturally sensitive in the primitive church. While Jesus preached the message of the kingdom of God in the Jewish cultural context, Paul's audiences were living in the Greco-Roman world. As vanThanh Nguyen indicates, Paul's sermon at the Areopagus is "an outstanding example of cross-contextual missionary preaching found in the New Testament."[37] Like Paul, the apostles who proclaimed the Christian message to racially and culturally different people were challenged "to contextualize and transpose the Gospel with care and creativity so as to engage with all sorts of listeners, even nonbelievers."[38]

Since Christianity achieved legal status in the Roman Empire with the Edict of Milan in 313, it spurred the process of inculturation in its rites. The adoption of Greco-Roman culture was the major force in the paradigm shift of Christian worship as the Christian church moved from an outlawed sect to an institutionalized state religion. For example, "Hellenistic mystery religions" were adopted in the formation of Christian spirituality, "civil and court rituals" in the revision of the eucharistic meal, "Roman cultural festivals" in the making of the Christian calendar, and so forth.[39] Preaching also changed its mode of communication according to the new cultural environment. It moved from "private exhortation" in the Jewish expository style to "public proclamation" in the Greco-Roman oratorical style, in order to preach to the educated "audience" in such public arenas as meeting halls and basilicas.[40] As Alden Bass recounts, "With the legalization of Christianity in the fourth century, preaching became a fully public affair, and preaching proliferated; people flocked to hear the great orators of the age such as John Chrysostom (d. 407),

---

[36] Bell, *Ritual*, 215.

[37] vanThanh Nguyen, "Preaching in the New Testament," in *A Handbook for Catholic Preaching*, ed. Edward Foley (Collegeville, MN: Liturgical Press, 2016), 49.

[38] Ibid., 50.

[39] Bell, *Ritual*, 216.

[40] Alden Bass, "Preaching in the Early Christian Church," in Foley, *A Handbook for Catholic Preaching*, 54–55.

Gregory Nazianzus (d. 390), Basil (d. 379), Ambrose (d. 397), Ephrem (d. 373), and Augustine (d. 430)."[41]

One of the most interesting changes in preaching in the Greco-Roman culture was that it was often understood as entertainment:

> Preachers often understood themselves to be one more form of entertainment in the city alongside the hippodrome, the circus, civic festivals, and the theater (Augustine, *Enarrationes in Psalmos.* 80.23). Sermons were calculated to give pleasure to the crowd and often concluded with applauses; at times claques were even hired to congratulate the preacher. According to Eusebius (d. ca. 339), the sermons of the bishop of Antioch, Paul of Samosata (d. 275), resulted in fans jumping up and down "as occurred in the theater" (*Historia Ecclesiastica* 7.30.9).[42]

Preaching was also influenced by the various cultural and linguistic backgrounds of the churches in the geographically different areas of the Greco-Roman world. For example, while Roman churches used the rhetoric of persuasion through argument that was popular in their culture, Syriac preaching was poetic and musical:

> Marrying theology and poetry, sermons were less argumentative and more poetic; sometimes verse homilies were sung to the accompaniment of instruments such as the harp. One of the greatest early Christian preachers was Ephrem of Nisibis (d. 373), the father of the hymnic homily. These sermons, called *madrashe*, consisted of stanzas sung by the preacher and a refrain given by the congregation. Ephrem also adapted the ancient genre of the dialogue poem (Syr., *memre*), which takes the form of an imagined argument between two biblical characters in order to highlight the dramatic tension within the biblical narrative. These verse homilies effectively explore the psychological dimension of the stories while simultaneously revealing the theological teaching of the passage. Ephrem became the model for fifth-century preachers such as Narsai (d. 503) and Philoxenus of Mabbug (d. 523). Jacob of Serug, known as the "flute of the Holy Spirit and the harp of the orthodox church," was famous for his nearly eight hundred homiletical poems. By

---

[41] Ibid., 51.
[42] Ibid., 55.

incorporating music and metrical verse into their homilies, the Syriac poet-preachers opened a new path in preaching which has yet to be explored in the Western church.[43]

The Medieval Era

In relation to liturgy, Michael S. Driscoll convinces us that a tremendous amount of liturgical divergence existed from the early period of Christianization to the medieval era. Churches in such different geographical regions as Gaul, Milan, Spain, the British Isles, etc., worshiped with "their own characteristic variations."[44] Yet, during the Middle Ages, when bishops and priests were educated with systematized liturgical and homiletical knowledge and skills, Christian worship became formalized as a public ritual performance and preaching as a public rhetorical event.

Still, local churches did not worship in a unified form. Rather, their worship was complexly diverse through inculturation with the practice of popular religion and devotions that had been developed in their particular historical and socio-cultural soil.[45] When Rome wanted to unify the liturgy and sacraments and fix the Roman Rite in order to bring forth "church unity that centered on absolute papal leadership" during the high-medieval era, local parishes and cathedrals, as well as monasteries, continued to use their particular liturgical forms, in protest against the clerical perpetration of the formalization of the liturgy.[46] Through numerous liturgical movements on small and large scales, they tried to interact with surrounding cultures to reach the racially and culturally diverse worshipers. In one effort, some medieval preachers used more than one language in preaching. As Carolyn Muessig illustrates:

> Preachers endeavored to preach in a language that their hearers would entirely understand. We see this with Bonaventure who,

[43] Ibid., 57–58.

[44] Michael S. Driscoll, "The Conversion of the Nations," in *The Oxford History of Christian Worship*, ed. Geoffrey Wainwright and Karen B. Westerfield Tucker (New York: Oxford University Press, 2006), 177.

[45] Ibid.

[46] Ibid., 202.

while giving a sermon before the people of Montpellier on Christmas, spoke in French, although his native language was Italian (*Sermo de tempore* 18). When preaching before the nuns of Saint-Antoine-des-Champs in Paris, he apologized most eloquently for his alleged poor French but stated that any language deficiency would not devalue the Word of God (*Sermo 1, de sancto MarcoEvangelista*). When he preached to his learned Franciscan brothers in Paris, he did so in Latin. Indeed, we have evidence from chronicles and saints' lives indicating that preachers were bilingual and sometimes trilingual. The French preacher Yves de Tréguier (d. 1303) was reported to have preached in three different languages—French, Breton, and Latin—using the language that best fit the needs of what his hearers required (Martin 1988, 26).[47]

In relation to racial issues, some medieval sermons included conflicts among racially different people, and some preachers "used sermons to convey prejudices, hatred, and violence":[48]

> Bernardino of Siena encouraged belief in witches and insisted that they be violently punished. In his tireless attempts to replace Jewish bankers with Christian ones, another Franciscan Observant, Bernardino of Feltre (1439–1494), preached against the Jews and their practice of usury. Part of his anti-Semitism included preaching the blood libel of the child Simon of Trent (d. 1475), whom many Christians believed had been killed by Jews.[49]

Timothy Thibodeau argues that, in Western Christendom, liturgical uniformity was realistically impossible until the end of the medieval era "when the printing press could codify and effectively impose what Klauser terms the rigid rubricism of the Counter-Reformation papacy and its Congregation of Rites."[50] As Susan White affirms, the practice of the rigidly unified Roman Catholic liturgy began as a result of the Council of Trent (1545–1563). The liturgical

---

[47] Carolyn Muessig, "Medieval Preaching," in Foley, *A Handbook for Catholic Preaching*, 66.

[48] Ibid., 69.

[49] Ibid.

[50] Timothy Thibodeau, "Western Christendom," in Wainwright and Westerfield Tucker, *The Oxford History of Christian Worship*, 230.

unification was actually a cultural unification, because the Council of Trent standardized public worship based on "the liturgical practice current in the city of Rome," ignoring "the diverse, local worship heritages of the rest of the church."[51] The Roman Catholic Church continued to use the unified liturgy until the Second Vatican Council, which initiated the renewal of worship in the middle of the twentieth century.[52]

It is worth noting that liturgical diversity persisted in the history of the Eastern Church too. Local churches in the city of Constantinople, as well as in Christianized countries in the East, kept their own uniqueness in worship. According to Alexander Rentel, even after the Byzantine Empire fell to the Ottoman Turks in 1453, liturgical diversity continued in monasteries in its various forms, though the church made an effort "to consolidate and codify the rite to maintain their identity."[53] Since the modern era, the change of worldview and cultural ethos has challenged the Eastern churches to keep renewing their liturgies in order to appeal to their contemporary worshipers.[54]

The Reformation Period

The movement of the Reformation in the sixteenth century was a historic landmark for the paradigm shift in Christian preaching and worship in Western Europe. Although it is often understood that the movement was a reaction to the "abuses" of the late medieval church, it was not merely a fight against the corruption of the church. Rather, it was a theological and liturgical response to the changing culture of the larger society. Sixteenth-century Western Europe was under the force of the cultural movement of the Renaissance. The philosophy, science, and art of the Renaissance challenged people to reconsider their Christian faith in a rational and humanistic way. In addition to

---

[51] Susan J. White, "Christian Worship since the Reformation," in Bradshaw and Hoffman, *The Making of Jewish and Christian Worship*, 189.

[52] Mark R. Francis, *Shape a Circle Ever Wider: Liturgical Inculturation in the United States* (Chicago: Liturgical Training Publications, 2000), 5.

[53] Alexander Rentel, "Byzantine and Slavic Orthodoxy," in Wainwright and Westerfield Tucker, *The Oxford History of Christian Worship*, 271.

[54] Ibid., 272.

the Renaissance movement, such cultural trends as the zeal for Christian mission into newly discovered parts of the globe, the emergence of a political sensibility for a new national consciousness, and the expansion of commerce and education with the invention of printing[55] made the renewal of preaching and worship inevitable.

Facing this changing cultural context, the late medieval church was impotent to deal with the liturgical crisis. According to Michael Aune's description,

> The Mass was hardly a communal act because it was offered by the priest alone, largely in silence, sometimes out of sight of the assembly, and in an unintelligible ritual language. . . . The locus of the sacred . . . was to be found in the professionally religious, the monks and the clerics, while ordinary lay life was a zone of spiritual underdevelopment.[56]

In order for Christian preaching and worship to be more relevant to the changing cultural contexts, the reformers, who were influenced by Renaissance humanism, instigated the religious reform by challenging the church to renew its theology and liturgical practice to be more authentic and intelligible. While they did not deny the fundamental importance of the liturgy and sacraments, they brought forth substantial changes in Christian worship, such as various rational approaches to sacramental theology, the translation of the Latin Bible into vernacular languages, the practice of worship in worshipers' native languages, more frequent administration of the Eucharist for the laity, and the revival of preaching, which had gradually disappeared in the Western liturgy since the death of Gregory the Great in 604.[57] Eventually, the Reformation changed Christian worship into a Bible-centered "preaching service."[58]

It is generally understood that Reformation worship in the sixteenth century was based on a rational approach, focusing on teaching the Christian faith through Bible-centered preaching. It is, however,

[55] James F. White, *A Brief History of Christian Worship* (Nashville: Abingdon Press, 1993), 105–6.

[56] Aune, *To Move the Heart*, 41.

[57] Edward Foley, "The Homily," in Foley, *A Handbook for Catholic Preaching*, 157.

[58] Aune, *To Move the Heart*, 51.

important to note that Luther and his followers tried to renew worship from external formality to inward experience of the Spirit and took music seriously as a significant liturgical component. Philip Melanchthon, according to Aune, emphasized that the church's worship should have the "power to move not merely the mind but to be also an instrument of God's spiritual work in changing the heart."[59]

While the Reformation contributed to the renewal of Christian worship by breaking the formality and banality of the late medieval liturgy, the reformers, who were geographically concentrated in Germany and Switzerland, were neither tolerant of nor open to embracing different theological and cultural voices. One of the outstanding examples is the death of the Spanish theologian, Michael Servetus. John Calvin and other reformers in Geneva condemned him for "spreading and preaching nontrinitarianism" and "anti-infant baptism,"[60] and he was eventually sentenced to death by burning. At his trial, one of the inquiries was the following:

> Whether he did not know that his doctrine was pernicious, considering that he favours Jews and Turks, by making excuses for them, and if he has not studied the Koran in order to disprove and controvert the doctrine and religion that the Christian churches hold, together with other profane books, from which people ought to abstain in matters of religion, according to the doctrine of St. Paul.[61]

The Age of Enlightenment

From the beginning of the seventeenth century, Western Europe went through modernization through Enlightenment rationalism. Protestant churches rooted in the Reformation tradition continued to renew their worship to appeal to human rationality through theological and liturgical disputes.[62] The substance of the liturgical components was critically reviewed to meet the rational standards, and

---

[59] Ibid., 64.

[60] https://en.wikipedia.org/wiki/Michael_Servetus. Accessed September 18, 2016.

[61] Ibid.

[62] Cf., Theodore M. Vial, *Liturgy Wars: Ritual Theory and Protestant Reform in Nineteenth-Century Zurich* (New York: Routledge, 2004).

worship was centered on preaching the Christian faith with moral instructions. Even in the case of the Roman Catholic Church, standing for the unified Tridentine rite as a countercultural approach to the secular culture of modernism, "Enlightenment figures downplayed many devotions and feasts emphasizing the simple service of God. Sermons became more didactic, drawing on Scripture and reason."[63]

During the modern period, Western churches were active in the world mission by the impulse of colonialism of the European countries and encountered racial, cultural, and religious diversity. These changing conditions were a challenge to Christian preachers about what and how to preach to non-European people. One of the examples is the practice of colonial preaching, which Robert Bireley offers a snapshot of, as follows:

> With regard to the Spanish Empire in the New World, there were fundamentally two types of preaching, one for the European population and one for the Amerindians. The former aimed at the exhortation of the people to live a better Christian life, and it did not differ greatly from what was employed in Europe. The latter envisioned the evangelization of the Amerindians. This made use of a much simpler style, and it required a great deal of linguistic ability in order to reach the many different Amerindian populations. Its more specific goal was to uproot the remnants of paganism and idolatry among the Amerindians.[64]

Stemming from the Reformation and the Reformed tradition, Protestant churches, particularly in the German lands, Scandinavia, and England, contributed to the diversity of Protestant worship by creating their own worship styles that appealed to their particular cultural ethos. The distinctive liturgical pattern of each denomination or each national church soon became formalized, and the fixed liturgical form was later considered its liturgical tradition. The United States, as an immigrant society, has been an arena for the rich diversity of Protestant worship and epitomized racial, ethnic, and regional divisions based on the immigrants' national origins. English pilgrims and other

[63] Robert Bireley, "Preaching from Trent to the Enlightenment," in Foley, *A Handbook for Catholic Preaching*, 82.
[64] Ibid., 84.

early Christian settlers from Europe brought with them strong connections to their homeland churches and worshiped in the new land as they did in their old lands. Sermon-centered worship that granted priority to the mind over the heart was the dominant liturgical style in the New England colony.[65]

Not all Protestant believers, however, were satisfied by the dry rationalistic and intellectual approach to worship. Baptists, Pietists, Methodists, and a variety of free-church groups in the seventeenth and eighteenth centuries attempted to renew head-oriented worship to be in balance with the heartfelt worship. Their liturgical movements against Enlightenment rationalism were supported by Pietist theologians like Friedrick Schleiermacher and church reformers like John Wesley. They promoted "theologies of the heart" and emphasized the significance of personal inward experience in worship. Their theological and liturgical renewal against formality and rationalism, on the one hand, shared an affinity with the contemporary secular culture of Romanticism.[66] On the other hand, their renewal movements were a sort of revival of the sixteenth-century Reformation in the sense that reformers like Melanchthon emphasized the renewal of worship "to move the heart."

The Era of Great Awakenings

The two Great Awakenings in the United States in the eighteenth and the nineteenth centuries brought about a radical paradigm shift in Protestant worship. They were so insurgent that they changed the landscape of Protestant worship, not only in worship style, but also in racial and cultural mixture. As Conrad L. Donakowski explains, these were mass movements that were countercultural to Enlightenment rationalism. Their changed worship style "featured emotional release" through heartfelt worship with "enthusiastic singing and the joyful tears of conversion experience."[67]

---

[65] Cf. Harry S. Stout, *The New England Soul: Preaching and Religious Culture in Colonial New England* (New York: Oxford University Press, 1986).

[66] Conrad L. Donakowski, "The Age of Revolution," in Wainwright and Westerfield Tucker, *The Oxford History of Christian Worship*, 368.

[67] Ibid., 371.

The first Great Awakening (1730–1740) in New England, led by Jonathan Edwards, George Whitefield, and others, made an effort to pull away the dry formality of Christian worship. They tried to revitalize worship to become an experience of a deep sense of spiritual conviction and redemption. Furthermore, the movement contributed to breaking down the walls of race and class by worshiping together with the converted, regardless of their race and social class, including black slaves.[68]

The Second Great Awakening, during the early nineteenth century, was a revival movement targeting the unchurched in the rural South and urban towns in upstate New York and other states. Many Methodist, Baptist, and Presbyterian ministers and lay leaders joined the movement and held camp meetings, recruiting people from a wide range of classes and races to evangelize the country. Worship in camp meetings was innovative in many respects. First, people worshiped together across the boundaries of denomination, language, race, and ethnic background, even though "Baptists, native peoples, and persons of African descent celebrated the Lord's Supper separately." [69] As James White comments, camp meetings were probably the "first ecumenical occasions" in the history of the Protestant Church [70] and absolutely a multicultural experience.

The second innovative aspect of worship in camp meetings was that music was used as the major liturgical component able to move the worshipers' hearts. As a result, new styles of church music were invented for that purpose. As Karen B. Westerfield Tucker describes,

> The presence at the camp meeting of persons of different ethnic and racial backgrounds provided an occasion for the sharing and mingling of musical forms, influencing the development, for example, of white and black spirituals. The camp in effect was a nursery for the gospel style of church song that became widespread in the late nineteenth century. Singing was an integral component of worship in black communities from the outset and was regarded as a me-

---

[68] Ibid.

[69] Westerfield Tucker, "North America," in Wainwright and Westerfield Tucker, *The Oxford History of Christian Worship*, 606.

[70] James White, *A Brief History*, 160.

dium of prayer, spiritual empowerment, and proclamation but also as a vehicle for inveighing against human injustices before God. The song could take the characteristically African form of call and response . . . inviting easy participation.[71]

The last, but the most innovative, aspect of worship in camp meetings was its unique liturgical style. In order to appeal to secular people who were unchurched and uneducated, the style of worship was intentionally designed to be a simple, extemporaneous, and emotion-driven service, rather than following the fixed liturgical forms of the established churches. In *Lectures on Revivals of Religion*, Charles G. Finney, the most prominent theologian and preacher of the Second Great Awakening, elaborated on details of revival worship.[72] For him, the purpose of worship was to increase the conversion experience, that is, to "harvest" sin-sick souls; consequently, the worship style had to be "the *most effectual* way, to make the truth stand out strikingly."[73] He insisted that any particular forms and modes of worship should not be regarded as absolute ways for Christians to worship: "God has *established no particular system of measures* to be employed and invariably adhered to in promoting religions. . . . It was left to the discretion of the church to determine, from time to time, what *measures* shall be adopted, and what forms pursued, in giving the gospel its power."[74]

With this liturgical freedom, Finney proposed his "new measures" as the effective way to achieve the purpose of worship, that is, the increase of the conversion experience. In order to have a conversion experience, explained Finney, worshipers must examine themselves, not looking "directly within to see what is the present state of [their] feelings," but looking "back over [their] past history," taking their sins up *"one by one"* and reviewing and repenting of them "one by one."[75] As the way to generate such feelings, Finney's series of new measures

[71] Tucker, "North America," 606–7.

[72] Charles G. Finney, *Lectures on Revivals of Religion*, ed. William G. McLoughlin (Cambridge: Belknap Press of Harvard University Press, 1960).

[73] Ibid., 251. Italics are original.

[74] Ibid., 250–51. Italics are original.

[75] Ibid., 40–41.

included singing for the benefit of sinners,[76] lay prayers in public,[77] extemporaneous preaching in a colloquial style,[78] and "the anxious seat" or an altar call for the repentant.[79] Tom Lawson analyzes the revival worship pattern based on the new measures in three connected stages—"the preliminary, the message, and the harvest"—with the climax on preaching.[80] The preliminary includes singing and prayers that lay the emotional groundwork for people to soften their hearts to hear the sermon; the message is supposed to aim for the conversion of sinners through extemporaneous and theatrical preaching without sermon manuscripts;[81] and finally, worship harvests by gaining new believers through an altar call at the end of the sermon.

Finney's pragmatic approach to Christian worship, which was a radical change from traditional Puritan worship based on rationalism, actually worked effectively to fulfill his liturgical purpose in his particular cultural soil of the early nineteenth-century United States. His new measures, however, have been criticized, not only by his contemporaries, but also by later church leaders and theologians. Lawrence R. Rast Jr. evaluates Finney's new measures as a mixture of the secular culture of "democratic individualism and market capitalism" linked to "Arminian theology." [82] Finney's worship style was also criticized for distorting the biblical and theological meaning of Christian worship, since he understood worship as an event of evangelism by focusing exclusively on the unchurched. Furthermore, the "decision theology" of salvation by individual work backing up Finney's new measures was disputed for being different from Reformation theology, *sola gratia* (by grace alone), which is the foundation of Protestantism.[83]

[76] Ibid., 133.

[77] Ibid., 257.

[78] Ibid., 216.

[79] Ibid., 267.

[80] Tom Lawson, "Adorate: Worship," http://www.adorate.org/2013/02/how-finney-ruined-worship-2-reviving.html. Accessed 10, 2013.

[81] Finney, *Lectures on Revivals*, 213, 216–17, 210.

[82] Lawrence R. Rast Jr., "Theological Observer: Charles Finney on Theology and Worship," http://www.mtio.com/articles/bissar52.htm. Accessed December 10, 2013.

[83] Ibid.

In spite of these criticisms, Finney's innovative worship style became quite influential on Protestant worship in the United States. One of the new waves after the Second Great Awakening was the "gradual proportional move away from the established liturgical churches," resulting in the birth of hundreds of new Christian communities such as Adventists, Disciples of Christ and other Holiness churches, and a number of evangelical free-churches.[84] Interestingly, a large number of these churches adopted for their Sunday worship services Finney's revival worship style along with the music written for revivals.[85] The revival style of worship also became the predominant form of Christian worship in other parts of the globe, where Protestantism was spread by missionaries who were the "harvests" of the Second Great Awakening.

From the Twentieth Century to the Present

The revival style of worship was eventually fixed as a liturgical pattern of the Christian church and became the liturgical tradition of free churches such as Pentecostalism, the Vineyard Movement, and other Church Growth Movements. Notably, this particular worship style is nowadays used even in mainstream churches as "Contemporary worship" style, whose popularity is growing as a supplementary style to their traditional denominational worship. Evangelical worship, Church Growth Movement worship, Contemporary worship, and Emergent Church worship, which is a recent liturgical movement, are all associated with the free-church liturgical tradition of the Protestant Church and contribute to the diversity of contemporary Protestant worship. The target of these worship services is either Christian believers who do not feel any authentic engagement in traditional Christian worship or spiritual "seekers" who are searching for a new religious experience.

Free-church worship services seem to be sensitive to the postmodern secular culture and intend to respond to that as a way to appeal to worshipers' emotions by adopting advanced information technology, currently popular music, and other cultural elements. However, they

[84] Donakowski, "The Age of Revolution," 371.
[85] Lawson, "Adorate: Worship."

are concerned with neither multiculturalism nor homiletical or liturgical issues emerging from the multicultural context. In other words, they pay little attention to the racial and cultural diversity within the congregation but simply believe that their worship style universally appeals to the worshipers' emotions, regardless of their differences in race, ethnicity, and culture.

In relation to the awareness of racial and cultural diversity, it is worth noting that the Second Vatican Council (1962–1965) stimulated the Roman Catholic Church to renew its liturgy by highlighting the racial and cultural diversity of the church. The Constitution on the Sacred Liturgy (*Sacrosanctum Concilium*), which was the first document produced by Vatican II, freed the rigid and unified Roman Catholic liturgy that had been practiced since the Council of Trent to be inculturated through interaction with local cultures.[86] Moreover, the Second Vatican Council encouraged preachers to reconsider their preaching ministry in a culturally diverse context and engage in dialogue to "[break] through established personal and social boundaries."[87]

It is also notable that the World Council of Churches has taken seriously the racial and cultural diversity within Christian churches

---

[86] Regarding liturgical inculturation, refer to Anscar J. Chupungco, "Methods of Liturgical Inculturation," in *Worship and Culture: Foreign Country or Homeland?*, ed. Gláucia Vasconcelos Wilkey (Grand Rapids: Eerdmans, 2014), 262–75. Chupungco defines liturgical inculturation as "a process whereby pertinent elements of a local culture are integrated into the worship of a local church," in order to "create a form of worship that is culturally suited to the local people," so that the worshipers may actively participate in worship. Based on his cultural analysis of Christian liturgy, he proposes three methods of inculturation—"creative assimilation, dynamic equivalence, and organic progression" (262). The method of creative assimilation "starts with what culture can offer" (266) and to integrate "pertinent rites, symbols, and linguistic expressions—religious or otherwise—into the liturgy" (264); the method of dynamic equivalence "starts with what exists in the Christian liturgy" (266) and "reexpresses the liturgical *ordo* in the living language, rites, and symbols of a local community" (267); and the method of organic progression is to supplement the existing liturgy by inserting new cultural elements into it (273).

[87] Guerric DeBona, "Preaching after Vatican II," in Foley, *A Handbook for Catholic Preaching*, 98.

and has organized the Commission on Faith and Order to search for the unity of the church, including the dimension of worship.[88] In addition, the Lutheran World Federation's Study Team on Worship and Culture researched the relationship between worship and culture and released "The Nairobi Statement on Worship and Culture" in 1996, which proposes four ways to relate Christian worship to culture.[89] These renewal movements were the result of the modern awareness of racial and cultural diversity by Christian churches that understood that the individual congregation is culturally homogeneous and that the cultural approach to worship concerned the unique culture of the individual congregation. Thus, their renewal movements were directly related to evangelism, that is, "the renewal and mission of the church around the world,"[90] rather than seeking an authentic worship experience for the multicultural congregation.

Mark Francis, however, reminds us that Roman Catholic churches in the United States are no longer "national parishes" built by immigrants of the same nationality; rather, they are becoming multiracial and multicultural.[91] This case also applies to Protestant churches in the United States. While it is true that, since the New England colony period, Protestant immigrants have brought with them strong connections to their homeland churches and worshiped according to those unique liturgical patterns, their congregations are now becoming more multiracial and multicultural, just as rapidly as American

---

[88] Thomas F. Best, "A Faith and Order Saga: Towards, *One Baptism: Towards Mutual Recognition*," in Wilkey, *Worship and Culture*, 304.

[89] The Nairobi Statement says that "first, it is transcultural: the same substance for everyone everywhere, beyond culture. Second, it is contextual: it varies according to the local situation (both nature and culture). Third, it is countercultural, challenging what is contrary to the gospel in a given culture. Fourth, it is cross-cultural: it makes possible sharing between different local cultures" (Lutheran World Federation, "The Nairobi Statement in Worship and Culture [1996]," in Wilkey, *Worship and Culture*, 138). In his essay, "A Fragile Future for the Ordo?" Stephen Burns provides an adequate critique of the four ways proposed in the Nairobi Statement (in Wilkey, *Worship and Culture*, 143–61).

[90] Lutheran World Federation, "The Nairobi Statement," 137.

[91] Francis, *Liturgy in a Culturally Diverse Community: A Guide Towards Understanding* (Washington, DC: Federation of Diocesan Liturgical Commissions, 2012), 46.

society is. This changing situation challenges preachers and worship leaders to take seriously how Christian preaching and worship should be transformed in order to appeal to racially and culturally diverse worshipers. Now is the time for Christian churches to embrace yet another renewal movement in preaching and worship.

Conclusion

The development of new homiletical and liturgical paradigms from the multicultural perspective is provisional and contingent on the particular cultural situation of a congregation and the degree of its awareness of cultural diversity. While it is unrealistic to present an absolute model for preaching and worship in multicultural contexts, the study of ritual theories and the historical review of the renewal movements in Christian preaching and worship in this chapter provide us with some direction for the homiletical and liturgical renewal. First of all, the renewal should be able to help the worshipers make meaning of the complex realities they face in a multicultural world. It concerns the process of interpreting or reinterpreting reality, and manifesting the presence and work of the Spirit, through which they may be empowered to live a meaningful and constructive life with people from a wide range of racial and cultural diversity.

Homiletical and liturgical renewal should also aim to make preaching and worship more relational and participatory. In order to help the multicultural congregation "participate fully, actively and consciously in the liturgy," [92] the new liturgical paradigm should be accessible to culturally and even linguistically different worshipers by incorporating proper ways of preaching, singing, praying, celebrating the sacraments, and other liturgical components. When worshipers fully participate in worship, they may experience "heightened emotional energy" [93] that enables them to transform their lives, individually and communally, with a new meaning of reality.

Most of all, renewed preaching and worship should appeal to "the deepest possible level of the human personality—'the heart,'" [94]

---

[92] Ibid., 103.
[93] Collins, *Interaction Ritual Chains*, 51.
[94] Aune, *To Move the Heart*, 68.

in which "intellectual precision and passionate force [have] been joined."[95] Aune explains the movement of the heart as follows:

> Being "moved," then, is not simply an elemental feeling or an "oh wow" matter. It does not happen or emerge *ex nihilo*. Rather, it is an interpretive process that engages the heart, "the whole, responsible self" in interaction with the indwelling Spirit. . . . It is not simply a mere registering of sensory data nor an individualistic, idiosyncratic "warm feeling." Rather, we see a process that entails both feelings and cognitive orientation. It provides . . . the catalyst that transforms knowledge into human understanding, thereby bringing intensity and commitment to human action.[96]

The movement of the heart happens when the liturgy appeals to the culturally diverse worshipers' "religious imagination and expression of the faith."[97] When liturgical symbols and nonverbal language, as well as words and music are used effectively, they are powerful tools to move the heart "from a state of uncertainty and doubt to a state of belief and trust in God's words and promises."[98]

The search for a new homiletical and liturgical paradigm for our multicultural context is spiritual work, for the renewal of preaching and worship is, in essence, the renewal of the Christian faith, as well as of the identity and role of the Christian church. In order to express the Christian faith appropriately and relevantly, Christian worship, as a religious ritual, needs to be continuously renewed through interaction with the surrounding culture. The renewal of preaching and worship is not a new but an old and vital task for every generation of the Christian Church. It is not only a human effort but also a divine gift that changes human hearts and empowers them to action for a new life together.

The sermon "Women on the Way," included in appendix 4, is an example of how preaching can be transformed in its content and style to appeal to racially and culturally diverse worshipers. It was prepared for the 2013 Asian Presbyterian Women's Conference.

[95] Ibid., 69.
[96] Ibid., 107–8.
[97] Francis, *Shape a Circle Ever Wider*, 108.
[98] Aune, *To Move the Heart*, 82.

Considering that the listeners would be Asian American female church leaders from different origins in Asia, I approached the complexity of Asian American culture from the postmodern point of view and critically analyzed it from the woman's perspective. I chose John 4:4-42, in which Jesus has a conversation with a woman of Samaria, as the sermonic text, and identified the Samaritan woman with three Asian women who had different life experiences in their particular social locations.

The sermon was designed with three vignettes representing the three women's lives, one of which was a YouTube video. Before and after the sermon and between the vignettes in the sermon, hymns were sung to provide moments of meditation. The sermon was performed as participatory preaching, like a skit. I contacted four conferees one day before the worship service to invite them to play the roles of Jesus and three Samaritan women, and my role was the narrator. We tried to memorize the lines as well as we could and had a dress rehearsal. The five of us participated in preaching by authentically playing our roles. When each Samaritan woman shared her story, a unique photo of a well symbolizing her story was shown on the background screen. The performance of the three women's stories touched the listeners' emotions and moved their hearts to engage in building a community of love and hospitality.

CHAPTER 6

Models of Multicultural Worship

Searching for a new model for preaching and worship in multicultural contexts does not result in the formulation of one unique pattern universally applicable to all worship services. Instead, the process is open to a variety of new possibilities for the transformation of preaching and worship. In the process of searching for new possibilities, it is important to keep in mind that not every situation demands the same change in preaching and worship, nor is every change constructive and productive toward providing a more meaningful and memorable worship service. So, a paradigm change in preaching and worship requires of the preacher and worship leaders critical discernment.

In *Preaching in an Age of Globalization*, I introduced four different images for the negotiation of cultural diversity—the melting pot, the salad bowl, the mosaic, and the kaleidoscope—and explored them in terms of homiletical models.[1] This chapter extends the conversation into liturgical models. The first section investigates the four cultural images in relation to developing models of multicultural worship. The second section proposes the new image of the metamorphosis with the possibility of being another model of multicultural worship.

Four Cultural Models

The four images—the melting pot, the salad bowl, the mosaic, and the kaleidoscope—represent different approaches to negotiating

---

[1] Eunjoo M. Kim, *Preaching in an Age of Globalization* (Louisville: Westminster John Knox Press, 2010), 104–9.

diverse cultures in society. In dealing with cultural diversity in liturgy, they are useful to articulate different cultural approaches to Christian worship. The four liturgical models evolving from the four cultural images are effective to critically evaluate current practices of worship in Christian churches and think creatively about the next level of change in the future Christian worship.

The Melting-Pot Model

From the early history of immigration, the image of the melting pot has been used as a motto for dealing with cultural diversity. The original intention of this view was that "ethnic differences 'melted' into a single 'pot' would produce a synthesis—a new homogeneous culture that was [neither] Anglo-Saxon, Jewish, Italian, nor Asian."[2] In reality, however, "what has happened in the melting pot conception of Americanization is that all varieties of ethnicities were melted into one pot, but the brew turned out to be Anglo-Saxon again."[3] In other words, contrary to the ideal of the melting-pot image, the racially and ethnically dominant culture absorbs other minority cultures in society and presents its cultural characteristics as the unified culture of society. As a result, racially and ethnically marginalized people are forced to reformulate their cultural identity by assimilating themselves into the dominant culture, in order to survive under the dominant cultural power.

When the melting-pot model is applied to worship, it can be explained as follows: An individual church or denomination has its dominant liturgical tradition rooted in its particular racial and ethnic history and tradition. The church seeks to maintain its liturgical and cultural identity, regardless of demographic changes in its membership, and does not admit cultural diversity in worship. Just as the premodern understanding of culture presents clergy or elite culture as high culture and considers the congregation passive receivers, melting-pot worship takes the dominant liturgical culture as the high culture that people of other races and ethnicities in the congregation

[2] Young Pai, *Cultural Foundations of Education* (Columbus: Merrill Publishing Company, 1990), 57.
[3] Ibid., 58.

must passively receive as their new liturgical identity. In this model, the diversity of the congregational subcultures is ignored by exclusively adhering to the dominant cultural identity. The consequence is that the church practices monocultural worship in a multicultural context.

In the United States, it is not hard to find churches that practice melting-pot worship. Although churches in the United States are gradually changing from racial segregation to integration in membership, many of them neither pay attention to changing congregational subcultures nor embrace cultural diversity among the worshipers with sufficient sensitivity to transform their liturgical culture. For example, many mainstream European American churches do not extend their theological and liturgical concerns to racially and culturally different people but instead understand their liturgical traditions as the best way to worship God. Ethnic minority Christians who worship in those churches as latecomers are forced to accept the dominant liturgical culture as their new identity.

Melting-pot worship is also found in ethnic minority and immigrant churches. In racist America, traditional African American worship has provided African American worshipers with a cultural and spiritual identity through their unique songs, sermons, and other liturgical components. First-generation Asian, Hispanic, African, and other immigrant congregations worship in their native languages in unique cultural forms that they have used in their homelands as a way to preserve their racial and cultural identity in the white-dominant American society. Offspring born and raised in the United States and racially different spouses, extended families, and friends are excluded from their worship unless they agree to be coopted by the dominant immigrant liturgical culture. Such examples show that melting-pot worship renders the church stuck in the midst of the rapidly changing currents of the congregational culture. It unwittingly contributes to the segregation of worshipers depending on their race, ethnicity, and culture.

The Salad-Bowl Model

While the melting-pot model expresses an exclusive attitude against different liturgical cultures in the congregation, the salad-bowl model acknowledges the diversity of the congregational subcultures, to a limited extent. "Each ingredient in a tossed salad retains its own color, texture, taste, individual identity."[4] This image of a salad bowl helps us understand multicultural society as one in which "the sum total of all the ingredients becomes a multi-ingredient national identity without the individual parts losing their identity."[5]

When the salad-bowl image is applied to worship, it may be understood that worship leaders are aware of the diversity of the congregational subcultures and are appreciative of racially and culturally different people coming together and worshiping together with their distinctive cultural identities. It is important, however, to remember that the salad-bowl ingredients are not served alone but rather require a salad dressing to blend the ingredients together. In fact, the salad dressing weakens the distinctiveness of each ingredient as it is added to the dominant flavor, taste, and color, resulting in a unique flavor and taste of its own. The salad dressing needs to be considered seriously in the salad-bowl model of worship. Like the salad bowl, salad-bowl worship blends the distinctiveness of the cultural ingredients with a liturgical dressing. In other words, the congregants come to worship with the colorful diversity of their subcultures, which is visible, but their cultural distinctiveness is blended with the dominant flavor, taste, and color of the liturgy, for example, the church's dominant group's worship style, liturgical tradition, and theological doctrine. Such liturgical dressings are so powerful that they dilute the subtle colors and tastes of the congregational subcultures and contribute to the preservation of the unified liturgical culture of the church.

Some examples of salad-bowl worship are part of my worship experience at a Presbyterian church my family and I have attended for over a decade. The worship team realizes that about 20 percent of the congregation is composed of racially and ethnically different people, and they respect the diversity of the congregational culture. So on a Christmas Sunday, for example, three congregants who were

[4] Grace S. Kim, "Asian North American Youth: A Ministry of Self-Identity and Pastoral Care," in *People on the Way: Asian North Americans Discovering Christ, Culture, and Community*, ed. David Ng (Valley Forge, PA: Judson Press, 1996), 205.
[5] Ibid., 206.

originally from Africa, Asia, and South America were invited to participate in preaching by sharing the stories of how Christmas was celebrated in their homelands. At Easter Sunday worship, the pastor encourages the congregants to shout "Christ is risen" in their native tongues. And for Sunday services, once or twice a year, non-Western hymns are selected as congregational songs or special music. The liturgical order and cultural ethos of the church, however, is firmly rooted in mainline white Presbyterianism.

Another example of salad-bowl worship is found in some joint worship services with subcongregations. These days, many churches in the United States share their buildings with ethnic minority groups by using the facilities in different time slots. Some perceptive church leaders feel that it is necessary for the landlord and the tenant congregations to worship together occasionally as an opportunity to affirm that they are one in the family of God. The problem with their good intention is that they do not know how to create a worship service that both congregations can fully appreciate. It is not easy to negotiate cultural differences in worship, including language, music, the sermon style, symbols, theological orientations, etc. As a result, the salad-bowl model is often used as the best solution for a joint service, in which the landlord congregation prepares and leads the service and the tenant congregation is invited to participate in some parts of the liturgy, such as a special song or scripture reading in their native tongue.

Compared with melting-pot worship, salad-bowl worship is sensitive to the diversity of the congregational culture and intends to celebrate cultural diversity in worship by trying out some new liturgical elements. Yet, as long as the leadership of worship remains the same, the celebration of cultural diversity in worship remains at a superficial level, rather than bringing deep change into worship with the desire of ending racial and cultural prejudice and inequality. Just as the problem of salad-bowl preaching is ideological, as I explained in my previous book,[6] so is salad-bowl worship. It leads the preacher and worship leaders to ask such critical questions as: Who has the power and authority to choose the liturgical dressing? Whose favorite

---

[6] Kim, *Preaching in an Age of Globalization*, 105.

is the dressing? What if some ingredients do not match that dressing? These questions imply that worship is a political act practiced through power dynamics within the church.

The Mosaic Model

The image of a mosaic has been favored by many theologians and sociologists as an effective model for dealing with cultural diversity in multicultural society. The mosaic, as a picture made of small, colored pieces of inlaid stone, glass, etc., gives an image of wholeness without any dominant centrality. According to this image, each racial and ethnic community is like a piece of the mosaic that is equally valued in achieving the overall harmony by coexisting with the others.[7]

Based on the image of a mosaic, mosaic worship can be described in at least two dimensions—one in a social context and one in a particular local church context. In our multicultural society, racially and ethnically different churches are considered pieces of the mosaic. They represent their own unique cultural elements and liturgical traditions while respecting other racial and ethnic churches as equally important for the entire picture of the Christian church. Their culturally distinctive worship services, such as African American worship,[8] Asian American worship,[9] and Hispanic American worship,[10] contribute to completing the mosaic of Christian worship. Mosaic worship plays a major role in preserving the worshipers' racial and cultural heritage and encourages the church to practice monocultural worship in a multicultural society. However, it sounds unrealistic to assume that all American Christians go to their own ethnic churches in order to preserve their liturgical tradition and culture. Rather, an increasing number of believers search for worship places beyond their

[7] Jung Young Lee, *Marginality: The Key to Multicultural Theology* (Minneapolis: Fortress Press, 1995), 98.

[8] Cf. Melva Costen, *African American Christian Worship*, 2nd ed. (Nashville: Abingdon Press, 2007).

[9] Cf. Russell Yee, *Worship on the Way: Exploring Asian North American Christian Experience* (Valley Forge, PA: Judson Press, 2012).

[10] Cf. Justo L. Gonzáles, ed., *¡Alabadle! Hispanic Christian Worship* (Nashville: Abingdon Press, 1996).

racial and ethnic boundaries, where they may experience meaningful and memorable worship.

In a local church context, the mosaic model is used as a way to handle cultural diversity within the congregation. Some local churches composed of more than one race and language face a dilemma in preparing worship, because the preparation of an integrated service with different cultures and languages is neither easy nor convenient. Their worship leaders often abandon efforts to offer an integrated service and, as a last resort, provide more than one service on Sundays, in different languages and at different times or places. For example, some urban white churches that have a substantial number of Spanish-speaking members hire a Spanish-speaking associate to offer the worship service in Spanish for that group. Moreover, most immigrant churches, though they are racially and ethnically homogeneous, offer two separate worship services on Sundays, one in their native language for the first-generation immigrants, and one in English for their children who were born and raised in the United States. The mosaic model convinces such churches that their separate services are like pieces of the mosaic that participate in completing the entire picture of their worship lives.

In many cases, however, separate worship services within a church results in separating the congregation, administratively and financially, as well as liturgically. One of the main reasons for the separation of the congregation is that the minor group resists its marginal place under the supervision of the major group. In other words, those who are located in the margins of the mosaic want not to remain in their designated marginal places but to freely move to different locations within the mosaic. In the mosaic model, however, dynamic interaction among culturally different worshipers is not supposed to happen. Just as the whole picture of a mosaic is already framed by a specific design that requires each piece to remain in its assigned place in order to complete the original design of the picture with its particular shape and color, so mosaic worship does not attempt to create culturally integrated beauty that crosses racial and ethnic boundaries.

This limitation of the mosaic model reminds me of a personal e-mail I received from the senior pastor of a United Methodist church located in a university town in Ohio. In his church, about 100 out of 700 members were Korean college students. In order to provide a culturally relevant service to the Korean members, his church hired a Korean-speaking associate pastor and created Korean worship for them. But the problem with this mosaic model, said the senior pastor, was that the two different worship services had no interaction with each other, despite his "continuous goal" to create worship "fully embracing each other so as not to be two or three churches within a church."[11] What kind of liturgical model, then, might work for this goal? The kaleidoscope model seems to be more effective for the creation of culturally integrated worship.

The Kaleidoscope Model

In *Women Preaching: Theology and Practice through the Ages,* I explained the image of a kaleidoscope as a viable metaphor for describing the connectedness and diversity of women's experience.[12] In addition, I proposed the kaleidoscope model to be a new homiletical model for preaching in an age of globalization.[13] The term "kaleidoscope," combining three words in Greek, *kalos* ("beautiful"), *eidos* ("shape"), and *skopein* ("to look"),[14] refers to a contoured optical instrument that illuminates beauty by a source of light. The kaleidoscope creates a multiplicity of symmetrical patterns from fragments of various materials through the use of mirrors and lenses set at different angles. When the kaleidoscope rotates, each element produces beautiful, clear, and various patterns through convergence and interaction with the others and with the light. When all of the pieces shift, tones seem somehow different in their altered positions, and we recognize a new pattern.[15]

When applying the image of a kaleidoscope to worship, kaleidoscope worship not only represents the cultural diversity of the worshipers but also creates new experiences of worship through dynamic

---

[11] A conversation with Rev. Mike Pratt on July 10, 2014.

[12] Eunjoo Kim, *Women Preaching: Theology and Practice through the Ages* (Cleveland: Pilgrim Press, 2004), 20.

[13] Kim, *Preaching in an Age of Globalization,* 106–9.

[14] Online Etymology Dictionary.

[15] Kim, *Preaching in an Age of Globalization,* 106.

interaction with different liturgical cultures among the worshipers. As Marjorie Suchocki explains, when the kaleidoscope turns,

> not only do all of the pieces shift, but it even seems that some new ones have been added. There is familiarity and some continuity, for the colors are still there—but their tones seem somehow different in the altered positions, and while at first we try to see them in their familiar form, we nevertheless find ourselves struggling to express the difference in the way of seeing. Finally, we must recognize the newness of the pattern, and we reach toward a familiarity with the new that can be as assuring as that which we remember—or project—as belonging to the old. But the kaleidoscope will never repeat exactly the same pattern.[16]

Like the kaleidoscope that does not repeat exactly the same pattern, but constantly shifts to a new pattern, kaleidoscope worship is dynamic, open to inclusiveness and creativity. Moreover, just as a kaleidoscope needs a light to create a beautiful panoramic picture, so kaleidoscope worship is not possible without the light that is the involvement of the Holy Spirit, to illuminate the beauty of diversity as the work of the Spirit. In order to create kaleidoscope worship, worship leaders need to increase their general and specific knowledge about and direct and indirect experience of other cultures. The kaleidoscope model also requires of them creativity and the skill to integrate different cultural elements of worship in harmony and beauty, since the ultimate goal of kaleidoscope worship is to reveal the intrinsic beauty of God, that is, God's benevolence, through the entire service. Through beautiful worship created by diverse cultural elements, the worshipers can appreciate the warm, personal loving-kindness and compassion of God; through beautiful worship, the spirits of the worshipers are connected to the divine Spirit that makes us live in unity-in-difference by building affinity and solidarity with others.

Kaleidoscope worship, creating kaleidoscopic beauty by using different cultural elements of Christian worship from different racial

---

[16] Marjorie Suchocki, *God, Christ, Church: A Practical Guide to Process Theology*, rev. ed. (New York: Crossroad, 1989), 3–4, quoted from Kim, *Preaching in an Age of Globalization*, 107.

and ethnic groups, aims to be appreciated by all worshipers in many different ways and eventually develop the beauty of a shared identity with others in the Spirit of God. More precisely, by sharing cultural elements in worship, worshipers also share others' suffering and pain and a common vision for the community and for the larger world beyond individual racial and ethnic groups' vested interests. Through kaleidoscope worship, we experience that God is beautiful (benevolent) for us, and we are inspired to be beautiful for others.

The sermons and liturgies included in the appendixes of this book illustrate the image of a kaleidoscope. The liturgies were designed as multicultural worship by using multiple languages representing the worshipers' native tongues, by carefully selecting songs and prayer styles in culturally sensitive ways, and by including in the sermons the diverse experiences of worshipers who are racially and culturally different. In this way, diverse experiences converge into engagement through common concerns and finally help them live out a vision for a better world from the multicultural perspective. Above all, these sermons and liturgies intend to move the hearts of the worshipers by appealing to their imagination, so that they might experience the worship service as inspiring unity-in-difference.

Of the four cultural models, the kaleidoscope model seems to be the most effective tool to create a culturally integrated worship service in multicultural contexts. Out of the convergence and integration of the cultural elements of worship emerges an ongoing transformation of worship, which enriches liturgical experience. Like other cultural models, however, the kaleidoscope model has its own limitation. When an artist makes a kaleidoscope, she has her own design and uses limited shapes and colors. As a result, the new patterns created in the kaleidoscope are limited to the original shapes and colors. Similarly, kaleidoscope worship represents only the limited number of different cultural components of Christian worship which have already been practiced in the Christian Church.

Can we imagine a radically different worship service beyond our current cultural practice of Christian worship? In other words, can we envision the future of Christian worship in a totally different model from the past and present practice of Christian worship? If so, what might it be like? I name this kind of visionary worship celestial worship and imagine it through the metamorphosis model.

The Metamorphosis Model

While the four liturgical models are based on recapturing the past and present practice of cultural elements, the metamorphosis model aims to demonstrate radical change for the future of Christian preaching and worship. Nancy P. Greenman, an advocate for radical change in American education, wrote an intriguing essay, "Not All Caterpillars Become Butterflies: Reform and Restructuring as Educational Change."[17] In her essay, she explains "three types of change: old or intraparadigmatic change, transitional or interparadigmatic change, and new change or metamorphosis." She then critically examines current practices of educational change, which are not sufficiently satisfactory to reform American education in our changing context. For her, change means "a making, or becoming, distinctly different,"[18] rather than "partial or moderate change" or "mirroring the logic of the existing system,"[19] and so she urges radical change, that is, metamorphosis, in American education.

Greenman's three types of change are applicable to understanding homiletical and liturgical models in multicultural contexts. The melting pot, the salad bowl, and the mosaic models represent intraparadigmatic change, in which "the same elements are simply rearranged; their validity is never questioned," while the kaleidoscope model illustrates interparadigmatic change that "contains elements of a new structure" through creative and integrative mutual interaction, "as parts of new and new parts," although "it is still anchored in the existing structure—the past"[20] or present cultural practices.

The next level of change, by which Greenman means metamorphosis or "transformation—a destructuring and restructuring to create a new level"[21]—challenges preachers and worship leaders to consider significant, radical change in preaching and worship, beyond existing

---

[17] Nancy P. Greenman, "Not All Caterpillars Become Butterflies: Reform and Restructuring As Educational Change," in *Changing American Education: Recapturing the Past or Inventing the Future*, ed. Kathryn M. Borman and Nancy P. Greenman (Albany: State University of New York Press, 1994), 3–32.

[18] Ibid., 4, quoted from *Webster's Seventh New Collegiate Dictionary* (1972).

[19] Ibid., 5.

[20] Ibid., 7.

[21] Ibid., 6.

cultural patterns. According to Greenman, "metamorphosis is represented by the disintegration of the box or container, whether porous or nonporous, and by the creation of a new, differently shaped container from some of the pieces or the energy, infused with newly constructed pieces of different fabric, and with new energy and assumptions . . . or paradigm shift." [22]

The history of Christian preaching and worship that was reviewed in the previous chapter shows how radical change has happened in particular historical and liturgical situations. Radical change from synagogue worship through the house church style of Christian worship to the institutionalized formality of the Christian liturgy throughout the early and medieval periods, from sacrament-centered worship to word-centered worship in the Reformation era, and from the head-oriented to the heart-oriented style of worship in the modern period, illustrates how the metamorphosis model has brought about new experiences of Christian worship. Without envisioning a new level of preaching and worship totally different from the practice in the past and present, metamorphosis does not happen in Christian worship.

The metamorphosis model is possible when it begins with a new vision for preaching and worship. One historical figure who helps us learn about the practice of the metamorphosis model is Hildegard of Bingen. Hildegard, a twelfth-century German abbess, was a visionary. She began to experience visions from her early childhood until her death, through which she could "see hidden things and foretell the future." [23] She recognized that her experience of visions was a gift that was ineffable and inexplicable to others. In her book, *Scivias* ("Know the Ways"), she said that what she spoke and wrote were "not by the invention of her heart or that of any other person, but by the secret mysteries of God she heard and received them in the heavenly places." [24]

Hildegard tried to understand what her visions meant to the church. She described them "as seeing the light of God through her

[22] Ibid., 8.

[23] Johanna Schllemat, "Hildegard von Bingen: Symphonia Armonie Celestium Revelationum," *Music History* 1 (Nov. 25, 2008): 4.

[24] Hildegard von Bingen, *Scivias*, trans. Columba Hart and Jane Bishop (New York: Paulist Press, 1990), 60–61.

five senses: sense of sight (*amat*), sense of hearing (*descernit*), the organs of taste (*sapit*), those of smell (*elight*), and those of touch."[25] Her works, including her music, paintings, and invented language, as well as her theological writings and sermons, present her life as a way of living on Earth with celestial visions. Her music is appreciated as a celestial chorus, her paintings as illustrations of the celestial terrain, and her invented language, *lingua Ignota* ("Unknown language"), as celestial words praising God. These are a few of the clues she provides us with which to understand and practice heavenly worship on Earth.

One concrete example is *Symphonia Armoniae Celestium Revelationum* ("Symphony of the Harmony of Celestial Revelations"), the collection of her seventy liturgical songs. All of the songs are her poems set to music,[26] inspired by divine revelation. They were sung by the nuns in her monastery and provided them with spiritual guidance. These songs illustrate her creativity toward radical transformation in liturgy by showing "a freedom of her ideas that went against the norm of music during that time." According to Joanna Schllemat,

> Many of these songs were full of many musical elements such as contrast, unity, resemblance, dynamic tension, and response. . . . This made her musical work sound different to the normal music of that time. Her music grasped musical compounds and rarely did you see much text with the music. . . . Hildegard provided new concepts of melody as a movement of the voice. . . . In her antiphon, "O Successores" from Symphonia she showed a lot of structural control. . . . Each of Hildegard's antiphons was unique in many different ways, but each showed a drive towards to the climax. It is interesting to understand that a woman of that century could have a profound impact on the development of music during that time.[27]

Hildegard expressed the inspirations of her visions not only through music but also through paintings. The Choirs of Angels, which is one of thirty-five miniature illustrations included in *Scivias*, describes her vision of celestial choirs as "armies arrayed like

[25] Schllemat, "Hildegard von Bingen," 6.
[26] Ibid., 7.
[27] Ibid., 8, 10.

a crown," "a mandala-like image of nine concentric circles ranged about a void to signify the ineffable Presence."[28] Scholars of Hildegard's works see this image as two-dimensional artwork and interpret the nine circles as the shapes of the hierarchical order of angels in heaven.[29] When we imagine the circles of angels as three-dimensional or four-dimensional, however, we can see the heavenly angels, not in a rigid hierarchy, but in a flexible, non-ranked array, praising God freely in harmony and beauty: *"And all these armies were singing with marvelous voices all kinds of music about the wonders that God works in blessed souls, and by this God was magnificently glorified."*[30] For Hildegard, the divine vision was the source of inspiration to create radical transformation in liturgy.

It is also remarkable that Hildegard invented the "alternative alphabet" of *lingua Ignota*, a "form of modified medieval Latin, encompassing many invented, conflated and abridged words."[31] She used it in her compositions for her lyrics and scripts. It seems that she intended to use it as an ideal language, that is, a spiritual or celestial language, in which all the worshipers could praise God together and increase solidarity among themselves.[32]

Hildegard enlightens us, enabling us to see that radical change in preaching and worship comes from above (a vision of heavenly worship) rather than below (our past and present practice of worship). Our earthly practice of a vision of heavenly worship leads us to experience radical transformation or divine creativity that overcomes divisions on Earth.

---

[28] https://en.wikipedia.org/https://search.yahoo.com/yhs/search?p=scivias&ei=UTF-8&hspart=mozilla&hsimp=yhs-002. Accessed December 15, 2015. To see the image of the Choirs of Angels, go to http://curiator.com/art/hildegard-of-bingen/scivias-i-6-the-choirs-of-angels. Accessed December 15, 2015.

[29] Cf., Annette Esser, "The Choirs of the Angels," *Scivias Meditation in December 2013*: http://www.oxfordgirlschoir.co.uk/hildegard/sciviassynopsis.pdf. Accessed December 15, 2015.

[30] Hildegard von Bingen, *Scivias*, book 1, vision 6.

[31] https://en.wikipedia.org/wiki/Hildegard_of_Bingen#cite_ref-19. Accessed December 15, 2015.

[32] Sarah L. Higley, *Hildegard of Bingen's Unknown Language: An Edition, Translation, and Discussion* (New York: Palgrave Macmillan, 2007).

While Hildegard lived during the historic pinnacle of Christendom and interpreted her celestial vision of worship for Christian believers, we live in a very different world, a pluralistic, multicultural post-Christendom world. Our particular historical situation challenges us to consider whether a celestial vision of worship should be interpreted exclusively for Christians or not. If God were the Creator of the universe, heavenly worship must not be owned by Christians alone. Conversely, it might be worship for everyone God has created, regardless of religious and cultural differences. This reminds us of what the prophet Isaiah proclaimed in a vision of future worship: "my house shall be called a house of prayer for all peoples" (Isa 56:7). It suggests that Christian worship should ultimately be transformed into worship for "all peoples" and that preachers and worship leaders who practice the metamorphosis model are called to become prophets and visionaries for this ultimate goal of Christian preaching and worship.

The metamorphosis model is open to the preachers' and worship leaders' vision for heavenly worship; the celestial vision may not be fully accomplished here and now. But, like the scenes of Jesus' transfiguration in the gospels,[33] the vision will function as a glimpse of the ultimate destination of multicultural worship, in which all peoples worship God together in harmony and beauty.

Like the four cultural models, the metamorphosis model also has some problems when it is used for preaching and worship. One is that the term metamorphosis, signifying a major, drastically transformative change, sounds too radical. In reality, radical change in preaching and worship often risks causing a high level of anxiety among the worshipers and confronts their stubborn resistance to that change with schisms and conflicts, rather than smooth transitions from the old practice to the new level of change. The tension between old mind-sets and a vision for the new practice of Christian preaching and worship challenges the church to consider seriously how to bring radical change in a constructive way. Communicating the celestial vision of worship with racially and culturally diverse worshipers and building a sense of common purpose of preaching

[33] Matt 17:1-8; Mark 9:2-8; Luke 9:28-36.

and worship among them might require some ideas to minimize the negative impact of congregational resistance. Such prerequisites for radical change call for preachers and worship leaders to have pastoral sensitivity to the power dynamics among the worshipers and leadership to help them transition from the old practice to a new level of change.

The other problem with the metamorphosis model is related to the common biological image of metamorphosis, which gives an impression that transformation from a caterpillar to a butterfly happens suddenly and permanently. In like manner, people may understand that the purpose of the metamorphosis model is to develop the ideal practice of Christian preaching and worship and fix it "once and for all." It is, in fact, unrealistic to assume that the ideal form of Christian preaching and worship exists, for our world is transient, requiring us to renew our practice of preaching and worship in order to keep it relevant in our changing context. Therefore, the image of metamorphosis should not be interpreted as the way to fix Christian preaching and worship once and for all but as a symbol of a deep, ongoing change that mirrors the ideal form or a celestial vision for preaching and worship that cannot be fully accomplished on Earth. The vision can be expressed and practiced in many effective ways in different historical and cultural contexts. In this sense, the metamorphosis model is open-ended, a journey toward the ultimate eschatological destination of Christian preaching and worship. A variety of practices of the metamorphosis model are "a series of markers rather than fixed end points,"[34] with "a leap of faith in possibilities—even if they do not appear to be possible from where we are standing."[35]

Conclusion

Once the preacher and worship leaders assess their worship by examining how they worship in which model, they can move to the next level of their worship by considering the strengths and weaknesses of each model. For example, the melting-pot worship can be improved in relation to how the diverse cultural elements of the litur-

[34] Greenman, "Not All Caterpillars," 14.
[35] Ibid., 25.

gical components can influence each other to create a unique flavor and taste for congregational worship. The salad-bowl worship can consider how the worshipers can share the variety of their liturgical salad dressings to establish a balance with one another. The mosaic worship can alternate with a joint worship service in which racially and culturally different subcongregations worship together in unity-in-difference. The kaleidoscope worship can expand its range of diversity beyond that of the local congregational culture to more diverse colors and patterns in order to represent the diversity of the larger society. And the metamorphosis worship can lead to education, as it helps the worshipers envision their worship as an experience of heavenly worship, which might be very different from their current experience of worship. Moreover, the five liturgical models are not mutually exclusive. For example, the kaleidoscope worship, when carefully and creatively designed, may be experienced by the worshipers as a metamorphosis.

Searching for a new paradigm for multicultural worship, therefore, is an ongoing challenge for preachers and worship leaders to imagine how their worship can be a manifestation of the glory and beauty of God. This means they need to be visionaries who can see the vision of celestial worship. Whatever their current liturgical model is, they are encouraged to strive to actualize the vision of heavenly worship on Earth, the eschatological destination of Christian worship.

PART 4

Practice in Multicultural Contexts

CHAPTER 7

Preaching and Worship
as Reflective Practical Theology

The previous chapters probed homiletical and liturgical issues from the multicultural perspective and presented theological, biblical, and historical insights, as well as liturgical models, for the renewal of Christian preaching and worship in multicultural contexts. This last chapter proposes a reflective practical theological method as the homiletical and liturgical process in an actual ministerial setting. Preaching and worship have been regarded as subdisciplines of practical theology, which is narrowly defined as one of the specialized theological disciplines along with systematic theology, biblical studies, and church history. The reflective practical theological method is, however, based on understanding practical theology in a broad sense by identifying Christian theology, in general, as practical theology, in which theory and practice are supposed to relate dialectically to each other. Its ultimate goal is to help the preacher and worship leaders discern what God is doing and what God is calling us to do today and inspire the worshipers to become agents of transformation for their churches and society. The following four sections develop a method of reflective practical theology in relation to the concept of practical theology, including the way to discern practical wisdom, an explanation of the four stages of the reflective practical theological method, and an exercise in the method in a liturgical context.

Practical Theology as the Essence of Christian Theology

In seminary education, it is generally assumed that preaching and worship courses teach would-be preachers and worship leaders "how" rather than "what" to communicate through preaching and worship. In other words, from their preaching and worship classes, students are expected to learn techniques and skills for communicating the theological substance they gained in systematic theology, Bible, and church history courses. Toward that end, some seminaries hire popular preachers, speech therapists, or theater people to teach basic "know-how." Even among seminary faculty members, it is often felt that preaching and worship can be taught by any of them.[1]

This trend for teaching and learning preaching and worship in seminaries reflects how practical theology has been understood in theological education. Since the late nineteenth century, many seminaries and theological schools have adopted the fourfold pattern of theology, the so-called "hagenbach type" that divides Christian theology into four areas: systematic, biblical, historical, and practical.[2] The first three areas in this pattern deal with the theory or the substance of theology, and the last area, including the fields of homiletics, liturgics, Christian education, pastoral counseling, evangelism, etc., deal with application. As a result, the fourfold pattern separates theory and practice in Christian theology and reduces practical theology to applied theology as merely a skill-oriented discipline.

Since the last quarter of the twentieth-century, however, such practical theologians as Edward Farley and Don Browning have questioned the dichotomy between theory and practice and rejected the concept of practical theology as a handmaid of the other three areas of Christian theology. In *Theologia*, Farley sharply criticizes the theological trend of the fourfold pattern for reinforcing a "hy-

---

[1] Alyce McKenzie, "The Company of Sages: Homiletical Theology as a Sapiential Hermeneutic," in *Homiletical Theology: Preaching as Doing Theology*, ed. David Schnasa Jacobson (Eugene, OR: Cascade Books, 2015), 87.

[2] Karl Hagenbach, et al., *Theological Encyclopedia and Methodology on the Basis of Hagenbach* (New York: Phillips and Hunt, 1884). Earlier than Hagenbach, Friedrich Schleiermacher divided theological education into three areas—philosophical theology (apologetics, polemics), historical theology (the Bible, church history, dogmatic theology), and practical theology (preaching, pastoral care, evangelism, church government) in *Brief Outline of Theology as a Field of Study* (Lewiston, NY: E. Mellen Press, 1830). He also expressed practical theology as "the crown of theological study" in *Christian Care: Selected from Practical Theology*, ed. James O. Duke, et al. (Philadelphia: Fortress Press, 1988), 99.

per-specialization" of Christian theology and ignoring the original role of Christian theology as guiding the daily life of the community of faith.[3] Browning also argues that Christian theology "as a whole is fundamental practical theology" that is involved in the four "sub-movements of descriptive theology, historical theology, systematic theology, and strategic theology."[4] Based on the view that Christian theology is itself practical, the essays in Bonnie Miller-McLemore and Mary Fulkerson's edited book, *Wiley-Blackwell Companion to Practical Theology*, demonstrate how various areas and fields of Christian theology can contribute to the integration of theory and practice and how theologians, whatever their specialties, can be practical theologians.[5]

The contemporary movement of recovering the significance of practice in Christian theology reminds us of the original nature and function of Christian theology. In the early Christian church, theology emerged as the knowledge of God from the interactive relationship between God and humanity. Its goal was to provide the community of faith with pastoral guidance and soteriological implications through doctrinal and biblical teachings for the daily practice of the Christian faith. In other words, the leadership of the church was the ultimate purpose of Christian theology. This implies that all theological reflection should be inherently practical.[6] As Randy Maddox reiterates, Christian theology is "the implicit worldview that [guides] the temperament and practice of believers' lives."[7]

Christian preaching and worship are practical theological disciplines in the broad sense of practical theology as the essence of Christian theology. More precisely, they are reflective of practical theological disciplines in which theory and practice correlate in

---

[3] Edward Farley, *Theologia: The Fragmentation and Unity of Theological Education* (Philadelphia: Fortress Press, 1983), 162.

[4] Don S. Browning, *A Fundamental Practical Theology: Descriptive and Strategic Proposals* (Minneapolis: Fortress Press, 1996), 8.

[5] Bonnie Miller-McLemore and Mary Fulkerson, eds., *Wiley-Blackwell Companion to Practical Theology* (Malden, MA: Wiley Blackwell Publishing Ltd., 2012).

[6] H. Richard Niebuhr, *Radical Monotheism and Western Culture: With Supplementary Essays* (Louisville: Westminster John Knox Press, 1993), 115–16.

[7] Randy Maddox, "The Recovery of Theology as a Practical Discipline," *Theological Studies* 51 (1990): 651.

the sense that "practice both actualizes and tests theory while also providing the data for ongoing theory."[8] Here, practice means not just any kind of human activity, but praxis, that is, "transformative practice," in which theory and practice are integrated and mutually critical to change each other. As Forester succinctly defines it, "Praxis involves making things (*poesis*) and changing things."[9]

Preachers and worship leaders, who are concerned with "the praxis of life,"[10] are not mere practitioners but practical theologians who critically reflect on theory based on practice and vice versa in their particular liturgical contexts. Their task, as practical theologians, is to give meaning and direction to the present and future life of the church and society by helping the worshipers discern what God is doing in order to make and keep human life more human in our multicultural world and to invite them to what we are called to do. In order to fulfill this practical theological task, the discernment of "practical wisdom" is prerequisite.

The Discernment of Practical Wisdom

Contemporary Christian theologians have understood practical wisdom as a rational activity that creates a new way of life, based on the meaning of Aristotle's term *phronesis*. As Alasdair MacIntyre explains, *phronesis* means "practical reasoning" that brings about "intelligent human action" "in each particular time and place."[11] David Tracy also understands it as the "prudent understanding of variable situations with a view as to what is to be done."[12] As Richard Osmer summarizes, therefore, practical wisdom means "practical reasoning about action, about things that change. It involves discerning the right

---

[8] Catherine Bell, *Ritual Theory, Ritual Practice* (New York: Oxford University Press, 1992), 75.

[9] Duncan B. Forrester, *Truthful Action: Exploration of Practical Theology* (Edinburgh: T&T Clark, 2001), 7.

[10] Ibid., 42.

[11] Alasdair MacIntyre, *After Virtue*, 2nd ed. (Notre Dame, IN: University of Notre Dame Press, 1984), 161–62.

[12] David Tracy, "The Foundations of Practical Theology," in *Practical Theology: The Emerging Field in Theology, Church, and World*, ed. Don Browning (San Francisco: Harper & Row Publishers, 1983), 73.

course of action in particular circumstances through understanding the circumstances rightly, the moral ends of action, and the effective means to achieve these ends."[13]

While contemporary theologians identify Christian practical wisdom as the Aristotelian concept of *phronesis*,[14] it is notable that Thomas Aquinas distinguishes them and understands practical wisdom from the uniquely Christian point of view. Like other theologians, he identifies *phronesis* as the virtue of prudence. For him, though, there are two different kinds of prudence: "infused prudence" and "acquired prudence." According to Aquinas, summarizes Pamela Hall,

> Infused prudence is "perfected in charity, enables a person to order himself or herself well with regard to what is necessary for union with God, as such, it confers understanding for what is conducive to becoming "citizens of the household of God," and it commands accordingly. Acquired prudence, on the other hand, is directed to achievements of the natural human good; it enables a person to know and choose what is good for the civil community to which the individual belongs. . . . Both activities are prudential, on Thomas's view, and both are ordered to the achievement of the human good. . . . The infused prudence [is] . . . the gift of the Spirit which corresponds to . . . the gift of counsel (*consilium*). . . . The gift of counsel perfects prudence by rendering it open to the movements of the Spirit, who has perfect and complete knowledge, and thus by allaying the anxiety of uncertainty; in this way human reason is perfected with regard to what should be done by being guided by divine reason . . . moved by the Spirit.[15]

Phronesis, as acquired prudence, has its limits, for human reasoning is based on human knowledge and experience, which are partial and fragmented. So, we cannot assume that it always leads us to right actions. To perfect human reasoning requires the intervention of divine grace, that is, the work of the Holy Spirit, which leads us to

---

[13] Richard Osmer, *Practical Theology: An Introduction* (Grand Rapids: Eerdmans, 2008), 84.

[14] Cf. Don Browning, *A Fundamental Practical Theology*, 10; McKenzie, "The Company of Sages," 95–96.

[15] Pamela M. Hall, *Narrative and the Natural Law: An Interpretation of Thomistic Ethics* (Notre Dame, IN: University of Notre Dame Press, 1994), 84–85.

the act of love. By being open to the movement of the Spirit, human reasoning can be guided by divine love toward "the common good of many."[16] In this way, practical wisdom, as infused prudence, is the product of a collaborative work between divine love and human reasoning. It is possible only where love is present and when human beings are able to have friendship with God and other fellows.[17]

The discernment of practical wisdom, therefore, is neither a mechanical process nor the application of simple clues, principles, or guidelines from Scripture, tradition, or elsewhere. It is a divine gift, granted through discerning the voice of the Spirit, accessible by listening attentively to others in love, especially to the voices of those who are marginalized—racially, ethnically, and socially—within and beyond the worship community. As Hall emphasizes, "From such friends, from their witness and their influence, believers can learn better what the life of grace requires—and what it promises."[18]

The Four Stages of Reflective Practical Theology

The ministry of preaching and worship, as reflective practical theology, involves not only discerning practical wisdom but also communicating it with the worshipers in a particular liturgical context. It is an imaginative act in the sense that it requires of the preacher and worship leaders an ability to do meaning-making through a certain mental process of imagination. While people tend to identify the term "imagination" with "artistic creativity, fantasy, scientific discovery, invention, and novelty," Mark Johnson criticizes this view as "a result of nineteenth-century Romantic views of art and imagination"[19] and argues that imagination is more than that. For him, it is not separate from reason, because it is "our capacity to organize mental representations (especially percepts, images, and image schemata) into

---

[16] Ibid., 81.

[17] Celia Deane-Drummond, *The Wisdom of the Liminal: Evolution and Other Animals in Human Becoming* (Grand Rapids: Eerdmans, 2014), 86; see chapter 1 of this volume.

[18] Hall, *Narrative and the Natural Law*, 91.

[19] Mark Johnson, *The Body in the Mind: The Bodily Basis of Meaning, Imagination, and Reason* (Chicago: University of Chicago Press, 1987), 139.

136

meaningful, coherent unities. It thus includes our ability to generate novel order."[20]

Like Johnson, Patrick Sherry also sees imagination as "an active power of the mind . . . an active combining power which brings ideas together."[21] Through imagination, asserts Sherry, we combine past memories and present experiences, and meditate on future action, events, and hope.[22] Unlike Johnson, however, Sherry understands the mind as more than just reasoning, "not part of the mind, but rather the whole mind working in a certain way, involving perception, feeling, and reasoning."[23] Through imagination, we can cultivate "mutual sympathies" by putting ourselves in others' places,[24] which eventually help us "see things from an unfamiliar point of view, and thereby perhaps stimulate them to lead deeper and richer lives."[25] In this way, imagination leads us to handle diversity in a constructive and creative way. This kind of understanding of imagination, claims Sherry, is attributed to God, and the Holy Spirit resides in it.[26]

In addition, it is crucial to recognize that imagination can be alienated from reality or corrupted as fantasy or illusion if it is "divorced from grace and truth."[27] It is also known that imagination depends both on our partial memories in the past and on fragmentary experiences in the present. In other words, it "permeates our embodied, spatial, temporal, culturally formed, and value-laden understanding"[28] and gives meaning by "[calling] to mind a set of related structures of understanding that are directed either to some set of structures in experience . . . or else to other symbols."[29] Accordingly, just as our memories and experiences are limited, so is our imagination. The practical wisdom we discern and manifest in preaching and worship

[20] Ibid., 140.

[21] Patrick Sherry, *Spirit and Beauty: An Introduction to Theological Aesthetics*, 2nd ed. (London: SCM Press, 2002), 111.

[22] Ibid.

[23] Ibid., 113.

[24] Ibid.

[25] Ibid.

[26] Ibid., 114.

[27] Thomas Troeger, *Imagining a Sermon* (Nashville: Abingdon Press, 1990), 107.

[28] Johnson, *The Body in the Mind*, 172.

[29] Ibid., 177.

through imagination is thus limited, neither holistic nor perfect, but partial and fragmented. It is not absolute but provisional and contextual, so that it is important for preachers and worship leaders to seek the wholeness of truth by opening themselves to new experiences in a changing context.

Despite such limits of imagination, it is not possible to discern practical wisdom without imagination. Imagination is the conduit of the method of reflective practical theology for preaching and worship in multicultural contexts. Practical theological reflection, in the preparation for preaching and worship, occurs not randomly but through a deliberate process. While a variety of methods are available for practical theological reflection,[30] the reflective practical theological method is unique in its spiral movement of four stages based on imagination: (1) empathetic imagination in interpreting the cultural context for worship; (2) prayerful and contemplative imagination in deepening the liturgical theme; (3) creative imagination in designing and performing preaching and worship; and (4) visionary imagination in evaluating the work of the previous stages. In each stage of the movement, racial and cultural diversity is regarded as the key concern.

Stage 1 is to understand the liturgical culture of the congregation through an empathetic approach to observation and critical analysis. In order to interpret particular cultural dynamics embedded in congregational worship, the preacher and worship leaders need to ask the following questions: Who are the worshipers, racially, socially, and culturally? Why do they worship in a particular pattern? What do they expect from preaching and worship? Who serves in the leadership roles? Which racial and cultural group is at the center and which racial and cultural groups are in the margins of congregational worship? How does the social structure contribute to such congregational dynamics in worship?

---

[30] Cf., Paul Tillich's "Correlational Method" in *Systematic Theology*, vol. 1 (Chicago: University of Chicago Press, 1973); Tracy's "Mutual Correlational Method" in *Blessed Rage for Order: The New Pluralism in Theology* (New York: Seabury Press, 1975); James and Evelyn Whitehead, "Three Stages in Method" in *Method in Ministry: Theological Reflection and Christian Ministry* (London: Sheed and Ward, 1980); and Osmer's "Four Tasks of Practical Theological Interpretation" in Browning, *Practical Theology*.

These questions can be answered from the knowledge and information gained from formal and informal research, including interviews with worshipers, reviews of church bulletins and denominational and congregational histories of preaching and worship, demographic surveys, ethnographic studies, and social analyses. These are useful tools to analyze the congregational culture and find out why such particular cultural dynamics are employed in that particular congregational worship. Empathetic listening to racially different worshipers about their personal and corporate experiences of worship can be especially helpful for the preacher and worship leaders to recognize what these worshipers think about worship and how they wish to practice it. In order to imagine how the worship service can be improved, it is important to look deeper into the cultural dynamics of those liturgical patterns that the worshipers have taken for granted.

Stage 2 is to select and meditate on a liturgical theme through prayerful imagination. For some churches, the liturgical theme is pre-assigned by the Christian calendar, the lectionary, or their local church calendars. If not, the preacher and worship leaders have freedom to choose the theme based on the particular congregational situation interpreted in stage 1. Once the liturgical theme is decided, they need to be open to any images that arise around the theme, rather than for its definition, and imagine feelings, biases, and apprehensions that may be revealed in those images.

Regarding the interpretation of the biblical text selected for preaching, the preacher needs to remember that the story of the Christian faith is still unfolding and has a surplus of meaning that will never be exhausted. As Thomas Groome convinces us, while "the story of God's love in and through Jesus is a theological paradigm" for Christians, it still continues to unfold "the story and vision of Christian faith" in new times and places by opening them to "the potential of every 'other' culture to bring new life to Christian faith through its inculturation."[31] One of the approaches to this unending hermeneutical task is to use multicultural hermeneutics, as explored in chapters

[31] Thomas Groome, "Inculturation: How to Proceed in a Pastoral Context," in *Christianity and Cultures*, ed. Norbert Greinacher and Norbert Mette (Maryknoll, NY: Orbis Books, 1994), 127.

3 and 4. Through a dialogue between biblical texts and other sacred texts and stories in relation to the liturgical theme, the preacher may imagine the meaning of the biblical text from a fresh, new angle and discern practical wisdom by deepening the theological and ethical meaning of the text.

Stage 3 is to manifest or communicate the discerned practical wisdom through preaching and worship. The main concern at this stage is how to effectively appeal to the worshipers' imagination, which has been impacted by diverse racial and ethnic cultures, so that they may be inspired to transform their ways of thinking and acting, personally and communally. Even though the worshipers are used to the existing liturgical pattern, the preacher and worship leaders need to be mindful of how this has often controlled and reined in congregational worship by confining it too closely within a particular culture or one ethnic group's ethos.

If the preacher and worship leaders are convinced that it is necessary to liberate the pattern from "provincialism and ethnic captivity,"[32] they should critically evaluate their congregational worship from a multicultural perspective and discern what is to be affirmed, questioned, and moved beyond the cultural elements embedded in the existing liturgical pattern. The five models explained in chapter 6—the melting pot, the salad bowl, the mosaic, the kaleidoscope, and the metamorphosis—are helpful in examining the current practice of preaching and worship and in creatively thinking about a new liturgical model for multicultural worship. It is also helpful to have a dialogue with those racially and culturally different worshipers to learn from them how Christian preaching and worship have been practiced in culturally different ways. When a new liturgical model will be used or when any changes in the liturgy are going to be made, it is a prerequisite that the congregation be informed in advance about the theological, biblical, and historical significance of the changes.

In changing the liturgical pattern, from the multicultural point of view, the one-size-fits-all approach to every worship service is not ideal, because the congregational culture is not static but dy-

---

[32] Forrester, *Truthful Action*, 101.

namic and fluid. Moreover, the level of consciousness of cultural diversity among the worshipers is always evolving. In this situation, flexibility is crucial to the mind-set of the preacher and worship leaders. Chapter 6 illustrated a variety of liturgical models based on different levels of cultural awareness of individual congregations. Likewise, the preacher and worship leaders must be sensitive to the particular situation of their congregational culture and renew the liturgical model to be the most effective. It is also equally important to prepare liturgical components such as sacred texts, stories, music, prayers, creeds, languages, verbal and nonverbal gestures, colors, space, time, etc., through careful discernment, from a multicultural perspective.

How, then, can liturgical change happen in the most effective and meaningful way? The answer is related to the following questions: How does the worship leadership team represent the culturally diverse worshipers, especially the racially and ethnically underrepresented, in congregational worship? How is their cultural diversity embraced in preaching and worship in a theologically constructive way? And how beautifully is racial and cultural diversity presented to stimulate the worshipers' imagination to appreciate the glory and beauty of God?

Stage 4 is to evaluate what was done in the previous three stages. This last stage would also be the first stage of the next cycle of the spiral movement of the reflective practical theological method. In general, criteria for evaluating preaching and worship include the coherence of the liturgical theme, the effectiveness of the use of the liturgical components, the flow of the liturgy, the movement in the sermon, the relevance of the biblical interpretation, the participation of the congregation, the presence of the preacher and worship leaders in the delivery, etc. In addition, sensibility to the cultural landscape of the worshipers is another important element in evaluating the worship service, from the multicultural perspective. When culturally embedded symbols and other liturgical elements are used effectively in preaching and worship, they encourage the worshipers to participate in the service, actively and fully; through participation, they experience worship as authentic.

The experience of authentic worship has the power to inspire the worshipers to transform themselves. As Sherry properly explains, the concept of inspiration, which literally means "blowing upon" or "breathing into,"[33] is closely related to the work of the Spirit:

> If . . . the Bible often envisages the spirit of God as a power which "blows through" or permeates people, giving or heightening certain capacities, particularly by producing a change of heart, then it would seem that inspiration was originally seen as an empowering of this kind (104). . . . St Thomas Aquinas . . . used the term *inspiratio* of the Gifts of the Holy Spirit, i.e. wisdom, understanding, knowledge, counsel, piety, fortitude, and fear of the Lord, in *Summa Theologiae*, 1a2ae.68.1; he says that they come through divine inspiration and that they dispose people to become readily mobile to this inspiration.[34]

Inspiration, as the empowerment of the Holy Spirit, happens when the preacher and worship leaders play the role of "an instrument of the Spirit" or "a co-creator" of inspiration.[35] This changes the worshipers' hearts and brings them to transformation by enhancing their "capacities in which their emotional and moral range is extended, giving rise to particular creative moral actions or to the perception of new patterns of goodness."[36]

Ultimately, all the criteria for evaluating preaching and worship converge into an assessment of how inspiring they are. Inspiration is, on the one hand, a subjective experience. On the other hand, it can be provoked as a communal experience, particularly in a liturgical context. Hence, listening to the worshipers' feedback through formal and informal channels, such as personal conversation, survey, or discussion with a feedback group, may improve the worship service by helping it to be more inspiring.

An Exercise in the Reflective Practical Theological Method[37]

In order to demonstrate how to use the four stages of the reflective practical theological method for preaching and worship in a concrete

---

[33] Sherry, *Spirit and Beauty*, 103.

[34] Ibid., 104, 107.

[35] Ibid., 77.

[36] Ibid., 108.

[37] The sermon and the order of the service that are used as samples in this section are included in appendix 5 and appendix 6.

ministerial setting, I chose the liturgical event of the assembly meeting of Denver Presbytery (PCUSA), of which I am a member. Denver Presbytery organized the Mosaic Diversity Workgroup to help member churches become aware of the significance of racial and ethnic diversity within and beyond the church, and educate and train the church leaders by providing counseling and resources. I have served on the Workgroup since it was launched. The Presbytery holds an assembly meeting every other month, at which the Workgroup is invited to prepare and lead a worship service. They also invited me to preach at that service.

Stage 1

I worked with seven other Workgroup members to prepare the service—two European American pastors serving predominantly white congregations, one in downtown and one in suburban Denver; one Hispanic American pastor serving a multiracial congregation, of which the majority was white, and sharing the church building with a Hispanic congregation; one Hispanic elder from that Hispanic congregation; one African American elder, whose congregation was predominantly black; and two Presbytery staff members, one Hispanic and one African from Zimbabwe. We met four times to discuss and prepare for the worship service.

Denver Presbytery has 10,500 believers on its membership rolls, with fifty-four congregations, including seven ethnic minority churches—one African American, one Korean American, one Myanmar American, one Vietnamese American, and three Latino American churches. The average attendance at the assembly meetings is between 150 and 200 people, consisting mostly of the pastors and elders of these congregations and retired ministers.[38] While more than 85 percent of the members of Denver Presbytery are white, Denver itself has one of the highest Hispanic or Latino populations in the United States. According to the 2010 US Census, Denver residents self-identified as follows: White (including 31.8% Hispanic/Latino), 68.9%; Black/African American, 10.2%; Asian, 3.4%; Native American/

---

[38] Denpres.org. Accessed November 7, 2016.

Alaska Native, 1.4%; Native Hawaiian/Pacific Islander, 0.1%; Other, 11.9%; Mixed Race, 4.1%.[39]

In this multiracial and multicultural environment, the member churches of Denver Presbytery are gradually becoming more diverse with the growing numbers of racially and ethnically different people as visitors and new members. Yet, they have not paid sufficient attention to them. For example, as I already mentioned in chapter 6, my family and I have attended Sunday worship services in a predominantly white church located in suburban Denver for more than a decade. When we first joined the church, my family was one of a few ethnic minority people in this three-hundred-member church. But, it has gradually changed to be more multiracial and multicultural, and now about 20 percent of the attendees at the Sunday service are non-white, and the number is increasing every year. While the pastor seems to be aware of our presence and attempts to acknowledge that by occasionally including our songs and native languages in the service, no comprehensive review or significant change in the worship service, from a multicultural perspective, has happened yet. Other Workgroup members also shared their own experiences, which were similar to mine. We discussed why our churches hesitated to welcome racially and ethnically different people and concluded that the main reason was a fear of "strangers" caused by our ignorance and lack of knowledge and information about them.

Stage 2

Based on the interpretation of the racial and cultural situations of Denver Presbytery, we decided to feature "Leading in Diversity" as the liturgical theme. As highlighted by this theme, the goal of the worship service was to challenge the worshipers who were leaders of their local congregations to critically reflect on their congregational culture and to help them reimagine their preaching and worship from a multicultural perspective. We also agreed to prepare the worship service as a good liturgical model, through which the worshipers might envision their own congregational worship to be a foretaste of

[39] http://censusviewer.com/city/CO/Denver; https://en.wikipedia.org /wiki/Demographics_of_Denver. Accessed November 8, 2016.

heavenly worship. Further, we agreed to offer a pre-assembly work-shop before the worship service, in order to provide the attendees with an educational opportunity to see how racial prejudice is caused by fear and how it can be overcome in positive and constructive ways.

I had the privilege of selecting biblical texts for preaching in rela-tion to the liturgical theme. Among many biblical stories related to racial and cultural diversity, I chose Matthew 15:21-28, the story of a Canaanite woman, as the main text, with the notion that Matthew's community was similar to the churches in Denver Presbytery in the sense that it was racially homogeneous and was challenged to open itself to people of other races and ethnicities. I also chose Isaiah 56:1-8 as a supporting text to help the worshipers imagine the celestial vision for worship. Based on the interpretation of these two texts, I titled the sermon "Leading toward Diversity."

In addition to studying the biblical texts, I was curious as to how other religions teach about racial and ethnic diversity. Remembering that there were three Asian American congregations—the Korean, the Vietnamese, and the Myanmar—in Denver Presbytery and that their pastors and elders regularly attended assembly meetings, I re-searched their religious backgrounds and learned that, even though they were Christians, Buddhist teachings were deeply embedded in their way of life and worldview. According to Buddhism, racial preju-dice and discrimination based on physical differences are against the way of humanity. During the Buddha's time, the caste system rooted in racism governed his society, but the enlightened Buddha denounced it by teaching his disciples that "the merits of people are to be judged not in terms of what they are born with but what they do with themselves."[40] In the *Metta Sutta*, he says:

> May all beings be happy.
> May they be joyous and live in safety.
> All living beings, whether weak or strong,
> in high or middle or low realms of existence,
> small or great, visible or invisible,

[40] G. P. Malalasekera and H. N. Jayatilleke, *Buddhism and Race Question*, online ed. (Kandy, Sri Lanka: Buddhist Publication Society, 2006). Accessed November 10.

near or far, born or to be born,
let no one deceive another, nor despise any being in any state;
let none by anger or hatred
wish harm to another.
Even as a mother at the risk of her life watches over
and protects her only child,
so with a boundless mind should one cherish all living things,
suffusing love over the entire world, above, below,
and all around, without limit;
so let one cultivate an infinite good will toward the whole world.[41]

Based on this teaching, Rosa Zubizarreta exhorts us, saying that "the Buddha left his father's castle to learn about the suffering of the world. How often do we extend ourselves outside the realms of our own privilege in order to become familiar with the suffering of others? . . . As long as we ourselves are not able to feel completely close to all other human beings, it is we ourselves who are living in illusion."[42]

Buddhist teachings on race and racial diversity correspond to what I perceived in the two biblical texts. Furthermore, they emphasize that love makes us overcome racial bias and discrimination, which is implicit in the biblical texts. Based on the understanding of the biblical texts through a dialogue with Buddhist teachings, the focus statement of the sermon was that Jesus was challenged by the Canaanite woman to demonstrate the love of God for humanity beyond racial and ethnic differences. The function of the sermon was to encourage the worshipers to love one another beyond our racial and ethnic boundaries, as Jesus did in the story.

Stage 3

In crafting the sermon, I followed the plot of the story in Matthew 15:21-28 and analogically connected each move to our contemporary

[41] Hozan Alan Senauke, "On Race & Buddhism" (http://www.patheos.com /blogs/monkeymind/2012/03/zen-teacher-alan-senauke-on-race-and -buddhism.html). Accessed November 10, 2016.

[42] Rosa Zubizarreta, "Making Invisible Visible," in *Healing Racism in Our Buddhist Communities* (https://www.dharma.org/sites/default/f RosaZubizarreta iles /Making%20the%20Invisible%20Visible.pdf). Accessed November 9, 2016.

experiences. The worshipers were invited to be active participants at the beginning of the sermon by acting out the story with the preacher in the role of the Canaanite woman, so that they might feel empathetically what she felt as a racially excluded person. Throughout the sermon, they would be encouraged to represent voices of the racially and ethnically marginalized people within and beyond their own churches and to lead their congregations to extend their love beyond people of their own race and ethnicity.

The liturgy was designed to follow the basic movement of the Presbyterian service for the Lord's Day,[43] since it was for a Presbyterian event. We were, however, careful to select words, music, prayers, and languages to represent the racial and cultural diversity of the worshipers. We also invited the racially and linguistically marginalized worshipers to play an active role in creating beautiful and inspiring worship. For example, five native languages of the worshipers—English, Spanish, German, Vietnamese, and Korean—were used in singing, scripture reading, prayers, and benediction, in tandem with English translations, both written in the worship bulletin and projected on the screen.

The flow of the service began with the invocation of the Holy Spirit, and then moved to the transforming moment of preaching, the experience of unity-in-diversity through communion, and celebration with a closing hymn and benediction at the end. I could imagine the climax of the service when the people sang the closing hymn, "We Are Marching," in three different languages, dancing to the sound of an African drum. The benediction following the dance could be the penultimate moving moment when the words of blessing from 2 Corinthians 13:13 were delivered by four racially and linguistically different people in their native tongues in harmony from the four corners of the sanctuary.

Stage 4

After the worship service, the congregation held a luncheon as a community meal. We, the Mosaic Diversity Workgroup, could have

---

[43] The Theology and Worship Ministry Unit (prepared), *Book of Common Worship* (Louisville: Westminster John Knox Press, 1993), 33–45.

informal conversations with the worshipers during the luncheon and receive their feedback. Although we intentionally designed the worship service as a beautiful kaleidoscope representing the cultural diversity of the worshipers, some of them said that such multicultural worship was a totally new, transforming experience for them through which they could imagine what heavenly worship might be like. Others commented that the sermon was invitational and powerful, moving their hearts to change their attitudes toward racially and ethnically marginalized people.

When I discussed the service with other members of the Work-group, one commented that the scripture reading of Isaiah 56:1-8 in Vietnamese was too long because he was not used to hearing a foreign language, although the Vietnamese pastor read it with enthusiasm. Others said that it was a wonderful experience to worship in many languages in harmony. Some also pointed out that the closing song could have been done with more musical instruments, such as tambourines and gongs, to generate a more celebrative mood and emotional energy.

In addition, I wondered if I could have been more explicit about Buddhist teachings on racial diversity in the service. I neither included a reading of the Buddhist texts in the order of the service nor referenced them in the sermon, but integrated their teachings in the interpretation of the biblical texts. If I had directly quoted them in the sermon or read them in conjunction with the biblical texts, how would the Presbyterian worshipers who have been raised by *sola scriptura* react to that?[44] Deciding whether to use other sacred texts in Christian worship for future liturgical events depends on the preacher and worship leaders' pastoral sensitivity to the level at which their worshipers appreciate cultural diversity.

An evaluation of the sermon and liturgy at this stage is a turning point, as it begins a new cycle of the spiral movement of the reflective practical theological method for the next worship service. The preacher and worship leaders are invited to the never-ending spiral movement to discern and communicate practical wisdom with the worshipers for the transformation of our multicultural church and society toward the eschatological vision of God's reign.

[44] See chapter 3 of this volume.

APPENDIXES

Sample Sermons and Liturgies

APPENDIX 1[1]

Sermon

"Can We Love Our Enemies?" (Luke 6:27-36)

The Responsive Song: "Come Now, O Prince of Peace"
(*The Faith We Sing* #2232)

The Text: Luke 6:27-36

The Liturgical Context: A Chapel Service at Virginia
Theological Seminary

I.

I'm very honored to preach at Virginia Theological Seminary,
particularly at the commemoration service
for the martyrdom of the Rev. Dr. Martin Luther King Jr.

When I read the gospel passage sent from the school
for the preparation of my sermon,
I said to myself,
"Oh no! I am not ready yet to preach this passage:
'Love your enemies, do good to those who hate you,
bless those who curse you,
and pray for those who abuse you.'"

---

[1] This sermon was prepared for the commemoration of the death of Martin Luther King Jr. and was preached at Virginia Theological Seminary on April 7, 2014. In the sermon, as was explained in chapter 1, the theology of diversity is presented as a response to racial conflicts and prejudices prevailing in our multicultural, globalized world. The sermon focuses on how difficult it is to love enemies, although Jesus commanded us to do so, and encourages the listeners to follow Jesus' footsteps to love even our enemies.

I think I am a good Christian (forgive my pride),
because I try my best to keep the greatest commandment that
"You shall love your God . . .
and your neighbor as yourself" (Luke 10:27).
I also know what Christian love means:
"Love is patient, love is kind, love is not . . . rude" (1 Cor 13:4-5).

When my next door neighbor makes loud noise at midnight
and sometimes litters on my front yard,
I am patient because he is my neighbor.
Even when the students in my class push me
beyond my level of patience,
I try to be kind and not rude to them.

What if, then, my neighbor turns out to be my enemy
who hurts me physically and financially,
just because I am racially different?
If he is violent,
striking me on the cheek and vandalizing my property,
can I offer the other cheek also and let him take away my goods?
Worst of all,
if anyone hurts my precious little son,
bullying, intimidating, and striking him,
just because his face is different and his skin color is different,
can I do to the bully as I would have him do to my son?
(No) . . .

II.

We live in a world of violence.
In our society,
thousands of race-biased violent acts occur every year.

Most of us still remember the Martin case:
Unarmed seventeen-year-old African American
high school student
Trayvon Martin was killed
by George Zimmerman,
a neighborhood watch coordinator
who was suspicious of this innocent black boy
walking on the street at night.

Like a voice "heard in Ramah,
Wailing and loud lamentation,"
Trayvon's parents "refused to be consoled" (Matt 2:18).
Who among us dare to tell them,
"Love your enemy, do good to him, bless him, and pray for him"?

I think that all of us in this room
have passion for social justice and
righteous anger against injustice.
So, when we read the gospel passage that says,
"if someone strikes you on the cheek,
offer the other also,"
we tend to identify with the innocent victim who was struck
and read the verse in that person's shoes.
Like us,
my students at Iliff are awesome people
who strive for justice and peace in the world.
About a month ago, however,
I had an unforgettable learning moment in my worship class.
I invited a guest lecturer
to teach us about African American worship.
He first asked the students,
who were all white,
about what the African American community needed.

Their answers were
"transformation," "liberation," "equality," "respect," and so on.
And I was proud of their answers.
Then, the guest lecturer asked them another question,
"What is your impression of African American men?"
Then, my students answered without hesitation,
"They are lazy, dangerous, violent;
they are predators."

I was shocked by these words
and was sad about such stereotypes of African American men.
But, on my second thought,
I asked myself,
"Am I different from my white students in my perception
of African American men?
Am I free of deeply rooted prejudice against them?"

153

Although I have personally experienced racial prejudice
against me
and have witnessed American racism against Asian American
communities,
I do see, deep in my mind,
my own prejudice against other ethnic minorities.
If I were George Zimmerman,
could I regard a young, hooded, black man
as an ordinary American teenager?

How many of us could be free
from the prejudice against African American and other ethnic
minorities,
that is deeply embedded in our society,
as well as in our individual minds.

Are we the ones who are struck on the cheek?
Or are we the ones who strike another's cheek?
. . .

As we know,
race-biased violence is by no means a US phenomenon alone.
We hear similar troubles from all around the globe.
Hate crimes against immigrants and minorities in Europe
and Asia,
ethnic genocide and horrific bloodshed in Africa,
and daily incidents of violence in the occupied West Bank.

Just a couple of weeks ago,
a violent incident, like the Martin case, happened in the West Bank:
A fifteen-year-old Palestinian boy was shot dead
by Israeli troops, guarding the separation fence in the West Bank.
The boy was foraging with friends
for gundelia, a thistle-type plant used in cooking,
but returned home as a cold corpse.

When I first heard this report,
my heart was broken,
thinking of the parents who lost their precious son,
and then I was outraged by the violence of the Israeli military.

But, you know,
the hands of American citizens are not clean of that innocent
blood.
Every year, billions of our tax dollars
are sent to Israel as its military assistance fund and,
willingly or unwillingly,
our money has supported its military strikes,
building the security wall and wired fences in the occupied
West Bank,
and violence against innocent civilians.

Shall we offer the Palestinian parents who lost their son
pastoral advice to forgive their enemy?
Or, are we among those who must seek forgiveness from them?

. . . .

Race-biased violence accompanies economic and social injustice.
Higher unemployment,
de facto segregation in housing,
an achievement gap in schools,
lower average wages for non-white workers,
and the operation of the criminal justice system,
what Michelle Alexander has called a "new Jim Crow" . . .
These are just a few examples in our society.

Neoliberal capitalism has widened the gap
between rich and poor internationally,
as well as domestically.
People in the southern hemisphere provide cheap labor,
cheap natural resources,
and cheap industrial products
for consumers in Europe and North America.
As a result, rich countries become richer and richer,
while the poor countries become poorer and poorer.

Many Americans are troubled by illegal immigrants and migrant
workers
and don't understand why they come to the United States,
particularly Mexicans

155

who cross the US-Mexico border
risking their lives.

In 2012 alone, 447 Mexicans
who were eager to cross to the United States illegally
died along the southwest border
and, in recent years,
millions of undocumented workers have been deported from the
United States.
We feel sympathy for them and wonder
why their countries are so poor that
their citizens have to endure such ordeals.
In fact,
their neighbor to the north, the United States,
has contributed to their poverty.

NAFTA (the North American Free Trade Agreement),
signed in 1994,
allowed huge American corporations
to capture Mexico's agricultural market with low prices,
some of whose costs are subsidized by the US farm bill.
One example is that of Smithfield Foods.
With headquarters in Smithfield, Virginia,
this American company sells 25 percent of all the pork in Mexico.
That makes it very difficult for Mexican farmers
to grow crops or raise animals and sell them at a price
that would pay the cost of producing them.
Unable to survive as farmers,
these Mexicans had to leave home to look for work.
Moreover, the Mexican farm families find it more difficult to live
where American agribusiness has polluted
their indigenous lands,
making it more difficult for Mexicans to stay home.
One example is the Perote Valley,
where Smithfield Foods raises one million pigs
whose animal waste has rendered the valley
almost uninhabitable because of the stink, flies,
water pollution, and diseases like the swine flu.

As a result,
many Mexicans had to leave their communities
and even cross the US-Mexico border
in order to feed their poverty-stricken families.[2]
Meanwhile, we Americans benefit from the global economy
with the low cost of food and other agricultural products.

Are we their good neighbor, or their enemy?
Are we the ones who should offer them mercy
or the ones who should be forgiven by them?

If we were undocumented migrant workers
who were victims of neoliberal capitalism,
if we were the Palestinians living in the occupied West Bank,
if we were African Americans
deeply branded with negative stereotypes
and suffering from discrimination and oppression,
could we forgive those
who hurt us physically, socially, and economically
and do good to them, bless them, and pray for them?

Honestly, we can love "good people"
who deserve our love,
but not the ones who harm us
with physical violence, economic damage,
or a violation of human rights and dignity.
In the name of justice,
we want retribution
with zero-tolerance.

III.

But, Jesus says that
we should love our enemies,

---

[2] Janet Sturman, "Neoliberal Capitalism and Forced Mexican Migration to the USA," *Socialism or Your Money Back: The Socialist Party of Great Britain's Official Blog,* http://socialismoryourmoneyback.blogspot.com/2013/09/neoliberal-capitalism-and-forced.html. Accessed March 28, 2014.

by offering the other cheek,
by giving them the shirt as well as the coat,
and lending whatever they ask for,
expecting nothing in return.

Why, then, does Jesus say this?
Is he a naïve idealist?

In fact, to the contrary!

Biblical scholars and historians agree that
Judea in the first century was a place of unprecedented violence.
Under the vicious power of the Roman Empire,
it was commonplace for the people to witness daily
racial and ethnic genocide of the colonized,
horrific, ruthless crucifixions as deterrents for rebels,
and the extortion from the poor of personal belongings needed for
basic human life.
According to the first-century historian Josephus,
not all the oppressed Jews were timid or passive in the face of
imperial violence.
Rather, uprisings against the Roman authority
occurred all over Palestine before the Jewish-Roman War
that resulted in the destruction of Jerusalem in 70 CE.
Some radical revolutionary groups, like the Sicarri
who attempted to expel the Romans and their partisans
from Judea through violence,
were originally based in Galilee,
the center of Jesus' ministry.

In this time of heightened violence in Jewish history,
Jesus witnessed the chain of violence,
that choked the life of the oppressed tighter and tighter
with a never-ending threat of death.
He could foresee that its consequence
would be the annihilation of Jerusalem and its people,
which actually happened forty years later
after his death.
The problem Jesus faced
under this threat of destruction was to ask,

"Could the reign of God come down on earth,
in which both the oppressed and the oppressors
are transformed and live together as the children of God?"

Unlike the Zealots
who were seeking justice and retribution through violence,
Jesus knew that only love for one's enemies
could end this violation and transform the people,
because only that love,
which is the intrinsic character of God,
has the power to bring repentance and forgiveness as true
reconciliation.
For Jesus,
in his urgent historical situation,
to love one's enemies was not optional but imperative,
not a cordial invitation with an RSVP,
but an urgent commandment,
because only the power of love
could make his people overcome the national crisis.

In the Gospel of Luke,
we find that
Jesus not only commanded his people to love their enemies,
but also he himself lived that out
by choosing nonviolent resistance against evil
and praying for his enemies even on his cross,
"Father, forgive them,
for they do not know what they are doing" (Luke 23:34).
Just as God is merciful,
an ever-loving God
who lets go of the anger against humankind
and offers the gift of unmerited forgiveness,
so the children of God are to be merciful
even to "the ungrateful and the wicked."

How grateful we are for the gospel message which reminds us
that even enemies can be loved
by their innocent victims
who are the children of the merciful God!

Then can we, forgiven enemies, love our own enemies?

IV.

According to some authoritative calculation,
the exact date of Jesus' crucifixion was April 3, 33 CE.
On April 4,
the same month, but one day later, in 1968,
Martin Luther King Jr. also died,
following in the footsteps of Jesus.
In one of the most chaotic and disturbing times of US history,
King and his people, who were convinced of the power of love,
demonstrated nonviolent resistance against racist America.

In his sermon "Loving Your Enemies,"
King was clear that loving enemies was
the "privilege" of the children of God
and that it was their urgent "obligation" to do so—
"before it [was] too late."[3]

Like Jesus,
King believed that
only the power of love for our enemies
makes reconciliation a reality:
by loving their enemies, the oppressed gain
"new self-respect . . . strength and courage
that they did not know they had,"
and their love "stirs the conscience of the opponent[s]"
and they, too, become the children of God.[4]

. . . .

Some contemporary people have shown us how that can
be realized:
sixteen-year-old Pakistani girl, Malala Yousafzai,
was shot by the Taliban
because of her advocacy of girls' education.
But, in her speech at the UN after her recovery,
she declared that she did not hate

[3] Martin Luther King Jr., *Strength to Love* (Philadelphia: Fortress Press, 1963), 56.
[4] Ibid., 151.

the Taliban and other terrorist groups,
but had compassion for them
and wanted that even their children could have education.

It is also remarkable that
a few years ago, concerning the war in Afghanistan,
the late Senator George McGovern suggested that
instead of spending money on more troops,
funding a school lunch program
would be a much more effective deterrent to more terrorism.[5]

As we know,
numerous humanitarian workers—
especially Christians—
serve people, both victims and enemies, with love
beyond racial and ethnic boundaries
on the US-Mexico border,
on the Israel-Palestine border,
even on the China–North Korea border,
and in Syrian, Sudanese, and other refugee camps.

I also find the spirit of love in Christian churches.
Half a century ago,
King deplored that
Sunday morning was the most segregated time of the entire week
in America.
How, then, about the church in 2014?
Although many agree that
Christian churches in the United States are still racially segregated,
I see slow change in their memberships toward integration.
And I witness to the fact that
some are trying to recapture
the prophetic spirit of Martin Luther King Jr.
and make their worship and preaching contribute
to breaking racial and ethnic prejudice
that is both deeply rooted in our minds
and systemic in our society.

[5] George McGovern, "Calling a Time Out," January 22, 2009.

V.

In the twenty-first century's globalized world,
we live in a web of interconnectedness.
We are like "the two sides of a coin."
On one side,
we are enemies of our innocent neighbors.
Consciously or unconsciously,
willingly or unwillingly,
we abuse their right to live as human beings
created in God's image,
and we hear Christ saying to us,
"You are forgiven by merciful God and your neighbor."

On the other side of the coin,
we are victims of racial prejudice—
physical, social, and economic violence,
and we hear Christ commanding us,
"Children of the Most High,
be merciful as your father is merciful."

. . . .

In this season of Lent toward Holy Week,
we are called to Christ's table
to share the cup of suffering
for the forgiveness of and reconciliation with our enemies.

Can we love our enemies?

May it be so,
as we believe that,
in our world of violence,
God is working among us, in us, and with us
for the breaking-in of "the beloved community."
Amen.

APPENDIX 2[1]

Liturgy
Worship at the Iliff Chapel

Prelude	Prof. Thomas Strickland
Welcome	President David Trickett
*Processional Hymn	"God, You Have Set Us in This Time and Place"

The New Century Hymnal #372

*Opening Prayer	Trustee Naomi Harris
Introduction to the Preacher	Dean Albert Hernandez
Psalmody (Korean)	Psalm 23:1, 2, 6 Joseph & Dorothy Lee, Carolyn Kuban (Guests)

The Lord is my shepherd, I lack nothing.
He makes me lie down in green pastures,
　he leads me beside quiet waters,
　he refreshes my soul.

---

[1] This worship service was designed to celebrate the installation of my full professorship on May 1, 2012. As was explained in chapter 2, the entire Iliff community—the students, the professors, the board of trustees, the staff, and friends of Iliff—was invited to the service. It was intentionally prepared to represent the racial and ethnic diversity of the community. For example, it used the community members' native languages, including Spanish, Korean, German, and Chinese with English subtitles. The worshipers actively participated in prayers, songs, dance, and preaching. Their participation created the joyful mood of a fiesta, an eschatological celebration.

Surely your goodness and love will follow me
all the days of my life,
and I will dwell in the house of the LORD forever.
(NIV)

Gospel Reading (Greek & English)   Matthew 13:24-30
Sarah Scherer & Brad Walston (MDiv Students)

Sermon"   The Weeds and the Wheat"   Prof. Eunjoo Kim
with Profs. Edward Antonio, Jacob Kinnard,
and Pamela Eisenbaum

Response to the Word   "One Love": Playing for Change
by Bob Marley
Dancers: Melissa Burgett, Thelma Flowers, Jenni-
fer Friedman, Jonathan Wallace, Joseph Greemore,
Alejandro Santiz, Sarah Scherer (MDiv Students).

Drummers: Vincent Tango, Joseph Greenmoore
(MDiv Students)

*Prayers of the People   Michelle Sisk (Staff), Prof. Ted Vial, R. J.
Hernandez-Diaz (PhD Student), Rachel Lei (R. J.'s Wife)

Facing the East:

All: O God of peace,
hear our prayer
for all the nations and peoples in the East
especially in Asia and the Middle East.

One (Rachel Lei in Chinese):

我们为朝鲜，西藏，叙利亚以及所有遭受不公正和压迫的人民
祷告

(We pray that the people of North Korea, Tibet, Syria
and those who suffer injustice and oppression)

愿他们在苦难里能知道你的存在。

(might know your presence in their troubling times.)

带领人们和平地表达他们的担忧以及政府领导者们和平地回应
他们；

(Guide the people to express their concerns peacefully
and government leaders to respond peacefully;)

激励人们仔细地倾听彼此的心声；
    (inspire all to listen to one another carefully;)
指引人们一同寻求公正与公义；
    (lead all to pursue justice together;)
从战争和仇恨中救赎他们。
    (redeem them from war and hatred.)

All: Healing Spirit, receive our prayer.

Facing the West:

All: O God of creation,
whose voice we hear in the winds,
and whose breath gives life to all the world,
hear our prayer
for all the nations and peoples in the West
especially in North America and all the things you have
    made.

One (Michelle Sisk):

Thank you God, for water, soil, and air.
Forgive our spoiling and abuse of them.
Forgive our greedy materialism and reckless consumerism.
Help us work for the justice created things need
and renew our spirit of stewardship.
Protect us from the evil of racial prejudice and conflict.

All: Healing Spirit, receive our prayer.

Facing the North:

All: O God of grace,
hear our prayer
for all the nations and peoples in the North,
especially in Europe.

One (Prof. Ted Vial in German):

Öffne einen Weg für sie, einander in Wahrheit und Liebe zu
begegnen.
    (Open a way for them to reach one another in truth
    and love.)

Ermögliche es ihnen, eine Gesellschaft zu errichten, in der alle dazu gehören können;

(Enable them to build a society where all can belong;)

ihre Habe in gegenseitigem Respekt zu teilen.

(to share their possessions in mutual respect.)

Verbinde sie im Gestalten und Schaffen von Werkzeugen des Friedens

(Unite them in the making and creating of the tools of peace)

gegen Ignoranz, Armut, Krankheit und Unterdrückung.

(against ignorance, poverty, disease, and oppression.)

Wir beten, dass sie nach der neuen Zukunft streben, in der sie als Schwestern und Brüder mit Menschen aus verschiedenen Teilen der Welt in Harmonie und Freundschaft wachsen.

(We pray that they seek for the new future
in which they may grow in harmony and friendship
as sisters and brothers with people from different parts
of the globe.)

All: Healing Spirit, receive our prayer.

Facing the South:

All: O God of the life-giving Spirit,
hear our prayer
for all the nations and peoples in the South
especially in Central and South America and Africa.

One (R. J. Hernandez-Diaz in Spanish):

Heridas del pasado, del colonialismo y del apartheid

(Wounds of the past from colonialism and apartheid)

permanecen, manteniendo sus dolorosos efectos.

(remain, affecting all they do.)

Cuando el hambriento y la pobreza, la enfermedad y la muerte

(Where hunger and poverty, illness and death)

hacen la vida insoportable,

(have made life an unbearable burden,)

escuche a su dolor y rabia

(listen to their grief and rage)

y sánelos, abráselos, cuídelos.

(and heal them by your touch and hold them in your care.)
Oramos que restablezca esperanza para la transformación
de las naciones

(We pray that you restore hope for change in the nations)
y la dignidad del pueblo.

(and the dignity of these people.)

All: Healing Spirit, receive our prayer.

Facing the Front:

One: O God of love,
open the eyes of the nations and peoples
so that they may walk in the light of love.

All: Amen.

*Hymn   "Hymn of Promise"   *The United Methodist Hymnal* #707

Commissioning and Benediction   Prof. Eunjoo Kim

One: Let us go forth into the new seasons of our lives.

All: We go forth into growing and changing and living.

One: Let us go with caring awareness for the world and all that
is in it.

All: We go to discover the needs and opportunities around us.

One: Let us go forth in peace and be led out in joy.

All: We go in God's continuing presence,
with the power to love and the strength to serve.

One: (Korean) 이제는 우리 주 예수 그리스도의 은혜와
하나님의 극진하신 사랑과
성령님의 감화 감동 교통하심이
아이리프신학교와 이곳에 모인 모든 분들위에
지금부터 영원토록 함께 하시기를 축원하나이다.
The grace of our Lord Jesus Christ,
the love of God,
and the communion of the Holy Spirit
be with us all who gather here
and with the Iliff School of Theology,
this day and ever more.

All: Amen.

*Postlude/Recessional: Prof. Thomas Strickland

*Please stand if you are able.

APPENDIX 3[1]

Sermon
"The Weeds and the Wheat" (Matt 13:24-30)

The Text: Matthew 13:24-30

The Liturgical Context: The Iliff Community Chapel

The Participants: Professors Edward Antonio, Pamela Eisenbaum,
Jacob Kinnard

I.

I still remember
when I first arrived at Denver International Airport
for a job interview at Iliff.
It was a snowy day in February 1998,
and my plane was delayed.
But, in the airport,
I was welcomed
with a big smile and a big hug
by Dr. Jean Miller Schmidt, professor of Church History,
at Iliff at that time.
On the way from DIA to the hotel near the school,
we talked about many things,
especially about the history of the Korean church.

---

[1] This sermon was prepared for the worship service to celebrate my full professorship and was preached at the Iliff Community Chapel. The listeners were the Iliff community members and their friends. As was explained in chapter 3, it is a product of multicultural hermeneutics. The text was interpreted in dialogue with the history of Korean Christianity and with theological perspectives of three Iliff faculty members who were from racially and culturally different backgrounds.

If I had another chance to talk with her,
I would want to continue our unfinished conversation
on the history of the Korean church,
because it is like a lens
through which we can discern
who we are
and what God is doing in the midst of our world.

II.

Korea is a multireligious country.
Buddhism, Confucianism, and Shamanism have coexisted there
for thousands of years,
and Christianity is a relatively new religion
for the Koreans.

When Christianity was first introduced to Korea,
it was done not by missionaries but by books.

According to one historical record,
in the summer of 1777,
a group of Confucian scholars went on a ten-day retreat
at a Buddhist temple in the mountains near Seoul
to study some new books brought from China.

In their reading list,
several Roman Catholic books, translated into Chinese,
were included.
At first, these Confucian scholars were
intellectually curious about Western philosophy and religion.
But, the more they studied the books,
the more they were fascinated by the new teaching about
God, humanity, and the way of life.
Eventually, they were converted to Christianity
and the number of Christian believers increased.
However,
eighteenth-century Korea was the field of Neo-Confucianism.
It taught
that the hierarchical order in class, gender, and age
should be the framework of social structure and relationships,

and its religious practice was centered on
the polytheistic ritual of ancestor worship.
In this field,
the gospel of egalitarian love and monotheism
that the early Korean Christians understood
through their self-study
did not look like good seed.
Instead, it was considered "weeds,"
dangerous and harmful to the field.

Unlike the householder in the parable of Matthew,
the ruling authorities of the country hastily made every effort
to pull the weeds out of the field
before they quickly spread
over the entire field.
As a result,
hundreds of thousands of early Christians in Korea
were persecuted
and many were beheaded.
Then, Christianity was banned in Korea
for more than a century.

Was the gospel of egalitarian love and monotheism
really weeds for the people?
Or, was it pulled up by mistake?

III.

As you may know,
Korea is a peninsula.
In the north, its land connects to China and Russia;
across the waters in the south and west,
it meets Japan and China.
If you sail from the east coast of Korea farther and farther,
you will cross the Pacific and reach San Francisco.

In the late nineteenth century,
Korean society was in chaos
because of constant military attacks
by these neighboring countries

and was under the threat of Western imperialists.
In 1882,
the government was forced to sign the Treaty of Amity
with the United States
and later with other Western countries,
and it had to allow their missionaries
to pursue their religious activities in Korea.

Moreover,
social unrest and religious corruption
made the ruling principles of Neo-Confucianism powerless.
No longer was the wheat
able to produce grain for the people.
The suffering masses yearned for new seed
that could grow and yield
their personal and communal well-being
in their changing soil.

At that time,
Protestant Christianity was one of the options
for them to choose as the seed of promise.
Most workers scattering that seed in the Korean soil
were American missionaries
who were a harvest of the Second Great Awakening.
They emphasized personal conversion and moral piety
as the core of the Christian faith.
They believed in biblical inerrancy,
and their theological approach was counter-cultural:
that is,
they regarded
all the Korean traditional religious and cultural practices
as "weeds"
that should be pulled up
in order to grow the so-called "good seed" in the Korean soil.
For example,
Korean Christians no longer celebrated
their traditional Thanksgiving Day,
but they observed the American Thanksgiving Day
as a way to weed out their old ways of life.

Is this kind of Christian gospel really "the wheat"
or the "weeds" in the sight of God?

. . .

This seed, however,
took root in the particular Korean soil
and has adapted to the changing environment of the field.
By overcoming hardships with Koreans
throughout their turbulent historical times,
the seed has evolved
to be a somewhat different plant
from the one that it was originally supposed to be.

During the period of Japanese colonialism in Korea (1910–1945),
Korean Christians resisted the Japanese emperor worship
since they thought it was against
the first and the second commandments
of the Decalogue;
many Christian leaders participated
in the national independence movement,
even at the cost of their lives.

During and after the Korean War (1950–1953),
churches in South Korea made unparalleled relief efforts
and preached the message of hope in God.
One prominent Christian leader was
Rev. Song, Chang-Kuen.
He was the first Korean student at Iliff.
After graduating from the doctoral program
in the New Testament in 1931,
he returned to Korea and founded a liberal theological school in
Korea,
named Hankook Theological Seminary,
and devoted himself to theological education
and the nurture of the Korean church
until he was abducted by the North Korean army during the war.

Hankook Theological Seminary later became
a base-camp for Minjung theology,
which is Korean liberation theology.

During the military dictatorship and the rapid social change
spurred by industrialization and urbanization,
Minjung theologians,
on the one hand,
gave a prophetic voice to the powerless
and fought for social justice and peace.

On the other hand,
the majority of church leaders,
who were conservative evangelicals,
invited Billy Graham and other revivalists
to hold national revival meetings
that provided the weary people
with emotional and psychological comfort.
Their evangelistic fervor contributed
to the numerical growth of the church.

. . .

Once, Christianity was in the margin of Korean society.
But now it has moved into the center.
About one-third of South Korea's forty-five million people
identify themselves as Christian.

However,
recent surveys show that
the quantitative growth of the Korean church has stopped
since the end of the last century,
and now it is decreasing
as a result of its long-term
internal and external problems,
such as
denominationalism,
dogmatism,
Christian triumphalism,
exclusionism of other religions,
sexism,
materialism,
consumerism.
Above all,

the lack of leadership of the church
in the twenty-first century.

. . .

Hmmmmmm. . . .
Don't you think
these problems are familiar to churches in the United States?
Actually,
contemporary American churches have been facing
these problems
longer than Korean churches,
and we have more serious problems
within and beyond the church,
such as
racial prejudice,
homophobia,
injustice to new immigrants,
and excessive individualism.
And,
an increasing number of Americans resist
institutionalized churches,
and the un-churched or the de-churched
are looking elsewhere
for insights and resources
to seek relevant meaning
for their spiritual lives.
Thoughtful theologians have already declared that
people in the West no longer live
in Christendom
but in Post-Christendom.

. . . .

Is the Christian gospel really "weeds"
for contemporary people?

Perhaps,
not all the seeds the church has planted were good!
Perhaps,
some of the good seed might have devolved into "weeds"
in the process of adapting to changing environments.

Or,
like the case in the parable in Matthew,
an enemy might have sneaked into the field
and scattered weeds!

Like the servants of the householder in the parable,
don't you think that
we should sort out the "weeds"
and pull them up
before they mess up the entire field?

But the problem is,
just as the history of the Korean church shows,
it is ambiguous and uncertain to judge
which seed would produce grain for the people
and which would produce no grain to harvest.

What if the gospel we believe to be good seed
eventually appears
as "weeds" without grain?
What if different religious and Christian groups
whom we believe to be weeds
unless they are converted to our theological orientation,
are in fact planting good seed in God's sight?

V

Imagine that,
with this ambiguity and uncertainty,
a group of seminary students and professors in Korea
want to have theological consultation
with some professors teaching in different parts of the globe.
And suppose that
they emailed the dean's office at Iliff
to request a Skype conference.

Fortunately,
Professors Edward Antonio, Jacob Kinnard,
and Pam Eisenbaum
are available
to participate in the long-distance conversation.
(These three professors come up to the chancel.)

On the opposite side of the globe,
a dozen Korean students and professors sit
in front of the camera.

On the screen, the moderator says,
"Professor Antonio, Professor Kinnard,
and Professor Eisenbaum,
it is our great pleasure
to have a conversation with you.
Even if you are not familiar with the Korean context,
we think
your profound theological knowledge and critical reflection
would help us discern directions of the Korean church
in the twenty-first century.
We are very uneasy
with the ambiguity and uncertainty
of the Christian gospel,
and we have one grand question for all three of you:
that is,
'What kind of Christian gospel shall we preach and teach
in the twenty-first century?'"

(Professor Antonio says on the microphone:)
"Your question reminds me of when Jesus was asked by a law
expert,
'Of all the commandments, which is the most important?'
Jesus answered,
'Love the Lord your God
with all your heart and with all your soul
and with all your mind and with all your strength.
The second is this:
Love your neighbor as yourself.
There is no commandment greater than these.'
As Jesus said,
We should preach and teach
how to love God and our neighbors as ourselves.
But, history shows us
churches in the West have failed to embody this good news
of Jesus Christ.

Instead of loving their neighbors,
they have built racial, cultural, and class barriers
in the name of Jesus Christ:
the Crusades,
the Inquisition,
the judicial murder of heretics,
the blessing of wars of conquest in the Americas,
genocide of the First Nations of North America,
the justification of slavery,
World War II with the Holocaust
and the use of atomic weapons as tools of terror against
civilians. . . .
These are part of the history of Western Christianity;
these are the corporate sins of the Western church.
So, the preaching and teaching of the Christian gospel in the
twenty-first century
must begin with the *repentance* of these sins in *humility*."

. . . .

(Prof. Kinnard says:)
"I teach religions in Asia.
So, the question about the preaching and teaching
of the Christian gospel in the twenty-first century
seems to be unrelated to my interest areas.
But, I would like to tell my Christian colleagues and students that
Western Christians have lived in Christendom
without learning how to open themselves
to diverse forms of religious faith.
If they want to live a life of love as Jesus has taught,
they must, first of all, *respect* other religious traditions
and learn from them,
because love begins with respect for otherness
and it has the power to stop religious violence and terror.
Christians have considered persons from other religions
candidates for conversion.
But, they are actually potential conversation partners
to think together and work together
toward a vision of the world
as a peaceable community of diverse communities."

. . . .

(Prof. Eisenbaum says:)
"What should we preach and teach
as the gospel in the twenty-first century?
In order to get the answer to this question,
I think,
we should read the Bible more *carefully* and *honestly*.
For example,
Christians have understood Paul as the first true convert to
Christianity.
But Paul was not a Christian,
but a Jew both before and after his experience of Christ.
In fact, such a word as 'Christian' had not been invented yet.
Paul was called by God,
rather than converted,
to fulfill a particular mission
to bring knowledge of the God of Israel
to all the nations of the world.
As a Jew,
Paul also believed
the resurrection of Jesus signaled
that it was time to reconcile non-Jews to Jews
because all people were potentially children of God,
part of the same family.
But, understanding Paul as a convert to Christianity
has contributed to gross misrepresentations of Judaism
and played no small role in the history of anti-Semitism.
How, then, can Christians embody the gospel of love?
Genuine *reconciliation* in God
with racially and ethnically different people
will be a significant way."

. . . .

Then, on the screen, one of the Korean students says,
"I am in confusion—
the history of Western Christianity sounds very disturbing."
Then, another student says,
"The word, 'Christendom' is alien to the Koreans."

Then, another says,
"Was Paul really NOT a Christian?"

(Prof. Edward says:)
"Well, they seem to be having trouble understanding us.
Maybe, long-distance learning is not so effective."

(Prof. Kinnard says:)
"Maybe, it is because of cultural difference!"

(Prof. Eisenbaum says:)
"Maybe, it's a language barrier.
We should have learned Korean and spoken to them in Korean!"

. . .

Then, on the screen,
the moderator says,
"Professor Antonio, Professor Kinnard,
and Profesor Eisenbaum,
thank you very much
for sharing your critical thoughts on Christianity.
I think
we need time to reflect on them
and have another conversation with you
in the near future.
Until that time, Good-bye."

(The professors go back to their seats.)

VI.

Now the Skype conference is over,
and the computer is turned off.

What do you think?
Studying at Iliff is not easy, right?

. . . .

What shall we preach and teach
in the twenty-first century?
How can we embody the gospel of love?
Through repentance in humility,
respect for otherness,

genuine reconciliation in God
with different racial and ethnic people,
for all of us are part of the same family of God.

. . . .

Friends,
what kind of gospel have you heard?
Or, what kind of seed have you planted
by preaching and teaching?

The Iliff School of Theology has planted
the seed of the Christian gospel
for one hundred and twenty years.
The rapidly changing world has constantly challenged us
to renew our theological education
to be good seed
in the sight of God.
And in the midst of ambiguity and uncertainty,
we have been sowing the renewed seed of the gospel,
in the faith that God is present among us
when we plant it in humility, respect, and honesty.

. . . .

In the parable in Matthew,
the servants urgently report to the householder
about weeds growing in his field
and request of him permission to get rid of them.
But the householder does not permit his servants
to pull them up immediately.
Instead, he allows the weeds to grow in his grain field
until harvest time.

And you know what?
Matthew says,
this parable of the gracious householder's grain field
is about
what the Kingdom of God is like.

. . . .

We cannot see a clear picture yet
of whether the seed we are sowing will produce
abundant grains of love or not.
But it is by grace,
it is nothing by but grace, that
you and I are called by God
to sow and grow the seed of love
in the field of God's reign.

In this field,
I believe,
the Spirit of God works with us
to yield
a harvest of thirty, sixty, or a hundred times.

Thanks be to God
who does not judge us now,
but is working with us
until the harvest day.

. . . .

(When the preacher turns back to the seat,
a drum sound is heard getting louder . . .)

Wait! Do you hear a sound?

(a group of dancers appear on the stage
to the music, "One Love")

Oh my! Aren't they Iliff people?
They are planting the seed of love
in the promise of God.
Hallelujah!
(The preacher goes back to her seat,
and the dancers dance at the chancel.)

APPENDIX 4[1]

Sermon
"Women on the Way" (John 4:4-42)

The Text: John 4:4-42 (paraphrased)

The Liturgical Context: The 2013 Asian Presbyterian Women's Conference

The Cast of Characters: Narrator (N), Jesus (J), Samaritan Woman 1 (SW1); Samaritan Woman 2 (SW2); Samaritan Woman 3 (SW3)

Hymn: "Blessed Assurance, Jesus Is Mine" (English and Korean)
The Presbyterian Hymnal #341

<u>Scene I</u>
(The background photo: "A Dry Well in the Desert")

(N, J, and SW1 come up to the front.)

N: Jesus left Judea and started back to Galilee. But he had to go through Samaria. So he came to a Samaritan city called Sychar, near the plot of ground that Jacob had given to his son Joseph. Jacob's well was there, and Jesus, tired out by his journey, was sitting by the well.

---

[1] This sermon was preached at the 2013 Asian Presbyterian Women Conference in Houston, Texas. As explained in chapter 5, it demonstrates shared (participatory) preaching as a new homiletical paradigm. The sermon includes four scenes based on the biblical story. Four conferees were invited to preach with me by playing a role in the sermon, and a YouTube video and a background screen were used for effective communication.

His disciples had gone to the city to buy food. It was about noon. A Samaritan woman came to draw water, and Jesus said to her,

J: "Would you give me a drink of water?"

SW1: "How come you, a Jew, are asking me, a Samaritan woman, for a drink?"

N: (Jews in those days wouldn't deal with Samaritans.)

J: "Well, if you knew the gift of God, and who it is that is saying to you, 'Give me a drink,' you would have asked him, and he would have given you living water."

SW1: "Sir, you have no bucket, and the well is deep. Where do you get that living water? Are you greater than our ancestor Jacob, who gave us the well, and with his sons and his flocks drank from it?"

J: "Everyone who drinks of this water will be thirsty again, but those who drink of the water that I will give them will never be thirsty. The water that I will give will become in them a spring of water gushing up to eternal life."

(Jesus and the Narrator go back to their seats.)

SW1:

I am thirsty . . . .
I come to the well every day to draw water.
But I am always thirsty. . . .
I remember my childhood life in the United States.
My parents were boat people who left their war-torn country
piled with corpses and bullet shells,
and crossed the ocean with a hope to escape hunger and death.
At the age of five,
I arrived with my parents in this new land,
first in a war refugee camp,
and then, in Little Saigon in Houston, Texas.
Since then, my thirsty journey began:
I have struggled to fit into the dominant European American culture;
I wished I had been born to white American parents,

who speak English perfectly,
and who work white-collar jobs from nine to five.
I've often felt inferior to my Caucasian friends
with white skin, tall and beautiful, with blonde hair.
I have tried my best to be like them.
Finally, I graduated from college
and now I've got a professional job.
My relatives and friends often say that
I am a so-called model minority.
But, I am still thirsty. . . .
I have constantly drunk the water
from the well of the American dream.
My immigrant ancestors gave me to drink from it.
But, water from that well has never quenched my thirst.
Like the Samaritan woman,
I wish someday I could meet Jesus at the well,
who understands my thirst
and helps me drink living water.

I am on the way to search for a well
where I can meet Jesus,
the source of life,
the living water.

At that well,
I can be who I am
with the pride of my Asian roots,
rather than trying to be someone else
that white America forces me to be.
Where can I find that well?

Solo: "Fill My Cup, Lord"   *The United Methodist Hymnal* # 641

Scene II

(The background photo: "A Broken, Discarded Well")

(J and SW2 come up to the front.)

SW2: "Sir, give me this living water, so that I may never be thirsty or have to keep coming here to draw water."

J: "Go, call your husband, and come back."

SW2: "I have no husband."

J: "You are right in saying, 'I have no husband'; for you have had five husbands, and the one you have now is not your husband. What you have said is true!"

(Jesus goes back to his seat.)

SW2:

Let me share with you the story of a Cambodian woman, Chanta:

https://www.youtube.com/watch?v=IEclmPZZKh8
("Sex Traffic in Cambodia—Short Version": 2 min. 50 sec.)

Two million children, like Chanta,
are forced into prostitution every year,
and half of them live in Asia.

The exploitation of Asian women's bodies in sex slavery
is not only recent history.
We know hundreds of thousands of Asian women
who were called "Comfort Women."
They were abducted by Imperial Japanese soldiers
from their homes
in Korea, China, Japan, the Philippines, and other countries in Asia
and coerced into Japanese military sex slavery
during World War II.

We do not know about the Samaritan woman's life.
The story does not tell us about that in detail.
But the conversation between Jesus and this woman implies a lot:
"Woman, you are right. . . . You have had five husbands,
and the one you have now is not your husband."

In a strictly patriarchal society
where the woman's body was valued only for procreation
and the satisfaction of man's sexual desire,
she had to have five husbands
and even the man she is serving now is not her husband!

I hear Jesus' reply to the Samaritan woman like this:
"Chanta, you are right.
None of the men you have served was your husband,
who is supposed to love you and treat you with respect.
Comfort Women,
I know your hardships and suffering,
your bloody tears shed because of your shame and the loss of
human dignity."

Do you know that
over 50,000 women, like Chanta,
are trafficked into the United States as sex slaves every year?

Have you heard about them?
Have you seen these Samaritan women near you?
Perhaps it is very hard for us to consider them as our sisters in
Christ,
because their lives are very different from ours,
I mean,
they are morally too sinful
according to our social and religious standards,
and we, consciously or unconsciously,
regard the Christian church
as a community of the righteous
rather than as one of sinners.

But, they are on the way to search for a well,
at which they can meet Jesus,
the giver of living water,
the spring of compassion and justice,
gushing up to eternal life.
Where can they find the well?

Congregational Hymn: "Fill My Cup" *The Presbyterian Hymnal* #350

Scene III

(The background photo: "An Empty Bucket by a Well")

(J and SW3 come up to the front.)

SW3: "Oh, so you're a prophet! Well, tell me this: Our ancestors worshiped God at this mountain, but you Jews insist that Jerusalem is the only place for worship, right?"

J: "Woman, believe me, the hour is coming when you will worship the Father neither on this mountain nor in Jerusalem. You worship what you do not know; we worship what we know, for salvation is from the Jews. But the time is coming—it has, in fact, come—when whether you are called a Samaritan or a Jew will not matter and where you go to worship will not matter. It's who you are and the way you live that count before God. Your worship must engage your spirit in the pursuit of truth. That's the kind of people God is out looking for. God is spirit, and those who worship him must worship in spirit and truth."

SW3: "I don't know about that. But, I do know that the Messiah is coming. When he arrives, we'll get the whole story."

J: "I am he, the one who is speaking to you."

SM3:

I still remember the day
I first arrived at John F. Kennedy Airport in New York City.
In my hand was an admission letter
from a seminary.
I was full of passion for learning about the Bible and the Christian
gospel
and wanted to be an ordained pastor
as a long-overdue response to God's calling.
As soon as I settled down in the new land of auspice,
I visited a Korean church near the school
and immediately was made to feel at home
by the members' warm-hearted hospitality.
It was precious to me
to get to be with people who shared my race and ethnicity every
Sunday.
Eating Korean food and talking in Korean at the church
helped me endure my homesickness
and overcome my fears about the strange new land.

However,
the more I learned about Korean and other Asian American
churches,
the more I felt that I was an alien to them.
They taught me about
Asian American practices of the Christian faith:
They said that women should be silent in the church
because the Bible, as well as the Asian culture, says so.
They also adamantly insisted that
women should not be ordained
to be elders or ministers
because women were not qualified
to be leaders of the community of faith.

But, the seminary taught me
feminist perspectives and the hermeneutics of suspicion.
Just as the Samaritan woman questioned
what she learned from her community
and asked Jesus to guide her with his wisdom,
so I questioned the teaching and practice of Asian American
churches
and asked Jesus:
Should Asian patriarchal culture and tradition,
embedded in Asian and Asian American churches,
continue to be the norm in the practice of the Christian faith?
I hear Jesus' answer to the Samaritan woman like this:
"But the time is coming—it has, in fact, come—
when you are no longer called a male or a female.
Your gender will not matter in the leadership of the church.
It's who you are and the way you live that count before God.
God is spirit,
and those who live out their faith in spirit and truth
will be the leaders of the church."

I pray that Asian and Asian American churches may listen to Jesus
and be free from their sexist traditions
to worship God in spirit and truth.
We Asian American women are on the way
to build our beloved churches
to become the true body of Christ.

Scene IV

(The background Photo:
"Overflowing Water from a bucket on a Well")

(All the readers come up to the front.)

N: Just then his disciples came. They were astonished that he was speaking with a woman, but no one said, "What do you want?" or, "Why are you speaking with her?" Then the woman left her water jar and went back to the city. She said to the people,

SW1, 2, 3: "Come and see a man who told me everything I have ever done! He cannot be the Messiah, can he?"

N: The people left the city and were on their way to him. . . . Many Samaritans from that city believed in him because of the woman's testimony,

SW1, 2, 3: "He told me everything I have ever done."

N: So when the Samaritans came to him, they asked him to stay with them; and he stayed there two days. And many more believed because of his word.

SM1:

Like the Samaritan woman,
millions of Asian immigrant offspring are thirsty.
Our children and grandchildren are on the way
to searching for a spiritual home,
in which their authentic self can be valued
and nurtured by the water of eternal life.

Where is the well
at which they can find a genuine dialogue partner
and engage in a life-giving conversation?
How about your church?
How about us?

SM2:

Like the Samaritan woman,
millions of Asian women and girls have been forced to exploit
their bodies.

Jesus has given us his body, torn apart on the cross:
"This is my body given for you.
Take it and do this in remembrance of me . . . ."

Can our church be the body of Christ—
a spiritual home for those
whose bodies were torn apart physically and spiritually?
Can we become their genuine dialogue partners
as Jesus did to the Samaritan woman?
How about your church?
How about us?

SM3:

It is time for us to build a well
at which we can encounter Jesus
and enter into dialogue with him
concerning our traditions and cultural heritages
and discern the will of God to reform our community of faith.

Like the people in the Samaritan village,
our Asian American churches are on the way
to search for the truth in Christ Jesus.

SM1: We are thirsty,
SM2: we are weary,
SM3: but, we do not give up on finding the way of the truth,
our Lord Jesus Christ.
We are on the way
of searching for living water
that can quench our thirst.

J: And Jesus is right there at the well.
N: Can our church be the well,
a fountain of water gushing up to eternal life?

Congregational Hymn: "Lord of Light, Your Name Outshining" *The Presbyterian Hymnal* #425

APPENDIX 5[1]

Sermon

"Leading Toward Diversity" (Matt 15:21-28; Isa 56:1-8)

The Texts: Matthew 15:21-28; Isaiah 56:1-8

The Liturgical Context: Denver Presbytery Assembly Worship

I.

This morning,
I feel very honored
to share the word of God with my Presbyterian colleagues
and friends.
Since the theme of the Assembly is "Leading in Diversity"
and the Mosaic Diversity Workgroup agreed
to focus on the racial and ethnic diversity in worship,
I chose the New Testament lesson from Matthew.
Some of you may wonder why I chose Matthew,
instead of the Pauline letters.

---

[1] This sermon was preached at the worship service for the August assembly meeting of Denver Presbytery in 2012. The listeners were the ministers and elders of the member churches. As I explained in chapter 7, both texts were interpreted through multicultural hermeneutics, explored in chapter 3, in dialogue with Buddhist texts. The focus and function of the sermon are grounded in the theology of diversity expounded in chapter 1. The focus statement of the sermon is that Jesus was challenged by the Canaanite woman to demonstrate the love of God for humanity beyond racial and ethnic differences. The function of the sermon is to encourage the worshipers to love one another beyond our racial and ethnic boundaries as Jesus did in the story.

As you know,
Paul the Apostle is explicit
when dealing with the issue of diversity in his letters,
since his audiences are ethnically diverse communities.
However, Matthew's audience is known
as a homogenous group, like our churches.
Matthew subversively reminds his Jewish Christian community
that God's salvation story in Christ has been formed
beyond racial and ethnic boundaries
by inviting many different people
to play a role.
The story of the Canaanite woman in chapter 15
is a surprising reminder of this.

Since the story is familiar to us,
I would like to act it out with you,
rather than read it by myself.

Please stand up and close your eyes;
imagine you are walking on a street in the Gentile region
near Judea in the first century.

There is a woman from that region following Jesus in the crowd.
She rushes to come to Jesus, desperately saying something to him.
Can you see her face?

. . . .

Can you hear what she says?

. . . .

Now, please open your eyes and see the bulletin.
The congregation's part you will play
is the role of the Canaanite woman,
and I will do the rest of the characters in the story.
Please feel free to use gestures:

One: Jesus left that place and went away to the district of Tyre and Sidon.

Congregation: Just then a Canaanite woman from that region came out and started shouting:
"Have mercy on me, Lord, Son of David; my daughter is tormented by a demon."

One: But [Jesus] did not answer her at all. And his disciples came and urged him, saying, "Send her away for she keeps shouting after us." [Jesus] answered [his disciples], "I was sent only to the lost sheep of the house of Israel."

Congregation: But she came and knelt before him, saying, "Lord, help me."

One: Jesus answered [her], "It is not fair to take the children's food and throw it to the dogs."

Congregation: She said, "Yes, Lord, yet even the dogs eat the crumbs that fall from their masters' table."

One: Then, Jesus answered her, "Woman, great is your faith! Let it be done for you as you wish."

All: And her daughter was healed instantly.

. . .

One: This is the Word of God for the People of God!

All: Thanks be to God!

II.
(You may be seated.)
Thank you so much for playing the Canaanite woman's role.
All of you were great!

. . . .

"I was sent only to the lost sheep of the house of Israel. . . ."
"It's not fair to take the children's food and throw it to the dogs."
Well, we know Jesus is a good guy.
But, in the story, don't you feel
he sounds like a man of prejudice?
This reminds me of one of my DMin students' dissertations
that I reviewed this summer.
She is serving a Lutheran church in Texas,
the members of which are 100% descendants of Norwegian immigrants.
As their pastor, she is expected to be very Norwegian;
she is supposed to help her congregation
continue their traditional religious and cultural practices
as a way to live life as Norwegian Lutherans in the United States.

In her dissertation, however,
she raised such a crucial question as:
"Has God called my congregation to be
pure, authentic Norwegian Christians,
whatever that means,
or to be inclusive by opening itself to love
even people of very different backgrounds?"

. . . .

I think two thousand years ago,
the Evangelist Matthew also raised that kind of question:
"Should my church continue to struggle to keep its Jewish identity
by limiting its ministry to Jewish people?
Or, should we extend our love to people of other backgrounds
living in our multiracial society of the Greco-Roman world?"
And Matthew knows his congregation's immediate answer to his
question
and takes a risk by putting it to Jesus' lips:
"I was sent only to the lost sheep of the house of Israel. . . ."

Perhaps my Lutheran student's congregation in Texas
would agree on this answer,
saying,
"Absolutely! Why bother us?
There are a variety of ethnic churches available for others—
Asian American churches,
Latino American churches,
African American churches, etcetera, etcetera. . . ."

This response echoes what I heard from a student in my class
who served a rural church in northeast Colorado.
He said,
"My church has been a white middle-class community for over
fifty years,
but these days almost every Sunday
Mexican migrant workers visit my church.
But I am very uncomfortable with them
because I don't know how to minister to them;
I don't know their language, their culture, or their life-style.

Above all, I am fifty-eight years old,
and I don't want to go beyond my comfort zone in my ministry."

. . . .

I remember a Korean friend of mine
who has lived in the United States for several decades.
He told me that
once he and his family visited a European American church near
their house.
His two teenage boys were fascinated by the live contemporary
music of the band.
But after the service, no one came to greet them.
The next Sunday, they tried that church again for the boys.
But again, no one even said "hi" to them.
On the following Sunday,
his older son said,
"Dad, we don't have to go to that church again.
They don't like us."

. . . .

I also heard an American who married a Korean woman, saying,
"I have gone to a Korean American church with my wife for ten
years.
However, whenever I attend the church,
I feel I am invisible.
They speak only Korean, eat only Korean food, and talk only with
Koreans.
Some of them are kind to me,
but they treat me as a permanent guest
rather than as a member of the church."

Like these,
many churches in the United States are racially segregated
either to stay in their comfort zone,
or because of conscious or unconscious racial prejudice,
or in order to preserve their racial and cultural identity.

For them, it is definitely unfair
"to take the children's food and throw it to the dogs."

III.

Yet, Matthew does not end his story here.
Instead, he has the Canaanite woman talk back to Jesus.
Regardless of his biased words,
she is persistent in her request for him to extend his grace
to her and her demon-possessed daughter,
saying,
"Yes, Lord. Yet, even the dogs eat the crumbs
that fall from their masters' table."
"Yes, Lord. Yet, my daughter and I also deserve to eat the food
that comes NOT from your children's table but from God's table."

Then, her words moved Jesus' heart,
and he embraced them
in his ministry of love and compassion
by healing her daughter.

. . . .

If you read the Gospel of Matthew more carefully,
you would learn that
the story of the Canaanite woman is
a turning point in Jesus' ministry.
That is, the rest of the chapter shows that
Jesus' ministry has changed its direction
beyond his racial and ethnic boundary toward the Gentile
believers:
In the following verses of the chapter,
he heals many sick people who have followed him
from the Gentile region
and feeds four thousand men plus women and children
who are non-Jews.

Yes, the Canaanite woman could receive the grace of God;
yet, Jesus could get a new vision for his ministry.

How masterful Matthew's literary skill is!
Through the story,
Matthew tells his racially and ethnically homogeneous community
that
"Like Jesus, we are good guys,

faithful Jews,
a chosen people,
descendants of King David.
But, like Jesus our Lord,
we are challenged to reconsider our identity and ministry
from God's point of view."

Hearing the story,
I am sure,
Matthew's community was challenged;
we are challenged.
And I hope
the Norwegian American church in Texas
and churches in Colorado and other parts of the United States are
challenged too.

IV.

If Jesus had been challenged and changed the direction of his
ministry,
our church, which was also challenged,
should also change the direction of its ministry.
How, then?

You know,
Matthew ends his gospel with Jesus' great commission to
"Go therefore and make disciples of all nations. . . .
I am with you always, to the end of the age" (28:19-20).
People often think that
in order to fulfill this commission,
Christian churches should send away missionaries to foreign
countries.
But, through the story of the Canaanite woman,
Matthew tells his community
that their church,
located in a local multiracial and multicultural environment,
should be the first place to make "disciples of all nations"
and be a prototype of this global ministry
by sharing the love of God
with people of different races and ethnicities.

About three weeks ago,
my Norwegian Lutheran student in Texas had
the oral examination of her dissertation.
At that time, one examiner asked her a question,
"If you think you and your congregation were called
to minister beyond your own people,
how can you lead your church in that direction?"
To this question, she replied that
she was still struggling with that issue.
Perhaps, she might need another six years
to give us a satisfactory answer
by learning from the practice of many creative ministerial
strategies.
But, since her dissertation committee did not want to hold her
so long,
we passed her,
and now her name is included in the summer graduate list.

. . . .

Interestingly,
Matthew does not propose to his church
any long-term and short-term strategies
to make his church a global community of faith.
Instead, he does just one thing, that is,
to let a Gentile woman
who visited his community
challenge his congregation:
"Yes, Lord, yet, even the dogs eat the crumbs
that fall from their masters' table."

Who is she?
She is an extremely marginalized person,
the stranger of the strangers to Matthew's community:
her ethnic profile doesn't match that of the majority of his
congregation;
her gender draws people to look down on her;
obviously she is not in a socially respected position;
perhaps, she is a single parent;
perhaps, as a Canaanite, she spoke to Jesus with a strong accent.

. . . .

Do you find a person with this kind of personal profile
among your congregants?

I see some of you nodding your head.
How, then, can their challenging voices be heard?
I am curious how your church has listened
to their desperate cries and responded to them with love.

I also see some of you shaking your heads in answer to my
question.
Maybe your congregation is racially, culturally, and socially
homogeneous.
Then, without the Canaanite woman,
who can challenge your church?

Hmmm . . .
If we don't have the Canaanite woman in our congregation,
who can PLAY the Canaanite woman's role
for our church?

Regarding this question,
I would like to remind you that
you were invited to play the Canaanite woman's role
for the performance of the New Testament Lesson.
Can you play this role again and again,
not just for scripture reading,
but for transforming your congregation,
through worship, preaching, pastoral care, Bible study,
and praying?

V.

I think it is not easy for most of us
to represent the voice of the Canaanite woman to the church,
because, first of all, we have to stand in her shoes
and identify ourselves with her
to understand who she is and what she needs.
Moreover, our congregations may not want to embrace her;
they may not want to change their racial and ethnic demographics,
since that requires them to give up benefits and privileges
that they have enjoyed as a homogeneous group.

How about us—clergy and lay leaders?
Do we want to transform the identity of our churches
into that of a racially, culturally, and socially diverse community?

If you hesitate to lead your church in that direction,
I understand that.
In fact,
church development strategists advise pastors to keep racial
homogeneity
if they want to grow their churches.
Even the Bible shows how controversial the issue of racial
diversity is.
Some passages in Ezra, Nehemiah and others
sternly instruct the community to exclude racially and ethnically
different people
and reckon them as enemies;
Acts 15 and Galatians 2 bear witness to divisions and schisms
caused by ethnic diversity
within the churches.
Why, then, should we go through such hardships?

However,
some prophetic oracles, like Isaiah 56:1-8,
anticipate the reign of God,
in which racially and ethnically marginalized people are welcome
to participate in temple worship,
because the temple should not be a place of preserving
conventional rituals and cultural practices,
but it should be a holy place,
"a house of prayer for ALL peoples."

What Paul and Matthew hoped for their churches
was to fulfill this vision in their communities,
"a house of prayer for ALL peoples,"
in which people diverse in race and ethnicity come
and joyfully participate in worship
and foretaste the fullness of life
with the risen Christ in the reign of God.

VI.

If we and our congregations really want to move
in this direction,
I think it is really a serious challenge.
Matthew also knows how serious it is.
He is not a starry-eyed dreamer
who thinks that human differences do not matter.
Rather, he is a man of faith who believes that
the identity of the Christian church is given
by the redeeming work of Christ,
through which God has called people
to strive for the kingdom of God,
like a tiny, little mustard seed
that has miraculously grown to become a tree,
so that many kinds of birds of the air come and make nests
in its branches (13:31-32).
To the tiny little mustard seed becoming a tree,
there would be many barriers.
But, Matthew believes that
they can be overcome by our faithful acts
and by the help of the Holy Spirit.

How, then, about us?

I really hope we have the same faith as Matthew's
and act faithfully by
listening attentively to the voice of the Canaanite woman
within and beyond our communities,
and creating space at the Lord's table
to share the grace of God in Christ Jesus with others
in humility.

Then, we can see more clearly
what the Spirit of God is doing in our communities
to make us whole.
By following the lead of the Spirit,
We make disciples of all nations
beyond our racial and ethnic boundaries.

(As soon as I finish the last sentence, organ or piano music ("Spirit," PH #319) comes on for a moment of reflection. Near the end of the instrumental music, I request the congregation to stand and sing the verses.)

Please, stand and let us sing together: . . .
Amen.

APPENDIX 6[1]

Liturgy: Worship
at the Denver Presbytery Assembly Meeting
August 25, 2015

Prelude	Marsha Marshall
Welcome & Passing of the Peace	Wanda Beauman
*Call to Worship (Spanish & English)	Raquel Yslas

Uno/a (One):   ¡Qué el Señor esté con ustedes! (The Lord be with you.)

All (Todo/as):   **And also with you. (Y también contigo.)**

Uno/a (One):   Vamos, postrémonos delante de sus pies (Come, Let us stand before God.)

All (Todo/as):   **Let us worship God, whose name be praised. (Vamos, adoremos a Dios, alabado sea su nombre.)**

Uno/a (One):   Dios nos ha llamado para ser mensajeros de las Buenas Nuevas de Cristo Jesús. (God has called us to be messengers of the good news in Christ Jesus.)

---

[1] This order of the service was designed as a model of multicultural worship at the request of Denver Presbytery. As I explained in chapter 7, it uses four different languages in addition to English—Spanish, German, Vietnamese, and Korean—with English subtitles, in praying, singing, benediction, and other liturgical components. Although the order followed the Presbyterian service for the Lord's Day, the content of each component was carefully prepared from the multicultural perspective.

All (Todo/as): **"How beautiful upon the mountains are the feet of the messenger who announces peace" (Isaiah 52:7). (<< ¡Qué hermosos son, sobre los montes, los pies del que trae las Buenas Nuevas, del que proclama la paz! >> (Isaías 52:17).)**

Uno/a (One): Alabemos a Dios con acciones de gracias, cantando cánticos de júbilo. (Let us worship God with thanksgiving, singing joyful songs of praise.)

All (Todo/as): **Halleluya! Halleluya! Amen. (¡Alleluya! ¡Alleluya! Amén.)**

*Hymn "Santo, Santo, Santo (Holy, Holy, Holy)" *LUYH* #47[2]

Prayer of Confession (German & English) Dietmar Fritsch

Gnädiger und barmherziger Gott, Du hast alle Menschen geschaffen, um der Funken Deines Gotteslebens zu sein, so dass Unterschiede unter Kulturen und Rassen Mehrfarbenmanifestationen Deines Lichtes sein können. (Gracious and merciful God, You have created all people to be the spark of Your divine life, so that differences among cultures and races may be multicolored manifestations of Your light.)

Verzeihe uns, Herr, denn unsere Herzen und Meinungen haben sich nicht völlig geöffnet, um die Ähnlichkeiten und Unterschiede von unseren Schwestern und Brüdern zu feiern; wir sind nicht fleißig gewesen, um außer unserem Niveau der Bequemlichkeit auszustrecken, um uns zu treffen und über andere zu lernen, ihre Geschichten zu hören und ihrer vollen Menschheit offen zu sein; wir haben es in unseren Gottesdiensten und Ministerien ignoriert, Ungleichheit und Rücksicht für andere in unseren Gebeten zu bringen. (Forgive us, Lord, for our hearts and minds have not fully opened to celebrate similarities and differences among our sisters and brothers; we have not been diligent to reach out beyond our level of comfort to meet and learn about others, hear their stories and be open to their full

---

[2] Linda White, ed., *Lift Up Your Heart: Songs for Creative Worship*, Pew Edition (Louisville: Geneva Press, 1999).

humanity; we have failed to bring diversity and respect for others into our prayers, our worship celebrations and ministries.)

Lehre uns Deinen Weg, Herr, daß wir in deiner Wahrheit wandeln können; hilfe uns aller Personen inklusiv bewusst zu sein, mit der Bekräftigung, den Wert von Vielfalt in deinen Augen und bau unsere Gemeinschaft des Glaubens in allen Rassen, Ethnien und Kulturen. (Teach us Your way, Lord, that we may walk in Your truth; help us be consciously inclusive of all individuals by affirming the value of diversity in Your sight and build our community of faith encompassing all races, ethnicities, and cultures.)

Silence

Assurance of Pardon

> One (One): Die Liebe Gottes ist größer als wir uns vorstellen können. Gottes Barmherzigkeit ist breit und tief genug, um unsere Sünden zu vergeben und unsere Kirchen zu erneuern . Wir können im Frieden in dem Wissen sein, dass wegen dieser Liebe und Barmherzigkeit, sind wir vergeben. (The love of God is bigger than we can imagine. God's mercy is wide and deep enough to forgive our sins and renew our churches. We can be at peace in the knowledge that because of this love and mercy, we are forgiven.)

> Many (Viele): **Thanks be to God through Christ our Lord! (Dank sei Gott durch Christus, Unseren Herrn!)**

First Scripture Lesson (Vietnamese and English)   Isaiah 56:1-8
                                                    Tú Bùi Minh

Đức Giê-hô-va phán nhu vầy: Hãy giữ điều chánh trực, và làm sự công bình; vì sự cứu rỗi của ta gần đến, sự công bình của ta sắp được bày tỏ. (Thus says the Lord: Maintain justice, and do what is right, for soon my salvation will come, and my deliverance be revealed.)

Phước thay cho người làm điều đó, và con người cầm vững sự đó, giữ ngày Sa-bát đặng đừng làm ô uế, cấm tay mình không làm một điều ác nào! (Happy is the mortal who does this, the one who holds it fast, who keeps the Sabbath, not profaning it, and refrains from doing any evil.)

Người dân ngoại liên hiệp cùng Đức Giê-hô-va chớ nên nói rằng: Đức Giê-hô-va chắc sẽ biệt ta ra khỏi dân Ngài. Kẻ hoạn cũng chớ nên nói rằng: Nầy, ta là cây khô. (Do not let the foreigner joined to the Lord say, "The Lord will surely separate me from the people"; and do not let the eunuch say, "I am just a dry tree.")

Vì Đức Giê-hô-va phán như vầy: Những kẻ hoạn hay giữ các ngày Sa-bát ta, lựa điều đẹp lòng ta, cầm vững lời giao ước ta, (For thus says the Lord: To the eunuchs who keep my Sabbaths, who choose the things that please me and hold fast my covenant,)

thì ta sẽ ban cho họ tại trong nhà ta và trong tường ta một chỗ, và một danh tốt hơn danh của con trai con gái; ta lại sẽ ban cho họ một danh đời đời chẳng hề dứt đi. (I will give, in my house and within my walls, a monument and a name better than sons and daughters; I will give them an everlasting name that shall not be cut off.)

Các người dân ngoại về cùng Đức Giê-hô-va, đặng hầu việc Ngài, đặng yêu mến danh Đức Giê-hô-va, đặng làm tôi tớ Ngài; tức là hết thảy những kẻ giữ ngày Sa-bát cho khỏi làm ô uế, và cầm vững lời giao ước ta, (And the foreigners who join themselves to the Lord, to minister to him, to love the name of the Lord, and to be his servants, all who keep the Sabbath, and do not profane it, and hold fast my covenant—)

thì ta sẽ đem họ lên trên núi thánh ta, làm cho họ vui mừng trong nhà cầu nguyện ta. Của lễ thiêu và hi sinh họ dâng trên bàn thờ ta, sẽ được nhận lấy; vì nhà ta sẽ gọi là nhà cầu nguyện cho mọi dân tộc. (these I will bring to my holy mountain, and make them joyful in my house of prayer; their burnt offerings and their sacrifices will be accepted on my altar; for my house shall be called a house of prayer for all peoples.)

Chúa Giê-hô-va, Đấng nhóm dân tan lạc của Y-sơ-ra-ên, phán như vầy: Dân nó đã được nhóm lại rồi, ta sẽ còn nhóm các dân khác lại về cùng nó. (Thus says the Lord God, who gathers the outcasts of Israel, I will gather others to them besides those already gathered.) (NRSV)

Second Scripture Lesson   Matthew 15:21-28   Eunjoo Kim

> One: Jesus left that place and went away to the district of Tyre and Sidon.
>
> Many: **Just then a Canaanite woman from that region came out and started shouting:**
>
> **"Have mercy on me, Lord, Son of David; my daughter is tormented by a demon."**
>
> One: But [Jesus] did not answer her at all. And his disciples came and urged him, saying, "Send her away for she keeps shouting after us." [Jesus] answered [his disciples], "I was sent only to the lost sheep of the house of Israel."
>
> Many: **But she came and knelt before him, saying, "Lord, help me."**
>
> One: Jesus answered [her], "It is not fair to take the children's food and throw it to the dogs."
>
> Many: **She said, "Yes, Lord, yet even the dogs eat the crumbs that fall from their masters' table."**
>
> One: Then, Jesus answered her, "Woman, great is your faith! Let it be done for you as you wish."
>
> Many: **And her daughter was healed instantly.** (NRSV)

Sermon   "Leading Toward Diversity"   Eunjoo Kim

Hymn   "Spirit"   PH #319[3]

Communion   Rob Wilson, Ashley Seaman, Kevin Olsen, et al.

Prayers of the People   Rob Wilson

*Closing Hymn   "We Are Marching/Siyahamba/Caminando"
(*Feel free to sing in any language;* v. 2: "We are singing . . .";
v. 3: "We are preaching . . ."; v. 4: "We are praying . . .")

*Benediction (Multilingual) Eunjoo Kim, Amy Mendez, Tú Bùi Minh,
                             Paul Neshangwe, Dietmar Fritsch

---

[3] *The Presbyterian Hymnal: Hymns, Psalms, and Spiritual Songs* (Louisville: Westminster John Knox Press, 1990).

Postlude

(* Please stand if you are able.)

Participants:

Wanda Beauman. Peoples Presbyterian Church.

Dietmar Fritsch. Eagle River Presbyterian Church.

Eunjoo Kim. Iliff School of Theology.

Marsha Marshall. Eagle River Presbyterian Church.

Amy Mendez. Denver Presbytery.

Tú Bùi Minh. Vietnamese Presbyterian Fellowship.

Paul Neshangwe. Denver Presbytery.

Kevin Olson. Strasburg Presbyterian Church.

Ashley Seaman. North Highland Presbyterian Church.

Rob Wison. Eagle River Presbyterian Church.

Raquel Yslas. First Presbyterian Church of Aurora.

Bibliography

Books

Aune, Michael B. *To Move the Heart: Rhetoric and Ritual in the Theology of Philip Melanchthon*. San Francisco: Christian University Press, 1994.

Bell, Catherine. *Ritual Theory, Ritual Practice*. New York: Oxford University Press, 1992.

———. *Ritual: Perspectives and Dimensions*. New York: Oxford University Press, 1997.

Bellah, Robert. *Religion in Human Evolution: From the Paleolithic to the Axial Age*. Cambridge: Belknap Press of Harvard University Press, 2011.

Bhabha, Homi K. *The Location of Culture*. New York: Routledge, 2004.

Blount, Brian K., and Leonora T. Tisdale, eds. *Making Room at the Table: An Invitation to Multicultural Worship*. Louisville: Westminster John Knox Press, 2001.

Boff, Leonardo. *Trinity and Society*. Translated by Paul Burns. Maryknoll, NY: Orbis Press, 1988.

Boyarin, Daniel. *Intertextuality and the Reading of Midrash*. Bloomington: Indiana University Press, 1990.

Bradshaw, Paul F. *The Search for the Origins of Christian Worship: Sources and Methods for the Study of Early Liturgy*. New York: Oxford University Press, 1992.

Brooks, Avery. *Healing in the Landscape of Prayer*. Harrisburg, PA: Morehouse, 1996.

Browning, Don S. *A Fundamental Practical Theology: Descriptive and Strategic Proposals*. Minneapolis: Fortress Press, 1996.

Buchanan, George. *Introduction to Intertextuality*. Lewiston, NY: Mellen Biblical Press, 1994.

Bultmann, Rudolf. *The History of the Synoptic Tradition*. New York: Harper & Row Publishers, 1963.

Calvin, John. *Institutes of the Christian Religion*. Edited by John T. Mc-Neill. Translated by Ford Lewis Battles. Philadelphia: Westminster Press, 1960.

Chandler, Daniel. *Semiotics: The Basics*. London: Routledge, 2004.

Cheng, Eileen Ka-May. *Historiography: An Introductory Guide*. New York: Continuum, 2012.

Collins, Randall. *Interaction Ritual Chains*. Princeton, NJ: Princeton University Press, 2004.

Costen, Melva W. *African American Christian Worship*. 2nd ed. Nashville: Abingdon Press, 2007.

Cotter, Wendy J. *The Christ of the Miracle Stories: Portrait through Encounter*. Grand Rapids: Baker Academic, 2010.

Davis, Kenneth, and Jorge Presmanes, eds. *Preaching and Culture in Latino Congregations*. Chicago: Liturgical Training Publications, 2000.

Deane-Drummond, Celia. *The Wisdom of the Liminal: Evolution and Other Animals in Human Becoming*. Grand Rapids: Eerdmans, 2014.

Dibelius, Martin. *From Tradition to Gospel*. London: Ivor Nicholson and Watson, 1934.

Duck, Ruth. *Worship for the Whole People of God: Vital Worship for the 21st Century*. Louisville: Westminster John Knox Press, 2013.

Farhadian, Charles E., ed. *Christian Worship Worldwide: Exploring Horizons, Deepening Practices*. Grand Rapids: Eerdmans, 2007.

Farley, Edward. *Theologia: The Fragmentation and Unity of Theological Education*. Philadelphia: Fortress Press, 1983.

Finney, Charles G. *Lectures on Revivals of Religion*. Edited by William G. McLoughlin. Cambridge: Belknap Press of Harvard University Press, 1960.

Forrester, Duncan B. *Truthful Action: Exploration of Practical Theology*. Edinburgh: T&T Clark, 2001.

Francis, Mark. *Liturgy in a Multicultural Community*. Collegeville, MN: Liturgical Press, 1991.

———. *Shape a Circle Ever Wide: Liturgical Inculturation in the United States*. Chicago: Liturgical Training Publications, 2000.

———. *Liturgy in a Culturally Diverse Community: A Guide Towards Understanding*. Washington, DC: Federation of Diocesan Liturgical Commissions, 2012.

Garfield, Jay L. *Empty Words: Buddhist Philosophy and Cross-Cultural Interpretation*. Oxford: Oxford University Press, 2002.

Geertz, Clifford. *The Interpretation of Cultures*. New York: Basic Books, 1973.

González, Justo L., ed. *¡Alabadle!: Hispanic Christian Worship.* Nashville: Abingdon Press, 1996.

Hagenbach, Karl, et al. *Theological Encyclopedia and Methodology on the Basis of Hagenbach.* New York: Phillips and Hunt, 1884.

Hall, Pamela M. *Narrative and the Natural Law: An Interpretation of Thomistic Ethics.* Notre Dame, IN: University of Notre Dame Press, 1994.

Hays, Richard. *Echoes of Scripture in the Letters of Paul.* New Haven: Yale University Press, 1989.

Hawn, C. Michael. *One Bread, One Body: Exploring Cultural Diversity in Worship.* Bethesda, MD: Alban Institute, 2003.

Heller, Roy L. *Conversations with Scripture: The Book of Judges.* New York: Morehouse Publishing, 2011.

Hendrickx, Herman. *The Miracle Stories of the Synoptic Gospels.* London: Geoffrey Chapman, 1987.

Henriksen, Jan-Olav. *Life, Love, and Hope: God and Human Experience.* Grand Rapids: Eerdmans, 2014.

Higley, Sarah L. *Hildegard of Bingen's Unknown Language: An Edition, Translation, and Discussion.* New York: Palgrave Macmillan, 2007.

Hildegard von Bingen. *Scivias.* Translated by Columba Hart and Jane Bishop. New York: Paulist Press, 1990.

Howe, Leroy. *The Image of God: A Theology for Pastoral Care and Counseling.* Nashville: Abingdon Press, 1995.

Huyssteen, J. Wentzel van. *Alone in the World: Human Uniqueness in Science and Theology.* Grand Rapids: Eerdmans, 2006.

Johnson, Elizabeth A. *She Who Is: The Mystery of God in Feminist Theological Discourse.* New York: Crossroad, 1993.

Johnson, Mark. *The Body in the Mind: The Bodily Basis of Meaning, Imagination, and Reason.* Chicago: University of Chicago Press, 1987.

Junker, Tércio B. *Prophetic Liturgy: Toward a Transforming Christian Praxis.* Eugene, OR: Pickwick Publications, 2014.

Kim, Eunjoo Mary. *Preaching the Presence of God: A Homiletic from an Asian American Perspective.* Valley Forge, PA: Judson Press, 1999.

———. *Women Preaching: Theology and Practice through the Ages.* Cleveland: Pilgrim Press, 2004.

———. *Preaching in an Age of Globalization.* Louisville: Westminster John Knox Press, 2010.

Kristeva, Julia. *Semiotike.* Paris: Éditions du Seuil, 1969.

Lindbeck, George A. *The Nature of Doctrine: Religion and Theology in a Postliberal Age.* Philadelphia: Westminster Press, 1984.

Lee, Jung Young. *Marginality: The Key to Multicultural Theology*. Minneapolis: Fortress Press, 1995.

Long, Thomas G. *Beyond the Worship Wars: Building Vital and Faithful Worship*. Bethesda, MD: Alban Institute, 2001.

MacDonald, Dennis. *The Homeric Epics and the Gospel of Mark*. New Haven: Yale University Press, 2000.

———. *Does the New Testament Imitate Homer? Four Cases from the Acts of the Apostles*. New Haven: Yale University Press, 2003.

MacIntyre, Alasdair. *After Virtue*. 2nd ed. Notre Dame, IN: University of Notre Dame Press, 1984.

Maddox, Randy. "The Recovery of Theology as a Practical Discipline." *Theological Studies* 51 (1990): 650–72.

Mckenzie, Alyce M. *Hear and Be Wise: Becoming a Preacher and Teacher of Wisdom*. Nashville: Abingdon Press, 2004.

Mead, Margaret. *Cooperation and Competition among Primitive Peoples*. New York: McGraw-Hill, 1937.

Melchert, Charles F. *Wise Teaching: Biblical Wisdom and Educational Ministry*. Harrisburg, PA: Trinity Press International, 1998.

Miller-McLemore, Bonnie J., and Mary Fulkerson, eds. *Wiley-Blackwell Companion to Practical Theology*. Malden, MA: Wiley Blackwell, 2012.

Mitchell, Henry. *Black Preaching: The Recovery of a Powerful Art*. Nashville: Abingdon Press, 1990.

Moltmann, Jürgen. *Theology of Play*. Translated by Reinhard Ulrich. New York: Harper & Row, 1972.

Niebuhr, Richard H. *Christ and Culture*. New York: Harper and Row, 1956.

———. *Radical Monotheism and Western Culture: With Supplementary Essays*. Louisville: Westminster John Knox Press, 1993.

Osmer, Richard. *Practical Theology: An Introduction*. Grand Rapids: Eerdmans, 2008.

Pai, Young. *Cultural Foundations of Education*. Columbus: Merrill Publishing Company, 1990.

Rappaport, Roy A. *Ritual and Religion in the Making of Humanity*. New York: Cambridge University Press, 1999.

Schleiermacher, Friedrich. *Brief Outline of Theology as a Field of Study*. Lewiston, NY: E. Mellen Press, 1830.

———. *Christian Care: Selected from Practical Theology*. Edited by James O. Duke, et al. Philadelphia: Fortress Press, 1988.

Schüssler Fiorenza, Elisabeth. *Jesus: Miriam's Child, Sophia's Prophet*. New York: Continuum, 1994.

Sherry, Patrick. *Spirit and Beauty: An Introduction to Theological Aesthetics.* 2nd ed. London: SCM Press, 2002.

Stout, Harry S. *The New England Soul: Preaching and Religious Culture in Colonial New England.* New York: Oxford University Press, 1986.

Suchocki, Marjorie. *God, Christ, Church: A Practical Guide to Process Theology.* Rev. ed. New York: Crossroad, 1989.

Sugirtharajah, R. S. *Asian Biblical Hermeneutics and Postcolonialism: Contesting the Interpretations.* Maryknoll, NY: Orbis Books, 1998.

Tanner, Kathryn. *Theories of Culture: A New Agenda for Theology.* Minneapolis: Fortress Press, 1997.

The Theology and Worship Ministry Unit. *Book of Common Worship.* Louisville: Westminster John Knox Press, 1993.

Theissen, Gerd. *The Miracle Stories of the Early Christian Tradition.* Translated by Francis McDonagh. Philadelphia: Fortress Press, 1974.

Thiemann, Ronald F. *Constructing a Public Theology: The Church in a Pluralistic Culture.* Louisville: Westminster John Knox Press, 1991.

Tillich, Paul. *Systematic Theology.* Vol. 1. Chicago: University of Chicago Press, 1973.

Tisdale, Leonora T. *Preaching as Local Theology and Folk Art.* Minneapolis: Fortress Press, 1997.

Tracy, David. *Blessed Rage for Order: The New Pluralism in Theology.* New York: Seabury Press, 1975.

Troeger, Thomas. *Imagining a Sermon.* Nashville: Abingdon Press, 1990.

Vanhoozer, Kevin. *Is There a Meaning in This Text? The Bible, the Reader and the Morality of Literary Knowledge.* Leicester: Apollos, 1998.

Vial, Theodore M. *Liturgy Wars: Ritual Theory and Protestant Reform in Nineteenth-Century Zurich.* New York: Routledge, 2004.

White, Hayden. *Tropics of Discourse: Essays in Cultural Criticism.* Baltimore: Johns Hopkins University Press, 1982.

White, James F. *A Brief History of Christian Worship.* Nashville: Abingdon Press, 1993.

Whitehead, James, and Evelyn Whitehead. *Method in Ministry: Theological Reflection and Christian Ministry.* London: Sheed and Ward, 1980.

Williams, Benjamin E. *Miracle Stories in the Biblical Book Acts of the Apostles.* Lewiston, NY: Edwin Mellen Press, 2001.

Witherington, Ben, III. *Jesus the Sage: The Pilgrimage of Wisdom.* Minneapolis: Fortress Press, 1994.

Woodward, Kenneth L. *The Book of Miracles.* New York: Simon & Schuster, 2000.

Yee, Russell. *Worship on the Way: Exploring Asian North American Christian Experience*. Valley Forge, PA: Judson Press, 2012.

Zizioulas, John. *Being as Communion: Studies in Personhood and the Church*. Crestwood, NY: St. Vladimir's Seminary, 1985.

Essays and Articles

Baldovin, John F. "Christian Worship to the Eve of the Reformation." In *The Making of Jewish and Christian Worship*, edited by Paul F. Bradshaw and Lawrence A. Hoffman, 156–83. Notre Dame, IN: University of Notre Dame Press, 1991.

Bass, Alden. "Preaching in the Early Christian Church." In *A Handbook for Catholic Preaching*, edited by Edward Foley, 51–61. Collegeville, MN: Liturgical Press, 2016.

Best, Thomas F. "A Faith and Order Saga: Towards, *One Baptism: Towards Mutual Recognition*." In *Worship and Culture: Foreign Country or Homeland?*, edited by Gláucia Vasconcelos Wilkey, 302–19. Grand Rapid: Eerdmans, 2014.

Bhabha, Homi, and Bhikhu Parekh. "Identities on Parade: A Conversation." *Marxism Today* (June 1989): 24–29.

Bireley, Robert. "Preaching from Trent to the Enlightenment." In *A Handbook for Catholic Preaching*, edited by Edward Foley, 74–83. Collegeville, MN: Liturgical Press, 2016.

Blount, Brian K. "The Apocalypse of Worship." In *Making Room at the Table: An Invitation to Multicultural Worship*, edited by Brian K. Blount and Leonora T. Tisdale, 16–29. Louisville: Westminster John Knox Press, 2001.

Buri, Fritz. "A Comparison of Buddhism and Christianity According to a History of Problems." In *Buddhist-Christian Dialogue: Mutual Renewal and Transformation*, edited by Paul Ingram and Frederick Streng, 15–34. Honolulu: University of Hawaii Press, 1986.

Burns, Stephen. "A Fragile Future for the Ordo?" In *Worship and Culture: Foreign Country or Homeland?*, edited by Gláucia Vasconcelos Wilkey, 143–61. Grand Rapid: Eerdmans, 2014.

Burke, Peter. "History of Events and the Revival of Narrative." In *New Perspectives on Historical Writing*, edited by Peter Burke, 283–300. 2nd ed. University Park: Pennsylvania State University Press, 2001.

Chupungco, Anscar J. "Methods of Liturgical Inculturation." In *Worship and Culture: Foreign Country or Homeland?*, edited by Gláucia Vasconcelos Wilkey, 267–75. Grand Rapid: Eerdmans, 2014.

Collet, Giancarlo. "From Theological Vandalism to Theological Romanticism? Questions about a Multicultural Identity of Christianity." In *Christianity and Cultures*, edited by Norbert Greinacher and Norbert Mette, 25–37. Maryknoll, NY: Orbis Books, 1994.

Cornille, Catherine. "Introduction: On Hermeneutics in Dialogue." In *Interreligious Hermeneutics*, edited by Catherine Cornille and Christopher Conway, vii–x. Eugene, OR: Cascade Books, 2010.

Crowder, Colin. "Wisdom and Passion: Wittgenstein, Kierkegaard, and Religious Belief." In *Where Shall Wisdom Be Found?*, edited by Stephen C. Barton, 363–80. Edinburg: T&T Clark, 1999.

DeBona, Guerric. "Preaching after Vatican II." In *A Handbook for Catholic Preaching*, edited by Edward Foley, 95–104. Collegeville, MN: Liturgical Press, 2016.

Delorme, Jean. "Intertextualities about Mark." In *Intertextuality in Biblical Writing*, edited by Sipke Draisma, 35–42. Kampen: Uitgeversmaatschappij J.H. Kok, 1989.

Donakowski, Conrad L. "The Age of Revolution." In *The Oxford History of Christian Worship*, edited by Geoffrey Wainwright and Karen B. Westerfield Tucker, 351–94. New York: Oxford University Press, 2006.

Driscoll, Michael S. "The Conversion of the Nations." In *The Oxford History of Christian Worship*, edited by Geoffrey Wainwright and Karen B. Westerfield Tucker, 175–215. New York: Oxford University Press, 2006.

Eckel, David. "Show Me Your Resurrection: Preaching on the Boundary of Buddhism and Christianity." In *Interreligious Hermeneutics*, edited by Catherine Cornille and Christopher Conway, 149–62. Eugene, OR: Cascade Books, 2010.

Foley, Edward. "The Homily." In *A Handbook for Catholic Preaching*, edited by Edward Foley, 156–68. Collegeville, MN: Liturgical Press, 2016.

Giroux, Henry E. "Insurgent Multiculturalism and the Promise of Pedagogy." In *Multiculturalism: A Critical Reader*, edited by David Theo Goldberg, 325–43. Cambridge: Blackwell, 1994.

Goldberg, David. "Introduction: Multicultural Conditions." In *Multiculturalism: A Critical Reader*, edited by David Theo Goldberg, 1–41. Cambridge: Blackwell, 1994.

González, Justo L. "Hispanic Worship: An Introduction." In *¡Alabadle! Hispanic Christian Worship*, edited by Justo L. González, 9–27. Nashville: Abingdon Press, 1996.

Gregersen, Niels Henrik. "Special Divine Action and the Quilt of Laws." In *Scientific Perspectives on Divine Action: Twenty Years of Challenges and*

Progress, edited by Robert J. Russell, et al., 192–200. Notre Dame, IN: University of Notre Dame Press, 2008.

Groome, Thomas. "Inculturation: How to Proceed in a Pastoral Context." In *Christianity and Cultures*, edited by Norbert Greinacher and Norbert Mette, 120–34. Maryknoll, NY: Orbis Books, 1994.

Greenman, Nancy P. "Not All Caterpillars Become Butterflies: Reform and Restructuring as Educational Change." In *Changing American Education: Recapturing the Past or Inventing the Future*, edited by Kathryn M. Borman and Nancy P. Greenman, 3–32. Albany: State University of New York Press, 1994.

Habermas, Jürgen. "Struggles for Recognition." In *Multiculturalism*, edited by Amy Gutmann, 107–48. Princeton, NJ: Princeton University Press, 1994.

Jenson, Robert. "The Praying Animal." *Zygon: Journal of Science and Religion* 18, no. 3 (September 1983): 310–20.

Harris, Murray J. "'The Dead Are Restored to Life': Miracles of Revivification in the Gospels." In *Gospel Perspectives: The Miracles of Jesus*, edited by David Wenham and Craig Blomberg, 301–20. Vol. 6. Sheffield: JSOT Press, 1986.

Hover, Robert W. "The Amen Corner." *Worship* 63 (1989): 462–64.

Juel, Donald H. "Multicultural Worship: A Pauline Perspective." In *Making Room at the Table: An Invitation to Multicultural Worship*, edited by Brian K. Blount and Leonora T. Tisdale, 42–59. Louisville: Westminster John Knox Press, 2001.

Kim, Eunjoo M. "A Theology of Preaching in Post-Christendom: Seeking a New Paradigm." In *Viva Vox Evangelii-Reforming Preaching*, edited by Jan Hermelink and Alexander Deeg, 263–80. Leipzig: Evangelische Verlangsanstalt, 2013.

Kim, Grace S. "Asian North American Youth: A Ministry of Self-Identity and Pastoral Care." In *People on the Way: Asian North Americans Discovering Christ, Culture, and Community*, edited by David Ng, 201–27. Valley Forge, PA: Judson Press, 1996.

Lee, Sang Hyun. "Worship on the Edge: Liminality and the Korean American Context." In *Making Room at the Table: An Invitation to Multicultural Worship*, edited by Brian K. Blount and Leonora T. Tisdale, 96–107. Louisville: Westminster John Knox Press, 2001.

Lutheran World Federation. "The Nairobi Statement in Worship and Culture (1996)." In *Worship and Culture: Foreign Country or Homeland?*, edited by Gláucia Vasconcelos Wilkey, 137–42. Grand Rapid: Eerdmans, 2014.

McKenzie, Alyce M. "The Company of Sages: Homiletical Theology as a Sapiential Hermeneutic." In *Homiletical Theology: Preaching as Doing Theology*, edited by David Schnasa Jacobsen, 87–102. Eugene, OR: Cascade Books, 2015.

Melanchthon, Monica Jyotsna. "Akkamahadevi and the Samaritan Woman: Paradigms of Resistance and Spirituality." In *Border Crossings: Cross-Cultural Hermeneutics*, edited by D. N. Premnath, 35–54. Maryknoll, NY: Orbis Books, 2007.

Moyaert, Marianne. "Absorption or Hospitality: Two Approaches to the Tension between Identity and Alterity." In *Interreligious Hermeneutics*, edited by Catherine Cornille and Christopher Conway, 61–88. Eugene, OR: Cascade Books, 2010.

Moyise, Steve. "Intertextuality and the Study of the Old Testament in the New Testament." In *The Old Testament in the New Testament*, edited by Steve Moyise, 14–41. Sheffield: Sheffield Academic Press, 2000.

Muessig, Carolyn. "Medieval Preaching," in *A Handbook for Catholic Preaching*, edited by Edward Foley, 62–74. Collegeville, MN: Liturgical Press, 2016.

Neusner, Jacob. "Shalom: Complementarity." In *Ministry and Theology in Global Perspective: Contemporary Challenges for the Church*, edited by Don A. Pittman, Ruben L. Habito, Terry Muck, 465–71. Grand Rapids: Eerdmans, 1996.

Nguyen, vanThanh. "Preaching in the New Testament." In *A Handbook for Catholic Preaching*, edited by Edward Foley, 41–50. Collegeville, MN: Liturgical Press, 2016.

Osmer, Richard. "A New Clue for Religious Education?" In *Forging a Better Religious Education in the Third Millennium*, edited by James Michael Lee, 178–205. Birmingham: Religious Education Press, 2000.

Parekh, Bhikhu. "Afterword: Multiculturalism and Interculturalism—A Critical Dialogue." In *Multiculturalism and Interculturalism: Debating the Dividing Lines*, edited by Nasar Meer, Tariq Modood, and Ricard Zapata-Barrero, 266–79. Edinburgh: Edinburgh University Press, 2016.

Presmanes, Jorge. "Prophetic Preaching." In *A Handbook for Catholic Preaching*, edited by Edward Foley, 210–20. Collegeville, MN: Liturgical Press, 2016.

Rentel, Alexander. "Byzantine and Slavic Orthodoxy." In *The Oxford History of Christian Worship*, edited by Geoffrey Wainwright and Karen B. Westerfield Tucker, 253–306. New York: Oxford University Press, 2006.

Ricoeur, Paul. "World of the Text, World of the Reader." In *A Ricoeur Reader: Reflections and Imagination*, edited by Mario J. Valdes, 491–97. London: Harvester Wheatsheaf, 1991.

Schllemat, Johanna. "Hildegard von Bingen: Symphonia Armonie Celestium Revelationum." *Music History* 1 (Nov. 25, 2008): 1–10.

Schroer, Silvia. "Transformations of Faith: Documents of Intercultural Learning in the Bible." In *Christianity and Cultures*, edited by Norbert Greinacher and Norbert Mette, 3–14. Maryknoll, NY: Orbis Books, 1994.

Searle, Mark. "Ritual." In *The Study of Liturgy*, edited by Cheslyn Jones, et al., 51–58. New York: Oxford University Press, 1992.

Smith, Wilfred Cantwell. "The Study of Religion and the Study of the Bible." In *Rethinking Scripture: Essays from a Comparative Perspective*, edited by Miriam Levering, 18–28. Albany: State University of New York Press, 1989.

Sugirtharajah, R. S. "Inter-faith Hermeneutics: An Example and Some Implications." In *Voices from the Margin: Interpreting the Bible from the Third World*, edited by R. S. Surgirtharajah, 306–18. 2nd ed. Maryknoll, NY: Orbis Books, 1997.

Thibodeau, Timothy. "Western Christendom." In *The Oxford History of Christian Worship*, edited by Geoffrey Wainwright and Karen B. Westerfield Tucker, 216–53. New York: Oxford University Press, 2006.

Tinker, George. "Decolonizing the Language of Lutheran Theology: Confessions, Mission, Indians, and the Globalization of Hybridity." *Dialogue: A Journal of Theology* 50, no. 2 (Summer 2011): 193–205.

Tracy, David. "Western Hermeneutics and Interreligious Dialogue." In *Interreligious Hermeneutics*, edited by Catherine Cornille and Christopher Conway, 1–43. Eugene, OR: Cascade Books, 2010.

———. "The Foundations of Practical Theology." In *Practical Theology: The Emerging Field in Theology, Church, and World*, edited by Don Browning, 61–82. San Francisco: Harper & Row Publishers, 1983.

Vroom, Hendrik. "Hermeneutics and Dialogue Applied to the Establishment of a Western Department of Islamic Theology." In *Interreligious Hermeneutics*, edited by Catherine Cornille and Christopher Conway, 203–27. Eugene, OR: Cascade Books, 2010.

Westerfield Tucker, Karen B. "North America." In *The Oxford History of Christian Worship*, edited by Geoffrey Wainwright and Karen B. Westerfield Tucker, 586–632. New York: Oxford University Press, 2006.

White, Susan J. "Christian Worship since the Reformation." In *The Making of Jewish and Christian Worship*, edited by Paul F. Bradshaw and Lawrence A. Hoffman, 184–206. Notre Dame, IN: University of Notre Dame Press, 1991.

Wolde, Ellen van. "Trendy Intertextuality." In *Intertextuality in Biblical Writing*, edited by Sipke Draisma, 43–49. Kampen: Uitgeversmaatschappij J.H. Kok, 1989.

Wright, Stephen. "Preaching the Miracles of Jesus." In *Preaching the New Testament*, edited by Ivan Paul and David Wenham, 59–72. Downers Grove, IN: IVP Academic, 2013.

Internet Citations

"Anecdote." Accessed October 22, 2014. http://dictionary.reference.com/browse/anecdote?s=t.

Census Viewer. "Denver, Colorado Population." Accessed November 8, 2016. http://censusviewer.com/city/CO/Denver.

Denpres.org. Accessed November 7, 2016.

"Demographics of Denver." Accessed November 8, 2016. https://en.wikipedia.org/wiki/Demographics_of_Denver.

Esser, Annette. "The Choirs of the Angels." *Scivias Meditation* (December 2013). Accessed December 15, 2015. http://www.oxfordgirlschoir.co.uk/hildegard/sciviassynopsis.pdf.

Hildegard of Bingen. *Scivias*. Accessed December 15, 2015. https://en.wikipedia.org/https://search.yahoo.com/yhs/search?p=scivias&ei=UTF-8&hspart=mozilla&hsimp=yhs-002.

———. "The Choirs of the Angels." Accessed December 15, 2015. http://curiator.com/art/hildegard-of-bingen/scivias-i-6-the-choirs-of-angels.

"Hildegard of Bingen." Accessed December 15, 2013. https://en.wikipedia.org/wiki/Hildegard_of_Bingen#cite_ref-19.

"Historiaprahy." Accessed October 22, 2014. http://www.britannica.com/EBchecked/topic/267436/historiography.

"Kisagotami Theri." Translated from the Pali by Thanissaro Bhikkhu. Accessed October 22, 2014. http://www.accesstoinsight.org/tipitaka/kn/thig/thig.10.01.than.html; http://www.clear-vision.org/Schools/Students/Ages-4-7/story-of-Kisa.aspx.

Lawson, Tom. "Adorate: Worship." Accessed December 10, 2013. http://www.adorate.org/2013/02/how-finney-ruined-worship-2-reviving.html.

Malalasekera, G. P., and H. N. Jayatilleke. *Buddhism and Race Question*, online ed. Kandy, Sri Lanka: Buddhist Publication Society, 2006. Accessed November 10, 2016. http://gxul.us/download/buddhism-and-the-race-question.pdf.

"Michael Seretus." Accessed September 18, 2016. https://en.wikipedia.org/wiki/Michael_Servetus.

"Multiculturalism." Accessed April 17, 2016. www.dictionary.com/browse/multiculturalism.

"Narrative." Accessed October 22, 2014. http://en.wikipedia.org/wiki/Historiography#Narrative.

Pew Research Center. "Religion and Public Life." Accessed October 22, 2014. http://religions.pewforum.org/reports.

"*Perichoresis*." Accessed June 28, 2016. https://en.wikipedia.org/wiki/Perichoresis.

Rast, Lawrence R., Jr. "Theological Observer: Charles Finney on Theology and Worship." Accessed December 10, 2013. http://www.mtio.com/articles/bissar52.htm.

Seattle, Chief. "Prayers to the Four Directions." In *Four Directions—Native American Prayers, Poems and Sayings*. Accessed August 16, 2016. www.starstuffs.com.

Senauke, Hozan Alan. "On Race & Buddhism." Accessed November 10, 2016. http://www.patheos.com/blogs/monkeymind/2012/03/zen-teacher-alan-senauke-on-race-and-buddhism.html.

"Sex Traffic in Cambodia—Short Version." Accessed January 5, 2013. https://www.youtube.com/watch?v=IEclmPZZKh8.

Sturman, Janet. "Neoliberal Capitalism and Forced Mexican Migration to the USA." *Socialism or Your Money Back: The Socialist Party of Great Britain's Official Blog*. Accessed March 28, 2014. http://socialismoryourmoneyback.blogspot.com/2013/09/neoliberal-capitalism-and-forced.html.

Tang, Thich Nguyen. "Buddhist View on Death and Rebirth." Accessed April 10, 2016. http://www.urbandharma.org/udharma5/viewdeath.html.

Zubizarreta, Rosa. "Making Invisible Visible." In *Healing Racism in Our Buddhist Communities*. Accessed November 9, 2016. https://www.dharma.org/sites/default/f Rosa Zubizarreta iles/Making%20the%20Invisible%20Visible.pdf.

Subject Index

222

Scripture Index

1 Corinthians			*Colossians*	
13:4-51	52		1:15-20	15
13:13	147			
2 Corinthians			*Hebrews*	
4:4-6	15		1:3	15
			5:5	15
Galatians			12:1	82
2	200		13:33	15
3:28	22			
Ephesians			*1 John*	
2:10	16		4:16	9
2:14	31			
Philippians			*Revelation*	
2:6-11	15		7:9	37

CPSIA information can be obtained
at www.ICGtesting.com
Printed in the USA
LVHW111606021221
705096LV00014B/1266

9 780814 663202